THE REVELS PLAYS

Former general editors
Clifford Leech, F. David Hoeniger, E. A. J. Honigmann
and Eugene M. Waith

General editors
David Bevington, Richard Dutton and J. R. Mulryne

A KING AND NO KING

THE REVELS PLAYS

THE REVELS PLAYS

A KING
AND NO KING

FRANCIS BEAUMONT
AND JOHN FLETCHER

edited by Lee Bliss

MANCHESTER
UNIVERSITY PRESS
Manchester and New York

distributed exclusively in the USA
by Palgrave

Published by Manchester University Press
Oxford Road, Manchester M13 9NR, UK
and Room 400, 175 Fifth Avenue, New York, NY 10010, USA
www.manchesteruniversitypress.co.uk

Distributed exclusively in the USA by
Palgrave, 175 Fifth Avenue, New York NY 10010, USA

Distributed exclusively in Canada by
UBC Press, University of British Columbia, 2029 West Mall,
Vancouver, BC, Canada V6T 1Z2

British Library Cataloguing-in-Publication Data
A catalogue record for this book is available from the British Library

Library of Congress Cataloging-in-Publication Data
A catalog record for this book is available from the Library of Congress

ISBN 13: 978 0 7190 8042 5

First published in hardback 2004 by Manchester University Press
This paperback edition first published 2009

Printed by Lightning Source

Contents

General Editors' Preface

Clifford Leech conceived of the Revels Plays as a series in the mid-1950s, modelling the project on the New Arden Shakespeare. The aim, as he wrote in 1958, was 'to apply to Shakespeare's predecessors, contemporaries and successors the methods that are now used in Shakespeare's editing'. The plays chosen were to include well-known works from the early Tudor period to about 1700, as well as others less familiar but of literary and theatrical merit: 'the plays included', Leech wrote, 'should be such as to deserve and indeed demand performance'. We owe it to Clifford Leech that the idea became reality. He set the high standards of the series, ensuring that editors of individual volumes produced work of lasting merit, equally useful for teachers and students, theatre directors and actors. Clifford Leech remained General Editor until 1971, and was succeeded by F. David Hoeniger, who retired in 1985.

Since 1985 the Revels Plays have been under the direction of four General Editors: initially David Bevington, E. A. J. Honigmann, J. R. Mulryne and E. M. Waith. E. A. J. Honigmann retired in 2000 and was succeeded by Richard Dutton. Published originally by Methuen, the series is now published by Manchester University Press, embodying essentially the same format, scholarly character and high editorial standards of the series as first conceived. The series concentrates on plays from the period 1558–1642, and includes a small number of non-dramatic works of interest to students of drama. Some slight changes have been made: for example, in editions from 1978 onward, notes to the introduction are placed together at the end, not at the foot of the page. Collation and commentary notes continue, however, to appear on the relevant pages.

The text of each Revels play, in accordance with established practice in the series, is edited afresh from the original text of best authority (in a few instances, texts), but spelling and punctuation are modernised and speech headings are silently made consistent. Elisions in the original are also silently regularised, except where metre would be affected by the change; since 1968 the '-ed' form is used for non-syllabic terminations in past tenses and past participles ('-'d' earlier), and '-èd' for syllabic ('-ed' earlier). The editor emends, as distinct from modernises, the original only in instances where error is patent, or at least very probable, and correction persuasive. Act divisions are given only if they appear in the original or if the structure of the play clearly points to them. Those act and scene divisions not in the original are provided in small type. Square brackets are also used for any other additions to or changes in the stage directions of the original.

Revels Plays do not provide a variorum collation, but only those variants which require the critical attention of serious textual students. All departures of substance from 'copy-text' are listed, including any relineation and those changes in punctuation which involve to any degree a decision between alternative interpretations; but not such accidentals as turned letters, nor necessary additions to stage directions whose editorial nature is already made clear by the use of brackets. Press corrections in the 'copy-text' are likewise collated. Of later emendations of the text, only those are given which as alternative readings still deserve attention.

One of the hallmarks of the Revels Plays is the thoroughness of their annotations. Besides explaining the meaning of difficult words and passages, the editor provides comments on customs or usage, text or stage-business—indeed, on anything judged pertinent and helpful. Each volume contains an Index to the Commentary, in which particular attention is drawn to meanings for words not listed in *OED*, and (starting in 1996) an indexing of proper names and topics in the Introduction and Commentary.

The introduction to a Revels play assesses the authority of the 'copy-text' on which it is based, and discusses the editorial methods employed in dealing with it; the editor also considers the play's date and (where relevant) sources, together with its place in the work of the author and in the theatre of its time. Stage history is offered, and in the case of a play by an author not previously represented in the series a brief biography is given.

It is our hope that plays edited in this fashion will promote further scholarly and theatrical investigation of one of the richest periods in theatrical history.

DAVID BEVINGTON
RICHARD DUTTON
J. R. MULRYNE

Abbreviations

Alden   *A King and No King*, ed. Raymond M. Alden, Belles-Lettres
   Series (Boston, 1910).
Bond   *A King and No King*, ed. R. Warwick Bond, in *The Works of Francis
   Beaumont and John Fletcher*. Variorum Edition, ed. A. H. Bullen et al.,
   4 vols, unfinished (London, 1904–12), I.
c   corrected.
Colman   *The Dramatic Works of Beaumont and Fletcher*, ed. George Colman,
   10 vols (London, 1778), I.
Dyce   *The Works of Beaumont & Fletcher*, ed. Alexander Dyce, 11 vols
   (London, 1843–46), II.
F2   *Fifty Comedies and Tragedies. Written by Francis Beaumont and John
   Fletcher, Gentlemen* (London, 1679). The second folio (text of Q5).
Glover and Waller   *The Works of Francis Beaumont and John Fletcher*, ed. A.
   Glover and A. R. Waller, 10 vols (Cambridge, 1905–12). Reprints F2
   text.
Langbaine   *The Works of Mr. Francis Beaumont, and Mr. John Fletcher* [ed.
   Gerard Langbaine the Younger], 10 vols (London, 1711), I.
Mason   John Monck Mason, *Comments on the Plays of Beaumont and
   Fletcher, with an Appendix, containing some further Observations on Shake-
   speare* (London, 1798).
OED   Oxford English Dictionary.
Q1   *A King and No King* (London, 1619). The first quarto.
Q2   *A King and No King* (London, 1625). The second quarto.
Q3   *A King and No King* (London, 1631). The third quarto.
Q4   *A King and No King* (London, 1639). The fourth quarto.
Q5   *A King and No King* (London, 1655). The fifth quarto.
Q6   *A King and No King* (London, 1661). The sixth quarto.
Q7   *A King and No King* (London, 1676). The seventh quarto.
Q8   *A King and No King* (London, 1693). The eighth quarto.
RenQ   Renaissance Quarterly.
SB   Studies in Bibliography.
SD   stage direction.
SEL   Studies in English Literature.
SH   speech heading.
Strachey   *A King and No King*, ed. J. St Loe Strachey, in *Beaumont and
   Fletcher*, The Mermaid Series, 2 vols (London, 1887), II.
Theobald   *The Works of Beaumont and Fletcher*, ed. L. Theobald, T. Seward,
   and J. Sympson, 10 vols (London, 1750), I.
Turner   *A King and No King*, ed. Robert K. Turner, Jr, Regents Renaissance
   Drama Series (Lincoln, NE, 1963).
u   uncorrected.
Walley-Wilson   *Early Seventeenth-century Plays, 1600–1642*, ed. Harold
   Reinoehl Walley and John Harold Wilson (New York, 1930), XII.

Weber   *The Works of Beaumont and Fletcher*, ed. Henry Weber, 14 vols (Edinburgh, 1812).

Williams   *A King and No King*, ed. George Walton Williams, in *The Dramatic Works in the Beaumont and Fletcher Canon*, gen. ed. Fredson Bowers, 10 vols (Cambridge, 1966–97), II, 1966.

Quotations from Shakespeare are taken from *The Riverside Shakespeare*, second edition, ed. G. Blakemore Evans and J. J. M. Tobin (Boston and New York, 1997). Quotations from other Beaumont and Fletcher plays are taken from *The Dramatic Works in the Beaumont and Fletcher Canon*, gen. ed. Fredson Bowers (Cambridge, 1966–97), with the exception of the Revels editions of Andrew Gurr (*Philaster*, 1969) and T. W. Craik (*The Maid's Tragedy*, 1988); commendatory verses to F2 are quoted from Glover and Waller.

Introduction

Although their plays are now seldom performed, Francis Beaumont and John Fletcher were two of the most important playwrights of the seventeenth century. Each wrote early solo work, but it is as collaborators that they found commercial success, and in the first decade of the reign of James I they worked out distinctive versions of the dramatic 'kinds'. Their form of tragicomedy, the fashionable new hybrid they helped to popularise, became canonical in the later Jacobean and Caroline theatre, and a modern critic concludes that 'No English dramatists before or since have had so extraordinary an influence'.[1] As early as 1612, in the epistle to *The White Devil* that lists the playwrights in whose light he wishes to be read, John Webster mentions 'Master Beaumont, and Master Fletcher' after Chapman and Jonson but before the 'copious industry' of Shakespeare, Dekker, and Heywood. When the first folio appeared in 1647, containing thirty-four plays and a masque, it was prefaced by thirty-seven commendatory verses, many of which laud Beaumont and Fletcher as twin halves of a single literary phenomenon. Sir George Lisle celebrates the merger by which 'still your fancies are so wov'n and knit, / 'Twas FRANCIS FLETCHER, or JOHN BEAUMONT writ', and Jasper Maine finds this 'Great paire of Authors, whom one equall Starre / Begot so like in *Genius*', to be 'so knit, / That no man knowes where to divide your wit'.[2] Ironically, while the title-page ascription and publisher's epistle to *Comedies and Tragedies written by Francis Beaumont and John Fletcher, Gentlemen* served to perpetuate this linkage for posterity, the volume contained almost nothing of Beaumont's. When the 1679 second folio added plays that had already been printed in individual quarto volumes, bringing the total to fifty, Beaumont's share was still small, since most of the previously printed plays had been written after Beaumont's marriage and retirement to Kent, in 1612 or 1613, by Fletcher alone or with his later collaborators. Over thirty years after his death in 1616, Beaumont's name still had a commercial cachet the publishers thought worth exploiting. Yet, although certainly open to charges of deceptive advertising, the publishers in another sense got it right. The distinctive styles in comedy and tragicomedy that were to sustain Fletcher until his death in 1625 were developed in this first collaboration, in which Beaumont was apparently the dominant presence, and the most famous (and in the seventeenth century most popular) plays in the 'Beaumont and Fletcher' canon—*Philaster*, *The Maid's Tragedy*, *A King and No King*, and *The Scornful Lady*—were indeed Beaumont and Fletcher collaborations.

John Fletcher was born in 1579, son of Richard Fletcher, whose meteoric career—chaplain to Queen Elizabeth, dean of Peterborough, bishop of Bristol, Worcester, then London—ended disastrously when his second marriage so displeased the Queen that she banned Fletcher from her presence and suspended his episcopal functions. He died in debt in 1596 and seems to have consigned his eight children to the care of his brother Giles, who had nine of his own and meagre financial resources. The 'John Fletcher of London' admitted in 1591 to Bene't College, Cambridge (his father's college), probably refers to the future playwright. After his father's death he presumably lived in London at his uncle's house, though certainly Giles was in no position to provide well for his or his brother's children. Implicated in the Essex conspiracy, Giles Fletcher received no significant patronage thereafter under Elizabeth and, despite early promises from James, nothing materialised under the new king. Whether or not John Fletcher agreed, Giles and his children blamed their poverty directly on King James.[3] Though his childhood had been spent in bishops' palaces, as far as is known John Fletcher as a young adult lacked any secure social or financial position. He went on, of course, to fame and relative fortune as dramatic collaborator with Beaumont, then Shakespeare, and he became Shakespeare's successor as principal playwright for the King's Men, the most prosperous and prestigious theatrical company of the time.

Francis Beaumont's social pedigree was more illustrious than Fletcher's. In the prefatory epistle to the 1647 folio, publisher Humphrey Moseley says he tried, unsuccessfully, to obtain a portrait of Beaumont from 'those Noble Families whence he was descended' as well as from his gentlemen acquaintances at the Inner Temple.[4] After the Reformation, in 1539, Francis's grandfather had acquired the recently dissolved priory at Grace Dieu, Leicestershire, that became the family seat where young Francis was born in 1584 or 1585. The dramatist's father, also Francis, became a lawyer, an influential member of the Inner Temple, and finally a justice of the Common Pleas. Young Francis matriculated with his two older brothers at Broadgates Hall, Oxford, in 1597 and, in the family tradition, followed them to the Inner Temple in 1600. By the time young Beaumont met Fletcher they may have been in analogous circumstances, for, although eldest brother Henry did not survive long after inheriting the family estate, brother John outlived Francis by many years. The dramatist remained a younger son, with that status's attendant financial insecurity. The family's finances were themselves threatened by persistent recusancy (apparently not shared by Francis). Francis's mother, several members of her family, his father before he became a judge, and his brother were known recusants. During the whole of Francis's playwriting career, two-thirds of the family land and goods were allotted to a Scots companion of King James, and brother John was confined to Grace Dieu.[5] Neither Beaumont nor Fletcher had reason to favour James's ideology or his court.

While their circle of friends presumably included lawyers and those participants in the struggle between James and Parliament who resided at the Inns of Court, both Francis and John showed more interest in literary pursuits than in legal studies. Francis composed a satiric 'Grammar Lecture' for one of the Inns' Christmas revels and in 1602 published (anonymously) an Ovidian narrative poem, *Salmacis and Hermaphroditus*, a late contribution to the gentlemanly fad for writing erotic epyllia, while John began his poetic career in the same year with the mock-heroic *Metamorphosis of Tobacco*. Such pursuits were not unusual, for the Inns of Court could boast a long and rich association with England's literary and theatrical life. When in his 1616 folio Ben Jonson dedicated *Every Man Out of His Humour* to the Inns, he recalled that even when the play was first performed in 1599 he 'had friendship with diverse in your societies'.[6] Beaumont may have turned his attention to the law for a few years, but he certainly followed the example of John Marston (Middle Temple), who turned from writing fashionable verse satire and his own witty epyllion in the late 1590s to writing satiric drama for the private theatres' children's companies, first for the boys of St Paul's and then for the Children of the Queen's Revels at the Blackfriars theatre. Even after turning playwright Beaumont presumably kept up his ties to the Inns, for he wrote *The Masque of the Inner Temple and Gray's Inn* to help celebrate the marriage of Princess Elizabeth to the Elector Palatine in February 1613.

The first certain record of Beaumont's turning to the stage, and perhaps of his friendship with Fletcher, is Beaumont's *The Woman*

Hater, a satiric comedy written for the Children of Paul's in 1606, possibly with some revisions by Fletcher for the 1607 quarto. They may even have known each other as early as 1602, if the prefatory verses to *Salmacis and Hermaphroditus* signed 'A. F.' in 1602 but 'J. F.' in the 1640 quarto refer to John Fletcher. At some point before 1607, when both Beaumont and Fletcher joined George Chapman in writing commendatory verses for the quarto of Ben Jonson's *Volpone*, the young men had become friends of Jonson as well as of Marston and Chapman. The warm, even jocular, tone of Beaumont's verse epistles to Jonson suggests intimacy as well as respect and, despite a later crusty private remark to William Drummond of Hawthornden, Jonson's epigram on Beaumont concludes on a note of unqualified admiration: 'where most thou praysest mee, / For writing better, I must envie thee'.[7] Whether or not we credit Dryden's rather surprising assertion that Beaumont was 'so accurate a judge of plays that Ben Jonson, while he lived, submitted all his writing to his censure', contemporary testimony supports both the closeness of the Beaumont–Jonson connection and his peers' respect for Beaumont's theatrical discernment.[8] Several of the 1647 encomiasts credit Beaumont with employing his sterner muse and firmer sense of dramatic construction to curb Fletcher's extravagance.

It may have been around the time of their acquaintance, or with their decision to work together on *Cupid's Revenge* (1608), that Beaumont and Fletcher also began their collaborative living arrangements, if John Aubrey's rather salacious assertion is to be believed: 'They lived together on the Bankside, not far from the playhouse, both bachelors; lay together; had one wench in the house between them, which they did so admire; the same clothes and cloak, etc. between them.'[9] Whether apocryphal or not, it does suggest the closeness of their literary collaboration. As today for movie scripts but not plays, collaboration in the late sixteenth and early seventeenth centuries was the mode of dramatic composition for half of all the plays written by professional playwrights, and closer to two-thirds of those mentioned in Henslowe's diary.[10] There are many ways to apportion responsibility in joint composition, but if the norm was 'loose partnerships or syndicates which worked together for short periods, and then broke up or reformed into other alliances',[11] Beaumont and Fletcher's close (until Beaumont's retirement, exclusive) partnership is unusual and produced almost seamless plays. Even Cyrus Hoy, author of the most comprehensive attempt to disintegrate the 'Beaumont and Fletcher' canon into individual contributions, admits that, while Fletcher is fairly easy to distinguish from his later collaborator Philip Massinger, in the true Beaumont and Fletcher compositions Beaumont's eclectic linguistic habits make it 'quite impossible' to identify with confidence his work 'wherever it might appear'.[12] Beaumont and Fletcher may have not only discussed the plot outline but read each others' drafts, even composed some scenes in concert; certainly there is a unity of conception and execution in their joint work uncommon in their contemporaries' collaborative plays. Thus while in *A King and No King* Hoy assigns Fletcher only 4.1–3, 5.1, and 5.3, I will treat the play as throughout composed by both authors.

DATE

Although *A King and No King* was not entered for publication in the Stationers' Register until 1618, Sir Henry Herbert records that it was 'allowed to be acted' in 1611 by Sir George Buc, and it was performed at court on 26 December 1611 during the Christmas revels season and again during the winter season of 1612–13.[13] *A King and No King* and *The Tempest* were both new to the court in the 1611–12 season; they were presumably first staged at the Globe or Blackfriars sometime after the 1610–11 revels season. After the King's Men took over the Blackfriars in late 1608 or 1609, their new plays would have been composed for performance at both theatres. The title-page of the first quarto (1619) of *A King and No King* lists the theatre as the Globe, that of the second quarto (1625) names Blackfriars. Six more quarto editions before its printing in the 1679 second folio attest to the play's popularity.[14] It is probably the last of Beaumont and Fletcher's most acclaimed collaborations, all for the King's Men, preceded by *Philaster* (c. 1609) and *The Maid's Tragedy* (1610 or early 1611).[15]

SOURCES

Although no single original for the plot of *A King and No King* is known, behind its composition lies a heterogeneous collection of certain and possible sources of inspiration. Chief among these is Xenophon's *Cyropaedia*, widely admired in the Renaissance as the portrait of a model warrior-ruler, and to it can be traced some of the names, relationships, and suggestions for the play's central inci-

dent. The play's title character—Arbaces, King of Iberia—does not
appear in Xenophon, but there is a Gobryas, whose murdered son
was to have married a king's daughter (bk 4, chap. 6); he sees Cyrus
as a substitute son and becomes one of his advisers. He lends his
name and ambitions for his son to the play's Gobrius, Arbaces's true
father. Cyrus's mother was Mandane, and her name appears in the
entry direction at 2.1, though in the play she remains speechless and
functionless and was dropped by later editors. More central to *A
King and No King*'s plot, though greatly altered by the dramatists,
are the *Cyropaedia*'s two great love stories. In the briefer story
Tigranes, son of a defeated Armenian king, becomes a loyal follower
of Cyrus after Cyrus releases his father and wife; Tigranes's newly
wed, devoted (and unnamed) wife bravely accompanies him
throughout the war (bk 3, chap. 1). Beaumont and Fletcher make
Tigranes himself the defeated King of Armenia, now secretly
betrothed to the devoted Spaconia, who follows him to Iberia after
his defeat and capture by Arbaces. Cyrus's act of pardoning
Tigranes's father may also have inspired the play's first scene where,
far from punishing his captured enemy, Arbaces insists that his own
sister must be Tigranes's bride. Xenophon's Tigranes also appears
in the chapter that first presents the captive Assyrian lady Panthea,
the most beautiful woman in Asia, and that again mentions Gobryas.
Panthea's inset story, the longest and most famous in the
Cyropaedia, is presented in instalments in books 5, 6, and 7.

Beaumont and Fletcher make their Panthea the young princess
of Iberia and apparent sister of King Arbaces with whom both he
and Tigranes fall passionately in love. Beyond Panthea's name, the
Cyropaedia suggests situational and thematic parallels. Cyrus refuses
even to see his beautiful captive, lest he be tempted, and entrusts
her to his friend Araspes to guard. In a joking discussion of beauty's
power, the primly self-confident Araspes argues that love is a matter
of the will and that beauty cannot 'compel a man against his will to
act contrary to his own best interests'; unlike thirst and hunger, love
is voluntary and, as proof, Araspes claims that 'a brother does not
fall in love with his sister or a father with his daughter' because 'fear
of God and the law of the land are sufficient to prevent such love'.[16]
Cyrus laughs at such certainty in man's rational self-control and
likens love to a disease to which men become slaves. Araspes's
naivety is soon demonstrated when he falls hopelessly in love with
his beautiful prisoner and even threatens to force her submission
when Panthea resists his courtship. In *A King and No King* both

Tigranes and Arbaces repeat, with variations, Araspes's attitude and fall, and Araspes's proof of the impossibility of unnatural love is wittily overturned by Beaumont and Fletcher's king's apparently incestuous longings. In larger terms, Xenophon altered his own sources to portray in his Cyrus an exemplar of the Persian virtues of justice and temperance. Beaumont and Fletcher's Arbaces is clearly created as an anti-Cyrus whose uncontrolled passions carry him beyond the law and into tyranny.[17] Xenophon may also have inspired the use of a narrative format offering both positive and negative examples as the most exciting and dramatic way of illustrating these virtues in practice, since Beaumont and Fletcher's Tigranes regains self-mastery even as Arbaces hastens towards political as well as personal disaster.

A possible source, in both tone and perhaps a verbal inspiration in one scene, is Ovid's *Metamorphoses*, a favourite and often imitated text among university students and Inns of Court men. Beaumont had already used it as the basis for his elaboration in *Salmacis and Hermaphroditus*, and Ovid's *Heroides*, X, had suggested the content of Aspatia's description of her grief in terms of mythological parallels in Beaumont and Fletcher's *The Maid's Tragedy* (2.2.29–43). In the story of Myrrha in Book X of the *Metamorphoses*, Myrrha's attempts to rationalise her incestuous feelings for her father by appealing to the 'natural' way other animals practise procreation (including as one of her examples the heifer sleeping with the bull who fathered her), as well as her protest that what nature allows human laws forbid, may lie behind Arbaces's complaints in 4.4. This pitting of nature against custom was common in Renaissance libertine writing, and Beaumont and Fletcher need not have gone back directly to Ovid; still, Myrrha's desire 'To touch him, speak with him, and kiss him too, / If nothing more's allowed' is certainly suggestive of the teasingly progressive physical intimacy of Arbaces and Panthea in 4.4.[18] In more general terms, the *Metamorphoses*'s refusal to stick to a single genre, its open form full of juxtaposed statement and counterstatement and surprising reversals, would have been congenial to Beaumont and Fletcher as writers of tragicomedy, as would Ovid's insistence that identity is as fluid and fluctuating as the other categories of life.[19] In *A King and No King*, Arbaces's sense of self shifts alarmingly: from king to beast to a different kind of king; from brother to husband; from son of the King of Iberia to son of Gobrius.

Other classical texts may have contributed in minor matters. Suggestions for Bessus, Beaumont and Fletcher's cowardly captain, as well as for Arbaces probably derive from the *Bibliotheca historica* of Diodorus Siculus. There a Median Prince Arbaces captures Sardanapalus; he is accompanied by the Babylonian captain Belesus who later tries to withhold some of the captured treasure but, surprisingly, receives forgiveness rather than beheading (bk 2, chaps 23–8). The name for Mardonius, Beaumont and Fletcher's sturdy soldier and honest adviser, may have been taken from Herodotus (bk 6, chap. 43; bk 7, chap. 51), where Mardonius is a Persian commander influential with Xerxes and son of another Gobryas, or from Plutarch's 'Life of Aristides', where a Mardonius commands an army under Xerxes. In Plutarch's 'Life of Lucullus' another Tigranes of Armenia appears, but this one in character seems closer to Beaumont and Fletcher's Arbaces: an insolent, overbearing monarch who demands flattery from his men and is self-described as 'King of Kings'. In addition, in *A King and No King* Ligones's contradictory advice—in his roles as father and as statesmen—about whether King Tigranes should marry Spaconia (5.2.68–72) seems modelled on ambassador Metrodorus's words to Tigranes in Plutarch: asked whether he would advise Tigranes to join Mithridates against the Romans, Metrodorus answers 'that as an ambassador he urged consent, but as an adviser he forbade it'.[20] More generally, Plutarch's habit of summing up the faults as well as the virtues of his subjects may have influenced Mardonius's often startlingly contradictory verbal portraits of Arbaces in *A King and No King*.[21]

Beaumont and Fletcher's titillating suggestion of an incestuous attraction between Panthea and Arbaces may derive from Araspes's confident assertion to Cyrus that such things do not happen, but a number of more modern works could have inspired the romance variation employed in *A King and No King*, where incest is averted by the timely discovery of true identity. The old Spanish tale of Abencerraje and Jarifa found its way into Montemayor's enormously popular *Diana*, and Beaumont and Fletcher had already used Perez's continuation of Montemayor for *Philaster*. In the *Diana* (bk 4) a supposed brother and sister tentatively declare a sinful passion but soon discover they are not related and can marry.[22] The first story of Juan de Timoneda's *El patrañuelo* (1567) and Alonso de la Vega's play based on it, *Tolomea*, tell of an 'incestuous' union that has produced a child before the penitent parents learn from the governess who switched babies that they are not siblings. Turner notes a possible additional link in that part of Timoneda's action takes place in Armenia.[23] A possible inspiration for *A King and No King*'s tidy explanation of why Arbaces and Panthea's attraction is not sinful and unnatural—that Arane, Queen of Iberia, fearing her husband too old to sire a child, accepts Gobrius's son as her own but then unexpectedly bears the old king a daughter—may lie in Masuccio of Salerno's fifteenth-century collection of tales, *Il novellino* (pt 5, 'novel' 42). In Masuccio's story the Queen of Poland exchanges her infant son for another (which she kills, though she had promised to raise him as future king of Poland); she assumes that her own son, too, is dead, but in a bizarre sequence of events the true prince of Poland lives, is exchanged again (now to the king of Hungary), and when grown up is unwittingly betrothed to his half-sister. Truth will out, incest is avoided, and the Hungarian king can marry his daughter to his erstwhile 'son', thus producing the paradox of regaining as son-in-law the new king of Poland he lost as blood heir. The Queen's bargain and the paradoxical final situation may bear relevance to *A King and No King* and, perhaps, to its riddling title.

English influences are also likely. Dramatic precedent for the 'incest averted' motif may be found in the sub-plot brother and sister who resist their illicit passion but finally discover they are changelings and their love 'natural' in John Lyly's *Mother Bombie* (Q2 1598). In fact, however sensational, incest was not a particularly unusual or outré motif in this period. Charles Forker finds thirty-eight dramatists 'who made various uses of the incest theme—mostly in plots but occasionally also in imagery'—in some sixty plays spanning all genres.[24] In Beaumont and Fletcher's sub-plot, Bessus and the Swordmen belong to the long-domesticated tradition of the *miles gloriosus*, though they may have a touch of popular recent incarnations: Jonson's Captain Bobadill in *Every Man In His Humour*, and Shakespeare's Pistol and Nym in *Henry V*, Falstaff in *Henry IV, Part 1*, and Parolles in *All's Well That Ends Well*. Beaumont and Fletcher's Bessus is not only, like Parolles, a braggart soldier publicly exposed but, as Turner points out, is played off against Arbaces as Parolles is played off against Bertram. Turner also suggests that Beaumont and Fletcher's title might have been influenced by the series of paradoxes near the end of *All's Well*: 'He lov'd her, sir, and lov'd her not', 'he's guilty, and he is not guilty', and especially 'thou art a knave, and no knave' (5.3.248, 289, 249).[25]

TRAGICOMEDY AND *THE FAITHFUL SHEPHERDESS*

Probably in the same year that Beaumont and Fletcher composed their first fully collaborative play, the tragedy *Cupid's Revenge* (1608), Fletcher wrote his first solo play, an experiment in 'Englishing' Italian pastoral tragicomedy titled *The Faithful Shepherdess*. Though Fletcher models his title on Giovanni Battista Guarini's *Il pastor fido*, and for his combative defence of tragicomedy in the prefatory epistle to the quarto (1609) borrows from Guarini's own justification of his controversial generic mixture, *The Faithful Shepherdess* is quite original.[26] *Cupid's Revenge* borrows its plot from Sidney's prose pastoral romance *Arcadia*, as well as the character types which represent the spectrum of love ranging from chaste devotion to lawless lust, but the play never manages fully to control its tone. Comic and tragic dramatic cues clash and, despite seven deaths, *Cupid's Revenge* is only technically tragedy. Fletcher retains the spectrum of lovers but more fruitfully employs Sidney's thematic patterning, so that *The Faithful Shepherdess*'s interest lies in its shifting configurations of lovers rather than 'plot' in any conventional sense. Turning from tragedy to a genre more suitable to this material also freed Fletcher to create a dramatic approximation of Sidney's witty, sophisticated, self-mocking tone that became a hallmark of his later tragicomic collaborations with Beaumont.

Finding a dramatic model for the structure of events also facilitated Fletcher's control of his material. Both direct allusion and more diffuse imitation show that Shakespeare's *A Midsummer Night's Dream*—the night in the magical wood of Acts 2 and 3—stands behind the serio-comic pairings and un-pairings of *The Faithful Shepherdess*. In tone, too, the Shakespeare of *Dream* reinforces Sidney as a model. Fletcher's delicate combination of gods and shepherds, lyricism and earthy humour, threatened loss and farce creates a sophisticated double view of love appropriate to the new hybrid genre. We are made to feel love's unique and individuating importance, the intensity and power that to the lover make every obstacle tragically significant; at the same time, we are asked to share the dramatist's amused appreciation of his young lovers' mortal folly. Fletcher lets us share sympathetically his characters' torments, as we do not in *Cupid's Revenge*, while distancing them by exaggeration and poetic stylisation: the characters' purposefully heightened emotions are simultaneously real and remote.

The kind of mixed mode *Cupid's Revenge* seems to strive for, against the chosen tragic genre, Fletcher captures with a different emphasis and smaller canvas. Instead of undermining each other, tragic potential is now subordinated to comedy's final reconciliations. He discovers in practice what the quarto's epistle 'To the Reader' defends in theory: a conception of tragicomedy as a sophisticated blend of genres that results not in the awkward yoking that Sidney had deplored in his *Defence of Poetry* but in a new genre, governed by tonal and thematic unity, with its own distinctive style and effect. That his first audience was unprepared to understand what it was offered is clear from what appears to have been a resoundingly negative reception and from Fletcher's own wish that his explanatory epistle 'had bene the prologue' (ll. 2–3).[27] The stage failure of *The Faithful Shepherdess* may indeed have been due to the audience's lack of sophistication, as Fletcher charges in his epistle. Yet Chapman's commendatory poem offers praise that may point to the real problem: 'A poem and a play too!'[28] The work may have been too long, too static (despite a few stageworthy surprises), too uncompromisingly pastoral—in short, too like a masque—for an audience that had come to see something more recognisably a 'play'.[29] Despite its initial failure, however, *The Faithful Shepherdess* and the epistle's theoretical defence were significant in helping to legitimise 'tragicomedy' as a theatrical form.

The play also looks forward to the essential shape and tone of Beaumont and Fletcher's very successful collaborative tragicomedies, *Philaster* and *A King and No King*. Yet while Italian theory and practice helped shape Fletcher's use of Sidney and Shakespeare, other native influences were already at work to suggest possibilities for the particular direction English tragicomedy was to take. Formal satire had become a literary fad in the late 1590s; although banned in 1599, its perspective lived on and transformed other modes because it was also a very real response to the disillusionment that marked Elizabeth's last years and that only intensified under her successor, since in James I's case familiarity seems quite rapidly to have bred contempt. It moved onto the theatrical stage in the early plays of John Marston and Ben Jonson (in his own term 'comicall satyres'), even down to specific characters like the satiric commentator and the already stereotypical parade of fools and social climbers he castigates. Satire's fondness for abstract, 'type' characters and tendency towards dialectic favour the creation of situations that display the beliefs and 'emotions of morally opposed, extreme types'.[30] More lasting were the effects of the satiric perspective on traditional theatrical fare. In tragedy, transformations move through *Hamlet* to what we now think of as 'Jacobean tragedy'—protagonists as often seen through the lens of satire as presented heroically, trapped in corrupt and corrupting political arenas. Comedy develops two offshoots: the rapacious economic and social (and sexual) free-for-all of city comedy, and a form of tragicomedy quite different from the Elizabethan 'mungrell' monster Sidney had condemned. Before the hastily arranged reconciliations and marriages, realistic social or political problems now throw in doubt the possibility of heroic action or easy solutions, while the darker forms of sexuality challenge romantic comedy's idealising love.[31] Indeed, a link is stressed between sexual licence and communal disorder. Even before Fletcher's domestication of Italian pastoral, plays such as Marston's *The Malcontent* and Shakespeare's *Troilus and Cressida* and *Measure for Measure* support John Shawcross's conclusion that seventeenth-century English tragicomedy 'has a synchronic relationship to the breakup in society, to a satiric view of the hollow political world'.[32]

These early efforts at blending generic effects were not all aesthetic successes (or commercial, the only known hit being *The Malcontent*), but they provide a wider—and less ethereal—context for *The Faithful Shepherdess* than the obvious continental inspiration of Guarini. The possibility of a closer engagement with contemporary concerns suggested by Marston's and Shakespeare's mixing of private and public, sex and politics certainly encouraged Beaumont and Fletcher's desertion of the purely pastoral, but the native examples probably also reenforced some of Guarini's arguments in the *Compendio* that did not appear in Fletcher's own very brief defence in the *Faithful Shepherdess* quarto. Guarini draws on Marsilio Ficino's translations of Plato to maintain the political significance of tragicomedy's apparently private focus on the control of the passions. The soul harmonised by Temperance is a figure for the happy and just political state, and as such it provides a model for using discussion of 'how to rule the body properly as a way for talking about the well-being of the commonwealth'.[33] The centrality of sex in Beaumont and Fletcher's joint tragicomedies thus has native precedent and but also Guarini's theoretical justification. The interdependence of public and private in literary theory also buttressed Renaissance political ideology, which held the family as model and microcosm for the state, and expressed the obvious fact—under the Tudors as well as the Stuarts—that in a monarchy the sovereign's personal life, perhaps even most centrally her or his sexuality, is political and private life inseparable from public rule.[34] Beaumont and Fletcher keep their politics safely distant, to be sure, although the locales in the joint tragicomedies are not much more exotic than Marston's Genoa or Shakespeare's Vienna (and their citizens are just as certainly contemporary Londoners as Mistress Overdone and Pompey Bum).

In immediate terms, Fletcher's experience in juggling the 'two tones' appropriate to the new hybrid form helped prepare for the more complex balancing act of *Philaster* and *A King and No King*. And different as Fletcher's *The Faithful Shepherdess* is from the satiric comedy of Beaumont's *The Woman Hater* and *The Knight of the Burning Pestle*, it displays a kinship in attitude extending beyond the Arcadian material used in *Cupid's Revenge* and suggests why this particular collaboration was so effective and, perhaps, why it produced plays of such even texture. They shared a taste for exploring the comic potential of emphatically theatricalised emotion. Each liked dramatic experiment, especially the innovative mixing of genres and dramatic conventions. That they found congenial the social and political implications of tragicomedy's challenge to dramatic hierarchies and conventions is clear in both *Philaster* and *A King and No King*.[35] The oscillation between conventional frames for interpreting experience—frames as opposite as satire and romance—is used to expose the instability and uncertainty of human judgement; conflicting generic cues throw into relief the conflicting social codes that produce the divided self so characteristic of Beaumont and Fletcher's naive young protagonists. Together they adapt the new form to explore the ways in which the private world of romantic love can suddenly threaten the health of the state and the public world's demand for respect for law, self-discipline, and subordination of self to community.

Finally, in Beaumont and Fletcher the dramatic techniques that create tragicomedy's characteristic aesthetic distance, and the transparent arbitrariness of the romance resolutions, focus our attention on the dramatists' craft. We are conscious not of the providential nature of a world that will itself work out comedy's ending, but of the artists who control this representation of that world by manipulating their fiction. In *A King and No King* they even posit their own representative within the story to save its characters from disaster and restore both family and state to order and the possibility of a prosperous future. Beaumont and Fletcher's popularity, then pre-

cipitous fall from grace after the Restoration, point to how perfectly
their tragicomedy answered the taste—and needs—of a post-heroic
age, one in which the kind of epic, martial (and aristocratic) heroism
celebrated by the great Elizabethan romancers was clearly not only
no longer possible but even, at least partially, acknowledged a myth.
With no 'modern' alternative clearly available, cynicism and nostalgia mix in ways that for a time conveyed its own sort of 'realism'.

THE PLAY

One of Beaumont and Fletcher's most popular plays, right through
the Restoration, *A King and No King* has lost the context that
inspired both critical acclaim and commercial success. Although
the authors have come to be seen as sensation-seeking dramatists
writing for a jaded, coterie audience, title-pages for the first and
second quartos attest to the popularity of *A King and No King* at
the public Globe theatre as well as the private Blackfriars. The play's
schematic patterning and relatively flat characters were at home in
an elite world that still admired the Elizabethan achievements in
epic romance, but they also appealed to the clientele for popularised
romance in chapbooks, ballads, and public theatre plays. Popular
drama often drew its plots from (or imitated) the numerous translations of Spanish prose romances;[36] it shared their predilection for
geographically and temporally ambiguous locales, riddling and
bawdy clowns, strong antitheses (in verbal texture and stage group-
ings as well as virtues and vices), and character 'types' inherited from
classical and medieval drama who tended to narrate rather than
seem to experience their emotions.[37] In contrast, modern audiences
are accustomed to a more realistic dramatic mode and trained to
demand the richly developed characters that ensured Shakespeare's
popularity through periods whose critical fashions condemned most
other aspects of his and his contemporaries' plays; without them,
Beaumont and Fletcher's ostentatiously artful construction can only
appear technically accomplished but lifeless. However admired then,
the heightened language, convoluted situations, and emphasis on
narrative suspense no longer fulfil our idea of serious theatre. And
since we no longer possess the 'cultural literacy' they assumed, their
allusions—theatrical and literary as well as social and political—
mystify instead of extending the play's dimensions.

Coleridge dismissed Beaumont and Fletcher as 'servile jure
devino Royalists', and John F. Danby's influential extension of

Coleridge charged them with opportunistically pillaging their
Elizabethan betters—the Great House tradition inherited from
Sidney and Spenser—to craft what are essentially theatrical pro-
paganda pieces for James I.[38] More recent historicist studies have
concluded that what we know of Beaumont and Fletcher's personal
friendships and patronage connections associates them rather with
members of the established, strongly Protestant country aristocracy
critical of courtly extravagance and corruption and appalled by
the rapid ascendancy of James's Scots favourites to positions of
power and influence.[39] Rather than debasing the idealism of high
Elizabethan literature from which they borrowed, they can be seen
as adopting Sidney's use of heroic lovers and romance narrative
for political ends, appealing now to the inheritors of the
Leicester–Sidney–Essex tradition with the same ideal of a monarch
surrounded by an aristocracy restored to its traditional role of counsellors to the king. In terms of commercial revival, the gap between
then and now is probably unbridgeable. Aside from the profound
shift in stylistic expectations, the causes of their protagonists' per-
plexity and anguish are today matters of only historical interest. Still,
their 'cultural moment' lasted for nearly a century, spanning a period
of traumatic upheaval in nearly every aspect of their audience's lives,
and it is worth considering the sources—political and social as well
as aesthetic—of that appeal.

Beaumont and Fletcher's kings may aspire to absolutist grandeur,
but in fact the joint plays offer no admirable or even truly regal
monarchs. Rather, their rulers display conventional traits of the
tyrant familiar from medieval mystery and morality plays—
boasting, 'ranting and self-glorification'.[40] In both tragedies (*Cupid's
Revenge*,[41] *The Maid's Tragedy*) and tragicomedies (*Philaster, A King
and No King*), these tyrants wilfully insist on allegiance while pursuing their own goals at the expense of their subjects and the good
of the commonweal. As a tragedy ending in regicide, *The Maid's
Tragedy* most clearly explores the limits as well as the rights of both
monarchs and subjects, and it demonstrates that Beaumont and
Fletcher could push the radical questioning to a fatal—and revolu-
tionary—conclusion if they chose. Deciding to write tragicomedy
does not necessarily mean determining to avoid such questions, nor
must tragicomedy's ending spinelessly negate the seriousness of
issues raised in Acts 1–4. Tragicomedy ends happily because that is
how comedy concludes: after the physical danger and psychological
torment, surprise revelations allow the conversion of tyrant kings

and marriage rather than death. Coleridge's verdict appears to
confuse generic characteristics with the authors' own politics and
imputes to their plays a 'message' of obedience to King James's claim
to absolute authority and acceptance of both the social and political status quo.[42] Rather, Beaumont and Fletcher express, as well as
play to, the crisis of authority that marked their times. Whether
the plays end with death or marriage, they pose the question,
'Where does authority lie?' With Leucippus, Philaster, Amintor, and
Melantius the dilemma is the subject's: all are plunged into situations in which fidelity to one's own truth conflicts with allegiance
to one's sovereign.[43] King Arbaces differs from Beaumoont and
Fletcher's other sovereigns in that he is the protagonist rather than
a subordinate figure (indeed, in the other joint plays the ruler is
merely a generic duke or king). His status is also more uncertain—
neither clearly a usurper nor merely a tyrant—and this indetermi-
nateness, combined with the fact that he rules legitimately at play's
end, shifts the political focus towards kingship itself and the qualities desirable in a ruler.

Both Plato and Aristotle characterised the tyrant as one who gives
in to excessive desire, thus dethroning the proper sovereignty of
reason. As in so much else, the Renaissance looked back to classical theory. Humanist treatises on statecraft held that a tyrant's aim
was his own pleasure while that of a true ruler was the general good,
and they set up clear oppositions: king/tyrant, reason/will and
appetite, natural/unnatural. In this they buttressed popular literature; both distinguished tyrant from true king 'primarily on moral
rather than constitutional grounds'.[44] King James often employed
the distinction himself (in his own favour) and adopted their right-
eous language; he reiterated it in his 1610 speech to Parliament: 'the
proude and ambitious Tyrant doeth thinke his Kingdome and people
are only ordeined for satisfaction of his desires and unreasonable
appetites'.[45] In a tyrant, reason cannot control appetite; the 'right-
full King' subordinates will to conscience. In the practical terms that
concerned his subjects, this theoretical difference did not matter,
since James also insisted that subjects owed obedience no matter
what their ruler's moral condition. Yet despite the *Homily Against
Rebellion and Willful Disobedience* and James's repeated admonitions,
some radical theorists justified resistance, even rebellion, against the
ungodly ruler on the very moral grounds that James's absolutist
theory of kingship found irrelevant. The subject's problem remained
because it was built into the contemporary theoretical discourse of

kingship. Questions of authority look quite different if, instead of assuming that lineal descent alone confers office and inherent superiority, moral probity becomes one of the standards for evaluating legitimacy. Beaumont and Fletcher play the sense that sovereignty must be demonstrated and allegiance earned against the claims of blood inheritance; their plays test how the subject might respond to a breaking of the implicit contract between moral king and loyal subject.

Lust provided a clear instance of ungovernable private passion leading to political misdeeds, yet was also sufficiently unspecific to keep the play out of the censor's crosshairs. Nor would a political valence for sexual transgression have baffled Beaumont and Fletcher's audience. Often citing biblical precedents, humanist treatises identify the 'tyrant's bestiality with his appetites and unbridled will, expressed in sexuality and cruelty'.[46] John Foxe's enormously popular Protestant hagiography, *Acts and Monuments*, reinforced this identification of licentiousness with misrule in such accounts as that of Edward II's politically disastrous love of his minion Gaveston (later dramatised by Christopher Marlowe). In dwelling on Arbaces's passion, Beaumont and Fletcher develop a tradition of sexualised politics in which a monarch's uncontrolled appetite 'became a symbol of lack of control that contaminated all aspects of governance'.[47] In *A King and No King* the question of legitimacy is metaphoric (the qualities proper and 'natural' to a monarch) as well as literal (the kingship itself).

The habit of seeing the monarch's private life as a microcosm of his mode of governance dovetails with the attraction to Xenophon's *Cyropaedia* as primary source.[48] Sidney had in his *Defence of Poesy* praised it for 'the portraiture of a just empire, under the name of Cyrus'.[49] It was widely admired as a primer for princes and had been used in the schooling of Edward VI as well as James I; at the King's request, it was translated by Philemon Holland for James's son and heir, Prince Henry.[50] Such an association suggests that the playwrights may have had a particular as well as a general political subtext in mind, for, although the literature on the education of princes is vast, two features particularly lauded in Cyrus—his preeminence as a peacetime ruler as well as warrior-king, and his chief virtue, temperance—would have been in 1611 especially pertinent. Prince Henry had recently established his own court and on 5 June 1610 had reached his political adulthood when invested as Prince of Wales (celebrations in fact stretched over the whole year). His association with a revival of chivalry was celebrated with great pomp and romantic medievalism in Ben Jonson's masque *Prince Henry's Barriers*. Henry devoted himself to the martial arts in part because from his youngest years in Scotland he had been groomed to fulfil the role of conqueror-hero, ordained to carry the Protestant cause to the battlefields of Catholic Europe; poetic tributes in Scotland, and after 1603 in England, invoked comparisons with Achilles, Hercules, Caesar and Alexander the Great.[51] To those opposed to his father's peace with Spain, Henry now carried the banner of militant Protestantism that had passed in Elizabeth's time from Leicester to Sidney to Essex, and as patron he received many of Essex's former clients, some of whom (George Chapman, Michael Drayton) were friends of Beaumont.[52] Beaumont composed the masque presented by the Inner Temple and Gray's Inn to celebrate the marriage of Henry's beloved sister Elizabeth to the Elector Palatine, current leader of the Protestant cause in Europe;[53] both Chapman's and Beaumont's masques were arranged for by Henry and probably composed before his death on 6 November 1612.[54] Respected as both chaste and austere, Henry's court also contrasted strongly with the extravagance and moral laxity for which his father's was famous. In short, the young prince was in 1611 a magnet for the hopes of those disgruntled with James, men who foresaw in Henry the return of a nostalgically idealised Elizabethan glory.[55]

Several features of *A King and No King*, then, would have carried special resonance with its first audience. In addition, romance comedy's generic concern with courtship and marriage is focused here on political match-making and the question of succession, both preoccupations of the early years of James's reign as he considered various possibilities for both Elizabeth and Henry that would enhance his own role in European affairs.[56] Matrimonial dilemmas had also preoccupied his predecessor, for, while her Privy Council urged marriage, they and Queen Elizabeth stumbled over the question of who—foreign prince or native peer?—would be both politically advantageous and politically safe. *A King and No King* provides a wish-fulfilment solution for the problems raised by dynastic royal marriages. Iberia gets a home-grown king (which prevents its becoming an Armenian annexe), yet, since Arbaces has already been fulfilling that position, there is no sudden 'elevation' to cause factional discord in his own country. The play's ending also provides satisfying substitutions and reunions in the private realm—achievements that could only be hoped for in the audience's own royal family. Arbaces loses a mother and a sister but gains a father and a wife (and mother-in-law); he loses a kingdom, but regains it, albeit in a slightly redefined relationship; the planned strategic marriage of Panthea and Tigranes falls through, yet events have turned out in ways that ensure peaceful future relations between Iberia and Armenia. In contrast, disintegration characterised England's royal family. After two of her children died in 1607, Queen Anne retreated to her own court; by that year James had alienated both his eldest children, Henry and Elizabeth; James's attention, and affections, turned to the new favourite, Robert Carr; and by 1611 Henry seemed almost to be competing with his father.[57]

With Henry newly installed as Prince of Wales, *A King and No King*'s 'education of a prince' subtext could have carried an additional, very precise application. If young King Arbaces, as victorious general and winner of a royal duel, could be seen as a flattering reflection of Prince Henry's own self-image and of the military glories generally expected for his reign, the play might also suggest that England's young prince could benefit from Arbaces's lesson in humility as well as the play's running thread of political commentary. In both public and private the virtue most conspicuously lacking in Arbaces is temperance. Although Prince Henry seemed on the right course to becoming warrior-king, even from a young age he exhibited an arrogance and rashness that drew rebukes (from his father) and more veiled admonition and advice from others (initially from tutors; later proffered in sermons, dedicatory epistles, masques, and plays).[58] To martial prowess Arbaces (and Henry) must add the virtues appropriate to peacetime rule. In terms of the romance plot that governs the play's structure, politics is a secondary concern, but the complications of that plot are delayed until Act 3, when Arbaces first meets his sister Panthea. Through internal commentary and implicit character comparisons, for two acts Beaumont and Fletcher develop a portrait of Arbaces as a king whose weaknesses are those incident to his position. They are exacerbated by the sensational addition of incest, not caused by it.[59]

Even before Arbaces enters, his lack of steadiness and self-control are detailed by Mardonius, the sturdy soldier-confidant and adviser who strives to moderate his king's wildness: 'he is vainglorious and humble, and angry and patient, and merry and dull, and joyful and sorrowful, in extremities in an hour' (1.1.84-6). One of these 'extremities', vaingloriousness, is illustrated in Arbaces's first speech, branded at once as bragging by the defeated Tigranes. Arbaces's

denial—'Far then from me / Be ostentation'—is belied by his immediate claim that he alone, 'propped' only by 'divinity', has 'the power
/ To teach the neighbour world humility' (1.1.125–6, 132–3). He
claims that patience prevents his being 'called a tyrant / Throughout the world' yet threatens death to any who 'offend' by not
flattering him (1.1.236–7). That he earns Bessus's observation
that 'The king / Rages extremely' further marks Arbaces as in part
a conventionally egoistic ranter (1.1.291–2). Narcissism initially also
defines Arbaces's relationship with the sister last seen when she was
nine. As 'Sister to such a brother', she must be equally irresistible
and able to 'do as much / In peace as I in war; she'll conquer too'
(1.1.164, 191–2). She becomes another figure in his drama of mag-
nanimous kingship—like Tigranes, the nobly treated enemy to
whom he will offer her in marriage, and Arane, the mother he repeat-
edly and ostentatiously forgives for seeking his death. Later, overwhelming desire for Panthea exacerbates Arbaces's mood swings,
pushing him to cancel the politically astute wedding and instead
alienate the intended groom with insults and sudden imprisonment,
an act Tigranes labels 'tyranny' (3.1.277). What had been vacillation
between noble magnanimity and insecure boasting descends quickly
into abuse of the royal power to silence and imprison.[60] Hubristi-
cally, he attempts to change reality by redefining it, denying the circumstances that make Panthea unattainable: 'Here I pronounce him
traitor . . . that names / Or thinks her for my sister' (3.1.161–3). He
even tries using the royal fiat to exorcize his own feelings: 'If thou
beest love, begone, / Or I will tear thee from my wounded flesh . . .
I know thou fearst my words. Away!' (3.1.86–93). Feeling omnipo-
tent, 'like a god incensed', he see himself wielding his 'unquestioned
word' like a force of nature, a wind so fierce that 'all it grapples with
/ Are as the chaff before it' (3.1.292, 267–8).[61]

In a tyrant's world, Panthea and Bessus are in their own ways both
model subjects. She is passive, adoring, obedient. As brother and
king he is as a god to her; when he accuses her of treason and impris-
ons her, she meekly accepts blatant injustice as though she were at
fault. Largely a comic 'type', an up-to-date *miles gloriosus* whose
attempts to redefine his cowardice as courage are played out hilari-
ously in separate scenes, Bessus expresses his ambition at court
chiefly through harmless flattery and transparently self-interested
lies. At two points, however, his behaviour significantly affects our
response to his king. When in 1.1 Arbaces enters boasting that 'They
that placed me here / Intended it an honour large enough / For the

most valiant living but to dare / Oppose me single, though he lost the day' (1.1.92–5), his conduct is the more demeaning because, despite his real bravery, he seems to echo the kind of outrageous claims Bessus has just been making to Mardonius.[62] When Arbaces later seeks help in obtaining Panthea, Bessus plays Bad Angel to Mardonius's Good Angel.[63] To gain his sovereign's favour he swears he 'will do anything without exception, be it a good, bad, or indifferent thing'; more ominously, his eagerness to break the incest taboo—indeed, 'if you have a mind to your mother, tell me, and you shall see I'll set it hard'—implies unquestioning acquiescence in any royal request (3.3.141–2, 171–2).

In contrast, Mardonius is the good king's ideal. He fights bravely for his king; as both friend and father-figure he counsels patience and prudence; he will not lie and refuses to carry out immoral requests. Mardonius grounds resistance to sycophancy in a soldier's values—'loyalty, integrity, masculinity'—and a knowledge that army and general, and by extension subject and ruler, are 'bound by mutual dependence and responsibility'.[64] He insists that the army's bravery deserves due acknowledgement, not the curt dismissal that does 'wrong to us / That daily ventured lives' (1.1.281–2). Betrayed by the request to propose Arbaces's unnatural 'suit' to Panthea, Mardonius can only cry, 'What have I done / Dishonestly in my whole life, name it, / That you should put so base a business to me?' (3.3.82–4). When Arbaces threatens death, both friendship and loyalty still demand that Mardonius should perform his half of the bond: 'Who shall then tell you of these childish follies / When I am dead? Who shall put to his power / To draw those virtues out of a flood of humours / Where they are drowned and make 'em shine again?' (4.2.178–81). Tigranes protested that his treatment by Arbaces broke 'the law of nature and of nations' (3.1.253); in pursuing his own sister Arbaces violates both in a more dangerously contagious way. Abandoning himself to desires both illegal and unnatural, Mardonius warns, will either lead to hypocrisy or set a precedent for civil anarchy: 'if you do this crime, you ought to have no laws, for after this it will be great injustice in you to punish any offender for any crime' (3.3.99–101). Such blind self-absorption also courts a fatal sense of security. After Arbaces has unjustly accused Bacurius too of treason, Mardonius reminds his king of the perhaps delayed but surely inevitable consequences of his abuse of power: 'you may talk, and be believed, and grow, / And have your too-self-glorious temper rocked / Into a dead sleep and the kingdom with you, / Till foreign swords be in your throats and slaughter / Be every where about you, like your flatterers' (4.2.183–7). When Arbaces denounces Bessus as one of the moral bankrupts who offer themselves as 'instruments' to realise their king's worst desires, what sounds like blame-shifting also makes the play's political point. Kings need strong counsellors to give sound advice and point out the failings to which absolute power is prone; kingdoms need rulers who know their limits and value such advice. The price of tyranny here is not regicide or revolt, as it is in *The Maid's Tragedy*; rather, temporarily blinded by divine right theory and threatening to 'O'erthrow . . . all moral laws', a young king must—and can—learn humility and accountability (3.1.200).

Mardonius remains constant and consistent. A solid rock amid the swirling torrent of Arbaces's passions, he is well qualified as commentator on the play's action but also outside it. As the bawdy raillery with Arbaces in 1.1 makes clear, Mardonius is too old to be swayed by amorous passion and in status only a captain (in this a foil for Bessus, not Arbaces). The decisive model in terms of temperance is Tigranes. Although the romance 'story' of Arbaces's life— the biography narrated by Gobrius in 5.4—does not include Tigranes, in the play he is nearly as prominent as the Iberian king. His attraction to Panthea provokes Arbaces's jealous wrath and so adds excitement and tension. It is irrelevant to establishing Arbaces's dilemma, since Panthea would still be his 'sister' without Tigranes as rival. In his response to apparently overwhelming passion, however, Tigranes is a crucial foil. He is like Arbaces in status and youth; his infatuation, too, is both unwanted and in its way illicit, since Tigranes is already betrothed to his countrywoman Spaconia. In 1.1 misplaced self-confidence implies that he shares the need for humility and self-knowledge, for he rebuffs Arbaces's proposed match with a boast: 'Perhaps I have a love where I have fixed / Mine eyes, not to be moved, and she on me. / I am not fickle' (1.1.184–6). Where Arbaces wishes he could reduce a word—'sister'—to meaningless sound, Tigranes briefly feels the same about his vow to Spaconia. Interestingly, it is Tigranes who is given the play's only long, meditative soliloquy (Arbaces's parallel reflection, at the beginning of 5.4, is hysterical and suicidal). Proving Spaconia's earlier insistence on the mind's ability to transcend the body's imperatives (1.2.18–21), he finally rejects his infatuation with Panthea as 'childish' folly and his desertion of Spaconia as 'unmanly, beastly, sudden doting' (4.2.28). He rededicates himself in part by recalling

Spaconia's numerous virtues, and this rational exercise of the will contrasts sharply with Arbaces's yielding to self-flagellation and feelings assumed to be ungovernable. In imposing the discourse of reason on that of self-rationalising passion, and in refusing to exploit his position by seducing Spaconia while intending to abandon her (as her father fears), Tigranes is the king who appears to fulfil the humanist ideal. His prominence suggests that Beaumont and Fletcher felt the need of a balancing figure, lest Arbaces's sense of helplessness be taken as a conclusive mark of the human condition.

However admirable, Tigranes is not the play's central figure. He gains self-knowledge—'I know I have / The passions of a man'—but its expression tapers off into a comically flat-footed jingle: 'if I meet / With any subject that shall hold my eyes / More firmly than is fit, I'll think of thee / And run away from it' (5.2.92–6). His story also, of course, lacks the piquancy, the almost compulsory thrills, of an 'unnatural' passion. And while Arbaces's royal status is important, at the play's emotional centre he claims attention as a young man suffering a personal anguish. Like Leucippus, Philaster, and Amintor, Beaumont and Fletcher's other young protagonists who feel their world slipping away, Arbaces finds himself helpless before raging forces that threaten to engulf him, even dissolve his individual self by leaving him 'as far without a bound / As the wild ocean that obeys the winds' (4.4.67–8).[65] If tyranny was often figured as transgressive sexual desire, incest in particular probes deeper, more private fears. At a level more fundamental than that of the monarch's rights and limits, it challenges our idea of what it means to be civilised beings.[66] Our rational faculties may lift us above other created beings, but classical and humanist philosophy as well as Christian theology viewed that status as precarious, ever in danger of sinking back into mere animal nature which was governed by the passions alone: 'wherever we look in early modern England, we find anxiety, latent or explicit, about any form of behaviour which threatened to transgress the fragile boundaries between men and the animal creation'.[67] At the same time, family, social, and political hierarchies all depended upon this fundamental distinction.[68] Incest shared with bestiality (indeed, was often included in the term) a sinful confusion and mixing of categories. When, in rehearsing the libertine arguments for total sexual freedom, Arbaces finds himself envying the bull in heat that need not 'Fearfully leave the heifer that he liked / Because they had one dam', he clearly sees his desire as violating proscribed limits, but under the sway of passion he concludes that man has bought his 'reason at too dear a rate' and is now 'accursed', 'bounded in / With curious rules when every beast is free' (4.4.131–8). Desiring to possess what he cannot have, he becomes possessed by his desire.[69] Such transgression turns upside down the ordered, rational, known and knowable world of which he seemed in such control as victorious warrior-king.

In the opening scenes, traditional gender and class roles, too, appear to be firmly in place. Men are warriors and rulers, rivals in both conflict and hospitality; women remain beautiful objects and tokens of political exchange. Soon, however, clear distinctions begin to blur. Arbaces's prediction of his sister-self proves unsettlingly true: the passive beauty becomes indeed the conquering warrior, subduing both kings. Practically from boyhood Arbaces has been off to the wars, proving his manhood and defining himself through his relation to men;[70] 'woman' and sexual passion now dissolve the inexperienced Arbaces into bewilderment, prayers, threats, tears, desire for death. Submission to his body effeminises Arbaces and cancels the one identity he seems to have earned. He feels unable even to walk without support, much less ever fight again (3.1.349–52).[71] Mardonius notes that his king is 'strangely altered' and now 'blushes like a girl and looks upon me as if modesty kept in his business'; two more days of this 'love' and 'a tailor may beat him with one hand tied behind him' (3.3.1, 5–6; 4.2.232–3). Initially, Arbaces seemed the ideal son and brother, stepping into the patriarchal breach to arrange an advantageous marriage for his sister; yielding to incestuous lust, he monstrously violates both roles.

The subservience of even the mighty to love's power, a staple of the Petrarchan love tradition, is exaggerated until kings are reduced not merely to abject subjects but to animals. Arbaces's language tries desperately to keep separate categories such as culture and nature, man and animal, self and other, sister and lover, but the distinctions keep collapsing. Genealogical confusion—she is not, then she is his sister—leads to confusion about his own identity: 'Am I what I was?' (3.1.81). Admitting he has 'lost / The only difference betwixt man and beast, / My reason', he strives by royal fiat to reduce relational designations fundamental to human social organisation—'brother', 'sister'—first to 'mere sounds', then to palpable enemies he can meet on his own martial terms: 'Where / Have those words dwelling? I will find 'em out / And utterly destroy them' (4.4.64–66, 113, 118–20). Yet he cannot alter reality by simply declaring Panthea no kin; in the sub-plot even the effort is mocked by Bessus's ludicrous attempts to bend language to his own wishes by manipulating the terms of honour so that cowardice becomes loyal integrity. Nor, as Richard McCabe notes, can Arbaces and Panthea replace conventional morality with 'an alternative morality centred on their own desires', as do Giovanni and Annabella in Ford's *'Tis Pity She's a Whore*.[72] This possibility, too, is burlesqued when, after a shameful beating by Bacurius, Bessus and the cowardly Swordmen defy the world with a private agreement that 'We are valiant to ourselves, and there's an end' (5.3.107). Lacking Tigranes's rational self-control, Arbaces fully understands the horror he faces but believes that committing murder, rape, and suicide is his unalterable fate: 'It is resolved. I bore it whist I could; / I can no more. Hell, open all thy gates, / And I will through them' (5.4.1–3). Anticipating a non-tragic outcome, however, he exhibits a 'double impulse', towards orthodoxy as well as revolt.[73] Because he cannot be amoral, he respects Mardonius's refusal to procure Panthea and is horrified at Bessus's eager compliance. Although he tries to justify desires that alienate him from the society he leads and theoretically represents, he also expresses the self-loathing that allows for comedy's ending, where marriage folds him back into the cultural commonalty.

To ensure a happy ending, the whole royal household needs reconstituting (and in a more acceptably patriarchal form). Arbaces apparently belongs to a family with no father and a murderous mother. During the course of the play we see brother disown sister, callously relegating her to the despair of a 'lost thing . . . only suffered to walk up and down / As one not worth the owning' (3.1.224–7), then relent but accuse her of treason and send her to prison. Worse yet, his perverse desire spreads like a contagion to pollute Panthea herself. Such monstrous relations prove mercifully untrue. The identities by which Arbaces has defined himself and which he seems to have defiled—king and brother—are exposed as illusions, though initially the underlying reality seems not much better, for we learn that, when the old king appeared destined to die without the heir that blood succession requires, Queen Arane faked a pregnancy and then procured a substitute 'son' who now sits on the throne, depriving the true heir (though only a woman) of her right and Iberia of a legitimate ruler.

The solution to both personal and national crises is Arbaces's true father, Gobrius. Events and relationships that had seemed out of control are transformed, and it is as son that Arbaces is reborn and redeemed. A 'word' of kinship, now 'father', calms rather than enrages him, and he 'will kneel / And hear with the obedience of a child' (5.4.185–6). Totally effacing his wife in his narration, Gobrius is teller and creator, author both of his son and of the plan by which his patriarchal ambition has shaped events to this desired outcome: 'Now when the time was full / She [Arane] should be brought abed, I had a son / Born, which was you. . . . She sware you should be king. / And to be short, I did deliver you / Unto her and pretended you were dead' (5.4.225–32).[74] By the kind of paradox characteristic of tragicomedy, a 'fortunate fall', the inverted moral world threatened by Arbaces's 'inevitable' sins and Bessus's cheerful amorality is avoided, and the cause of Arbaces's despair and self-loathing becomes the means to his rescue. The monstrous interloper, a fake royal son who usurps the highest political and social office and endangers the true heir, now can properly ascend the throne, since proving not to be king by blood allows him to become legitimate king by marriage. Tyranny and incest—violations of the 'law of nature and of nations'—transmogrify into generosity and love, and comedy's symbol of resolution is underlined by doubling the number of weddings. As loving father who has choreographed the whole sequence, Gobrius would appear to validate an ideology that stressed the family as the foundation of the state and the *pater familias* as masculine paradigm.[75]

That we feel misgivings at the apparent restoration of the traditional order is in part a function of the hybrid form.[76] As with tragicomedies such as *Measure for Measure*, the signs of comic closure are quite flagrantly just that—signs, generic markers that encourage us to disregard the less reassuring realities the play has taken care to establish.[77] Arbaces's movement towards discovering any kind of tragic interiority—a possibility signalled by his questioning 'Am I what I was?' (3.1.81)—is aborted, and a social identity becomes entirely sufficient: Gobrius's son and eligible groom for a princess. A gaping moral abyss appears to have been closed by the discovery that incestuous lust was 'really' the natural attraction of an appropriately nubile young couple. Yet naturalising this passion cannot fully erase what it has revealed. If a universal cultural taboo distinguishes between the human and the bestial, that distinction is not upheld by a plot-solving discovery, since, when he believed Panthea to be his sister, Arbaces was sure he could not keep himself from killing his best friend, raping her, and committing suicide—three sins that index a widening circle of violence produced by the initial surrender to passion.

The sudden turn to romance is thus also less than satisfactory for the public outcome, for it legitimates a king at the mercy of his passions and therefore prone to tyranny. Arbaces certainly has not been 'well beaten', the schoolboy humbling Mardonius says he needs to make him 'temperate' (4.2.121). At the end, Arbaces's giddy elation at his uncrowning and grand gesture to the departing Tiigranes and Spaconia—he will 'have the kingdom / Sold utterly and put into a toy / Which she shall wear about her carelessly' (5.4.326–8)—are appropriately funny and even charming, but they indicate no new maturity or sudden access of moderation. By emphasising the tidy 'literariness' of its solution, the ending acknowledges itself as no solution at all for a real world where kings might prove—as one had in *The Maid's Tragedy*—to be both legitimate and perverse. One of the play's many ironies is that although both the political estate passed on from his 'father' the old king and moral inheritance from his 'mother' (that 'spacious world / Of impious acts' for which he berates Arane when he thinks her an adulteress (5.4.168–9)) prove illusory, from his true father, who has ruled so effectively as Lord Protector, Arbaces may acquire—by inheritance or schooling—the temperance and sure command of Machiavellian statecraft that will leave the kingdom in good hands after all.

The concluding narrative's focus on ingenious plotting differentiates *A King and No King* from Beaumont and Fletcher's preceding tragicomedy *Philaster* (and Shakespeare's *Pericles*, *Cymbeline*, and *The Winter's Tale*) and helps account for the narrowed scope of this play and, perhaps, the charge of cynicism often levelled at its authors.[78] An inscrutable but benevolent Providence that provides a wondrous deliverance is replaced by human agency and psychological motivation—first in Arane's efforts to secure herself a position as queen mother, then in Gobrius's manipulations for himself and his house. What often goes unnoticed in *A King and No King* is that the supposedly 'royalist' ending has not reproduced the traditional social and political hierarchy; rather, Gobrius has effected a quiet palace coup. Arbaces is king because his father seized an opportunity to put his son on the throne, then accommodated to the unexpected birth of a true heir with an elaborate intrigue, all the while keeping his son safe from an equally ambitious (and equally treasonous) queen mother whose own murderous plots he apparently foiled through the use of spies or intelligencers.[79] Gobrius is willing to restore only so much of Panthea's 'right' as is consistent with, and can be made to contribute to, the advancement of his own son: 'I sought to kindle / Some spark of love in you to fair Panthea, / That she might get *part* of her right again' (5.4.251–3; emphasis mine).

A King and No King is thus Janus-faced. It partakes of the nostalgia associated with its genre, yet the emphasis on human agency and ambition also looks ahead toward the new world rather than back to a stable social order and better times under Elizabeth.[80] Contamination of the political and social hierarchy is 'naturalised' by allowing Arbaces to rise legitimately, but that this violation of Degree sharply challenges the status quo is made clear in Spaconia's rise as Tigranes's queen in the sub-plot, where her own father voices uneasiness at his king's choice: 'If I shall speak now as her father, I cannot choose but greatly rejoice that she shall be a queen. But if I should speak to you as a statesman, she were more fit to be your whore' (5.2.68–72). Such social mobility receives implicit sanction from the very flaws the action has revealed in 'king' Arbaces. Gobrius's plan, after all, depended on Arbaces's *in*ability to exercise rational self-control, the very failure that calls in question his fitness for royal office. The point seems not to be that legitimation will necessarily transform the intemperance that Mardonius in 1.1 declared part of Arbaces's nature, but rather that, king or no king, he is first of all human—a perhaps trite, yet still fundamental, truth that the natural king Tigranes recognises when he acknowledges he has the 'passions of a man'.[81] Passion is, like death, a great leveller; the fragility of human ideals is itself an answer to absolutism. That royal blood does not create beings of a different order is even clearer in the women. The naive and retiring Panthea is ideology's perfect wife and subject, and may prove an anchor for Arbaces's moody changefulness, but, though of the old king's blood, she seems to have inherited no talent for rule. Spunky and independent Spaconia, who for her beloved 'lost her liberty, her name, / And country' and carried out her own stratagems in a strange land, would appear quite able to rule Armenia should her royal husband die (4.2.23–4).

If a belief in sovereignty linked to patrilineal inheritance is gently mocked by this unorthodox portrayal, the allied fantasy of sovereign omnipotence and magnificence praised by and reflected in a cheering populace is replaced by Beaumont and Fletcher's version of a victorious royal return in 2.2. Like the intrusion of the Woodmen or Country Fellow in *Philaster*, this calculated appearance of earthy dialogue and rude physicality highlights by contrast the artificiality of romance's heightened emotion and strained rhetoric in the adjacent main-plot scenes: Spaconia's plea in 2.1 for Panthea to promise not to fall in love with Tigranes; in 3.1 Arbaces's horrified reaction to his sudden 'incestuous' passion. Instead, 2.2 offers us 'real' citizens and a generic shift, now to satiric city comedy. Act 2, scene 2 is actually two scenes, each proceeding along a different trajectory. At its centre is an ideologically perfect royal triumph. Arbaces declaims an unexceptionable Good Prince speech, humbly offering the peace he has won as his 'account' rendered 'For all the love you have bestowed on me, / All your expenses to maintain my war' (2.2.85–6, though even here he slips into self-praise at 119–23). At appropriate pauses the people shout 'God bless your majesty!' The way the citizens interact among themselves encloses this monarch/subject exchange, however, and it mockingly implies that each side has been playing its role in a known and practiced political charade. It also reveals concerns not so different from those motivating their social superiors. The proud, status-conscious Citizens' Wives want to claim superiority over both their rural counterparts and the apprentices and servant on stage. These menials show no deference, however, and both sides display an obsession with honour and readiness to quarrel that echo in a vulgar key the central business of the Bessus sub-plot and even Arbaces's boasting and anxiety in Act 1 to demonstrate (and have publicly applauded) his royal magnificence. Relevant too is the randy, free-floating sexuality of the men's bawdy jokes and the First Citizen's Wife's interest in the 'normal' illicit lust of casual adultery. These subjects are gathered for a rare holiday sight, but both before and after the royal procession they are absorbed in the excitements of their own little world. International peace means nothing to them. They mishear their king, yet depart quite satisfied at his having brought each of them a peck of peas from the war.

The boisterous good humour of the citizen scene suggests one way in which *A King and No King*, more than *Philaster*, leans towards the 'comedy' half of its hybrid genre. Another is the expansion of Bessus's role from conventional foil character, a standard of comparison who affects our response to Arbaces both negatively and positively, into the nucleus of a fully developed farcical sub-plot. Its burlesque of manipulating language to substantiate private desires has been mentioned. These scenes of verbal contortion and slap stick humour (3.2, 4.3, 5.3) are also calculatedly positioned to precede main-plot swatches of impassioned rhetoric and psychic anguish.[82] In addition, the scene in which Arbaces and Panthea declare their

love for each other (4.4), itself a comic oscillation between seriousness and farce, is framed by Bessus comedy, not only 4.3 but
Bessus's thrashing by Ligones in 5.1.[83] Finally, in terms of dramatic
rhythm, Act 5's sweep to the denouement is halted for the last and
funniest sub-plot scene (5.3), where Bacurius pummels not only
Bessus (his third beating) but the Swordmen as well. In main-plot
scenes, too, Bessus often punctuates serious courtly business with
his comically inane or transparently self-serving comments.

There are other ways in which shifts in perspective and linguistic
register suddenly break off any unwavering involvement with the
lovers' intensity. Both Mardonius and Tigranes publicly criticise
Arbaces's boasting and arbitrary decrees, and in one scene Bacurius
joins Mardonius in indicating the extent to which Arbaces is trying
the limits of his honourable subjects' loyalty (4.2). Extensive use of
the 'aside' creates a further oscillation between viewpoints in several
key scenes. At its dizzying extreme, in 3.1, the 'asides' of Mardonius,
Tigranes, and Spaconia create a series of framing voices—each with
a different critical stance—interpreting the first meeting of Arbaces
and Panthea, an encounter in which much of what Arbaces's says is
also to himself. Inner torment is flanked on all sides by external
commentary. This means that, despite his centrality to the play's
main action, Arbaces is not really the focal point at the dramatic
moment when the shocking possibility of incestuous love is first
introduced. That Arbaces's expression of his own emotional states
tends to the descriptive—both abstract and self-consciously rhetorical—reinforces our detachment.[84] Such unsettling juxtaposition of
perspectives and self-conscious switching between conventions cor-
responds to the generic alternation of satire and romance whereby
Arbaces is one moment the object of ridicule and the next offered
as worthy hero, if not of tragedy at least of romance.[85] It also con-
tributes to that mixing of the sentimental and sensational so characteristic of Beaumont and Fletcher's tragicomedies. The technique
admits that 'plot' is simultaneously everything—the cliffhanger
aspect of 'How will Arbaces and Panthea be rescued?'—and
nothing.[86]

To the possibilities of shock, delight, and evasion offered at the
narrative level of tragicomedy, Beaumont and Fletcher thus add a
distinctive presentation style. Sophisticated and self-mocking, it
complements the emphasis on ingenious plotting; aesthetic distance
contains the play of sexual fantasies and suppressed desires.
The nature of the play's concerns as well as its style suggest that
Beaumont and Fletcher's primary audience was young, male, and

at least relatively well-educated and theatrically aware. The characteristic emotional effects are developed through protagonists whose youth and naive idealism at least in part justify their extreme responses to the apparent gulf separating received ideology from the realities with which they are faced. The apparent instability of character and moment-to-moment emotional shifts, often now discounted as superficial, seem to have been part of *A King and No King*'s attraction at a time when traditional, stable status identities had become disconcertingly fluid. While intellectual and emotional confusion may be natural to adolescence, four hundred years of cultural change now stand between a modern audience's empathetic response and Arbaces's particular bewilderment, triggered by the sudden failure of an identity assumed unassailable because inherited at birth and endorsed by the natural order. It did resonate with audiences in 1611 and for the rest of the century, perhaps because it reflected the experience of several generations consumed with uprooting and redefining familial and social as well as political relationships. In *A King and No King* they could confront that confusion, distanced by artistic form and further cushioned by a wish-fulfilment resolution.

STAGE HISTORY

The first recorded performance of *A King and No King* was 26 December 1611. It is listed in the Office of the Revels accounts for the Christmas season of 1611–12, which names five of the plays in the King's Men's twenty-two performances.[87] By 1611 the King's Men had two playing venues, the public open-air Globe theatre and the recently acquired indoor Blackfriars, and *A King and No King* could have premiered at either.[88] Like other King's Men properties at this time, *A King and No King* was written to be acted at both theatres, and title-pages of the first two editions confirm this flexibility: Q1, 1619, advertises 'Acted at the Globe'; Q2, 1625, touts 'Blacke-Fryers'. Although the pattern of summer playing at the Globe and winter performances at Blackfriars may not yet have been firmly established, it is likely that the play was performed at both theatres in its first year, for there was as yet no distinction in prestige between the theatres and playing was uninterrupted by plague closures for both this and the 1612–13 season.[89]

We tend to separate and elevate the King's Men from other dramatic troupes because it was Shakespeare's company and because several of the other dramatists we value also wrote for it—Jonson,

Middleton, and Webster as well as Beaumont and Fletcher. Certainly it had become London's most prestigious company, and its distinction was enhanced when it became the only one with two playhouses and the possibility of year-round performances. Yet, with the exception of Shakespeare, these playwrights also wrote for other companies, and those companies also played at court. Like them, the King's Men was a commercial enterprise, capitalising on theatrical fashions as well as helping to create them. It became successful in part because of an astute commercial strategy that produced a repertory of broad appeal. In addition to a range of new works, revivals of popular old plays helped fill out their roster, and some of these throw light on the dramatic context that influenced Beaumont and Fletcher's choices. The revival of *Mucedorus*, that 'mouldy old tale', around 1605–6 (Q2, 1606) may have encouraged Beaumont and Fletcher as well as Shakespeare to think of contributing something in the pastoral–romance–tragicomedy vein. It was again revived around 1610, for it was offered to the King in the 1610–11 revels season, and its influence on at least *The Winter's Tale* has long been accepted.[90] The Revels Account for 1611–12, noted above, and two records from the Office of the Chamber for 1612–13 suggest that *A King and No King* was very much at home with other fairly lurid tales of aberrant love and violent passion that apparently qualified as fashionable and likely to please—in 1611–12, Caliban's lust for Miranda in *The Tempest*, the twisted and deadly eroticism that pervades *Cupid's Revenge*, and in *The Winter's Tale* Leontes's murderous jealousy and attempt to force the world to the 'level of his dreams', so like Arbaces's in *A King and No King*. *The Rape of Lucrece* perhaps speaks for itself, while the lost *Proud Maid's Tragedy* certainly sounds promising in this regard. The 1612–13 records list many more plays and so give an even better idea of what the Revels Master thought royal entertainment. *A King and No King* played not only with the King's Men's *Winter's Tale* and *Tempest* again, but also with their revivals of Shakespeare's *Othello* and Beaumont and Fletcher's own *Philaster* (probably twice) and *Maid's Tragedy* and, by other troupes, *Cupid's Revenge* (twice this season) as well as several comedies of piquant sexual intrigue (*The Coxcomb*, *The Widow's Tears*, *The Dutch Courtesan*).[91]

Reprintings of *A King and No King* in 1631 (Q3) and 1639 (Q4), as well as performances at court in the 1630–31 and 1636–37 Christmas seasons, suggest sustained popularity through the Caroline years.[92] It was one of the Red Bull actors' stock plays before the Civil

War.[93] Despite Beaumont's retirement in 1613, the continued high repute in which he as well as Fletcher was held is clear from the fact that a volume of his *Poems*, as well as one of Shakespeare's, was issued in 1640 (Beaumont's reprinted, with additional poems, in 1653). Although the theatres were closed during the Commonwealth period, a few clandestine performances are on record as having been broken up by the authorities, including one of Beaumont and Fletcher's comedies of manners (*The Scornful Lady*) at an unknown theatre in the summer of 1647 and another of *A King and No King* announced for 6 October at the Salisbury Court the same year.[94] English refugees in Holland proposed playing *A King and No King* before the Princess Royal in the spring of 1654.[95] It was during this official cessation of playing that Humphrey Moseley brought out the Beaumont and Fletcher first folio (1647), a commercial venture apparently also intended as both a plea for reopening the theatres and a gesture of royalist solidarity by the Cavalier poets who contributed its enormous number of commendatory verses.[96]

Monarchy returned with Charles II in 1660 and with it London's theatrical life, now in the form of a duopoly in which Thomas Killigrew and William Davenant managed the two licensed theatres. Between them they also split the prewar repertory, of which a substantial number of Beaumont and Fletcher plays fell to Killigrew; he is responsible for most of the Restoration revivals of their plays and seems also to have had a near monopoly on Jonson.[97] Understandably, old plays dominated the first seasons. In 1660–61 and 1661–62 Killigrew's company presented sixty-eight pre-Restoration plays; twenty-seven were by Beaumont and Fletcher, three by Shakespeare, three by Jonson.[98] Not only were new plays scarce, but many in the early Restoration audience had lived during the heyday of Jacobean theatre, and they remembered both plays and playwrights they had enjoyed. The most popular revivals were of Beaumont and Fletcher's comedies and tragicomedies (many, of course, being actually Fletcher or Fletcher–Massinger compositions).[99] *A King and No King* was performed on 14 August 1660 at the Red Bull Theatre by Killigrew's company, usually referred to as 'the King's', and again on 3 December at their new theatre at Gibbons' Tennis Court;[100] Pepys saw it performed twice in 1661 by this company, on 14 March and 26 September, and deemed it 'well acted' and 'very well done'.[101] The King's Company acted it again the next year, as a performance of 15 February 1662 appears in Sir Henry Herbert's records.[102] It was played frequently enough in the

early 1660s that in an elegy on the actor Walter Clun, murdered on
2 August 1664, the anonymous writer recalls the part of Bessus as
among Clun's most famous roles.[103] Downes termed it a 'Principal
Old Stock Play' and gives the cast list for a performance with
Charles Hart as Arbaces that must have taken place before summer
1667, when Nell Gwynn, who played Panthea, left the Theatre
Royal.[104]

Although Beaumont and Fletcher's lighter fare proved in the end
more durable, in the seventeenth century the production history of
A King and No King (as well as of their other famous tragicomedy
Philaster) kept pace, though it must be borne in mind that before
the eighteenth century records of performance are scattered and
almost certainly incomplete. In 1668 Dryden reports that Beaumont
and Fletcher's 'plays are now the most pleasant and frequent
entertainments of the stage; two of theirs being acted through the
year for one of Shakespeare's or Johnson's [*sic*]'.[105] Beaumont and
Fletcher remained the favoured prewar dramatists through the
1660s, but their towering dominance gradually faded. Tastes began
to change and new dramatic works became available. In the 1667–68
season to which Dryden alludes, Renaissance and Restoration plays
were evenly represented, with thirty-three old plays and thirty-two
new works (of which twelve were new that season).[106] Thereafter,
new plays provided most of the theatrical offerings, and Renaissance
plays increasingly needed altering to retain popularity (sometimes
so dramatically as to become operas).

Tragicomedy in particular suffered a dwindling popularity as the
century neared its close, Beaumont and Fletcher's as well as those
newly written during and just after the Civil War.[107] Nancy Klein
Maguire argues that it is no coincidence that 'the major serious
genre of post-regicide England is tragicomedy', for 'the dual perspective of reality characteristic of tragicomedy' proved particularly
well suited to 'a society which yoked together political and psychological absolutes as contradictory as regicide and restoration'.[108] The
production history of *A King and No King* may be explained in part
by the relaxation of such earlier anxieties. The king saw a performance on 6 May 1669 at the Bridges' Theatre (the first Drury Lane
Theatre), but the next recorded production is another royal attendance of 23 April 1675;[109] the cast list published in the 1676 edition
of the play (Q7) may be from one of these productions. Edward
Kynaston, who had received great praise for his women's parts at
the reopening of the theatres, now as an adult took the part of

Tigranes, while Hart again played Arbaces.[110] Although in *The Tragedies of the Last Age* (1677) the critic Thomas Rymer lambasted the play itself, Hart's delivery received high praise. The 'sort of men' who judge merely by what they like say

> a King and no King, pleases. I say the Comical part pleases. I say that Mr. Hart pleases . . . and what he delivers, every one takes upon content; their eyes are prepossest and charm'd by his action, before ought of the Poets can approach their ears; and to the most wretched of Characters, he gives a lustre and brilliant which dazles the sight, that the deformities in the Poetry cannot be perceiv'd.

In a later section complaining of indecorum, since 'all crown'd heads by Poetical right are Heroes', Rymer buttresses his case with a bit of stage business that suggests that Arbaces's boasting in 1.1 was played for comedy: 'Arbaces . . . no sooner comes on the Stage, but lays about him with his tongue at so nauseous a rate, Captain Bessus is all Modesty to him, to mend the matter his friend shaking an empty skull, says "Tis pity that valour should be thus drunk".'[111] Pathos, however, was apparently also a Hart specialty, for an anonymous elegy on 'that Worthy and Famous Actor, Mr. Charles Hart, who departed this Life Thursday August the 18th, 1683' includes in its praise the observation that 'when Arbaces wept by sympathy, / A glowing Tide of Wo gush'd from each Eye'.[112]

The handwritten cast list in a copy of Q7 reported by Genest apparently refers to another production, perhaps in 1683, in which Betterton played Arbaces to Kynaston's Tigranes.[113] *A King and No King* was presented before Queen Mary on 20 October 1685. Early the next year (23 January), Peregrine Bertie wrote to the Countess of Rutland that 'To day will be acted *King and noe King*, by the King's command; everybody is sending to keep places'.[114] The next season it was played at Whitehall on 9 December 1686 and at Drury Lane 6 January 1687; a playbill announces a further performance for 22 February 1687 by the United Company at the Theatre Royal.[115] Although the record lapses after this cluster of productions, in 1691 Langbaine could still describe it as 'a Tragi-Comedy, which notwithstanding its Errors discover'd by Mr. Rymer in his *Criticism*, has always been acted with Applause, and has lately been reviv'd in our present Theatre with . . . great success'.[116] It may have enjoyed a further run in the 1692–93 season, for Q8 appeared in 1693. *A King and No King* also had the dubious honour of being one of the several old plays pillaged for new Restoration works, in this case by no

Dryden or even Otway. James Howard in 1667 borrowed the main plot for *All Mistaken, or the Mad Couple*. Jealousies and misunderstandings remained intact, but the central incest problem was avoided, and there was no violation of decorum or elevation of a non-royal groom.[117]

Because it was initially so popular and admired, *A King and No King* allows us to trace the seismic shift in aesthetic criteria that within fifty years had virtually forced it from the stage. Early in the Restoration, Dryden praised Beaumont and Fletcher in general terms as surpassing Shakespeare, since in their case a like natural wit had been 'improved by study'. Their plots were 'more regular', their language was more natural because they 'understood and imitated the conversation of gentlemen much better'; indeed, the 'English language in them arrived to its highest perfection', while Shakespeare was already 'a little obsolete'.[118] By 1677, as we have seen, Thomas Rymer attacked *A King and No King* precisely because it was one of 'the choicest and most applauded English tragedies of this last age' and so an excellent example of popular error needing his correction.[119] Not only did it offend against decorum in both poetry and character (Panthea as well as Arbaces); it also violated the classical unities, piled improbability on improbability, and in every respect failed to uphold morality. Nature should be imitated, as Aristotle prescribed, but as it ought to be, 'not the obscenities, not the blindsides of Nature'.[120]

Prompted in part by Rymer's critique, Dryden in 'The Grounds of Criticism in Tragedy' (1679) reconsidered *A King and No King* in the light of neo-classical principles and nearly abandoned his earlier evaluation. Although it is still the 'best of their designs, the most approaching antiquity, and the most conducing to pity', Dryden can no longer 'wholly ascribe to the excellency of the action'; trying to locate a reason the play still moves him, he now finds it only in 'the lively touches of passion'.[121] Moreover, Beaumont and Fletcher are now guilty on another front—what he calls 'manners'—and Dryden here delineates the changed conception of character that helped damn Beaumont and Fletcher and so favoured Shakespeare that he could be forgiven defects of plot and language. Dramatic character should no longer be representative; rather, 'character' approaches its modern meaning of 'personality', the totality of a man's manners and 'that which distinguishes one man from all others'.[122] The intricate plotting so much admired in the encomia prefacing the 1647 folio and only a decade ago praised by Dryden himself is now a defect: 'manners can never be evident, where the surprises of fortune take up all the business', for then 'the poet is more in pain to tell you what happened to such a man, than what he was'.[123] Beaumont and Fletcher's failure is in this moral as well as artistic: with Arbaces, as with their other characters, 'you know not whether they resemble vice or virtue, and they are either good, bad, or indifferent, as the present scene requires it'.[124]

Such sentiments voice at least some of the reasons Beaumont and Fletcher fell from favour, to which might be added that the 'conversation of gentlemen' that had sounded contemporary and wittily risqué in the 1660s, when Shakespeare was already 'a little obsolete', was beginning to lose its currency. By the later 1690s Beaumont and Fletcher's plays were not only offensively improper in terms of social decorum—none more so than *A King and No King*'s flirting with incest and cross-class marriages—but also linguistically antiquated and in need of expurgation. Then too, while the eroding social and political foundations of the first half of the seventeenth century remained uncertain after the war, that time passed.[125] And to the competition from new playwrights was added that of new forms, such as burlesque, pantomime, and opera. Changing conditions of performance also militated against the successful revival of prewar plays. The length of time needed to change sets required adaptation of plays constructed for rapid changes of location on a bare stage, so practical necessity as well as neo-classical theory imposed unity of place and reduction in the number of scenes. The proscenium-arch stage also curtailed the sense of intimacy important to the effect of the older drama.

Shakespeare survived these changes (with omissions and alterations), but as his star rose Beaumont and Fletcher's declined, and by the late eighteenth century only two comedies remained 'stock plays' in the Renaissance revival repertoire, *The Chances* and *Rule a Wife and Have a Wife*. *A King and No King* virtually disappeared, though it did enjoy a cluster of productions in the first decade. Described as 'not acted for several years', it was staged at Drury Lane on 15 June 1704 as a benefit for Captain Griffin, who may have acted Mardonius; Wilks starred as Arbaces, and the play was followed by dancing.[126] It was played at Drury Lane on 14 April and 10 October 1705, the latter advertised as 'At the Desire of several Ladies of Quality'; no cast lists survive, but both performances were again concluded with dancing.[127] On 28 March 1706, double-billed with 'The Masque of *Acis and Galatea*', it was staged at the Queen's

Theatre in a benefit performance for Betterton; again at the Queen's Theatre, 'by subscription', it was performed on 21 January 1707.[128] The funding of plays by seasonal subscription followed this method's success with Italian opera; according to Colley Cibber, the Queen's management used it in this instance for 'Reviving three Plays of the best Authors' and soon was able to offer *A King and No King*, *Julius Caesar*, and the comic scenes of Dryden's *Marriage a la Mode* and *Maiden Queen* 'put together'.[129] For the rest of the century the records indicate few and largely scattered productions. *A King and No King* played on 26 March 1724 at Lincoln's Inn Fields, where the presence of leading actor James Quin as Bessus suggests the comic underplot's importance to the production.[130] After a decade's lapse, it appears again on 31 October and 1 November 1733 at Goodman's Fields Theatre.[131]

Speaking generally of the Beaumont and Fletcher corpus, Theophilus Cibber at mid-century could confirm that 'however it might be when Dryden writ', their popularity relative to Shakespeare 'is now reversed', for 'Beaumont and Fletcher's plays are not acted but above once a season, while one of Shakespeare's is represented almost every third night'.[132] The aversion felt by a London critic in 1757, advising a young actress of the difficulties faced in performing the 'old plays', indicates the extent of the shift in language and manners: 'The great ladies of Ben. Johnson [*sic*], are north country chambermaids in point of breeding, Beaumont and Fletcher the same.'[133] For the most part, as the number of Beaumont and Fletcher plays performed declined, the number of alterations increased for those that remained. Thomas Davies reports that in the early 1760s actor-manager David Garrick planned a production in which the main parts were clearly to be Arbaces (Garrick himself) and Bessus (Mr Woodward). Textual cuts and alterations had been decided and rehearsals begun, yet 'at every reading of it in the green-room, his pleasure instead of increasing, suffered a visible diminution', and he gave over the project. Conjectures about Garrick's decision included the possible offence of the title, since 'a young and beloved prince had just ascended the throne', and the 'impropriety of the story'. The moralistic Davies favours the latter reason, for 'A play founded on incest, or any thing repugnant to nature, even in supposition, can never please an English audience'.[134]

Although *A King and No King* had finally seemed beyond saving to Garrick, a more thoroughgoing revision by Thomas Harris attempted to revive the play's fortunes in 1788. Promising the novelty of 'Never acted at this Theatre', Covent Garden offered a version on 14 January 1788 in which the alterations, consisting 'of many curtailments, the last scene of Act IV being entirely omitted', allowed for the addition of singing in Act 2 (a 'Grand Chorus') and the inclusion on the bill of *The Dumb Cake*.[135] The cursory review in *The Morning Post* approved such 'alterations as the nature of present manners necessarily required' but judged the result a 'motley drama' with manifold 'improbabilities' only partly offset by 'many noble sentiments, much forcible imagery and powerful language and in the comic scenes, a considerable share of humour'. Of the actors, the reviewer seemed most impressed by the 'laughable poltroonery' of Mr Ryder's Bessus.[136] Harris's adaptation was not revived, although it did not sink wholly without a trace: many years later Dyce recalled that its having been 'coldly received' justified Garrick's decision to abort his production.[137] If there was a performance history for the German adaptation, transferring the scene to England and Scotland in Saxon times, it is not recorded; the text was published at Dessau and Leipzig in 1785 under the title *Ethelwolf oder der König Kein König. Ein Schauspiel in fünf Aufzügen*.[138]

Scholarly editions continued to appear, but at this point the performance history of *A King and No King* goes blank. Expurgation and emphasis on Bessus and the comic sub-plot proved insufficient to restore it to the stage. Fully aware that the popularity of a dramatic writer required frequent theatrical production, George Colman fought a losing battle for sustained revival of the 'old dramatists'. Asked to contribute an essay to the 1761 edition of Massinger, he used the opportunity to challenge Garrick to look beyond Shakespeare: 'Under your Dominion have not Beaumont and Fletcher, nay even Johnson [*sic*] suffered a kind of theatrical Disgrace?'[139] Seventeen years later, in the headnote to *A King and No King* in his own edition of Beaumont and Fletcher, Colman lamented that 'Notwithstanding its prodigious merit, it has not been performed for many years past'.[140] Still defending Beaumont and Fletcher against Rymer, Colman in his endnote maintains that the play 'abounds with the highest dramatic excellencies'.[141] At the end of the century, after noting that fame's tide 'has flowed in favour of Shakespeare' for thirty years, Monck Mason expresses wonder and sorrow that this has not 'induced his admirers to pay some attention to his contemporary poets, Beaumont and Fletcher'. Instead, they are 'now so totally neglected, that many copies of the last

edition of their plays [i.e. Colman's] still remain unsold'.[142] The saga
of neglect continues in Henry Weber's 1812 edition, where Weber
deplores the lack of a stage production of *A King and No King* 'for
more than fifty years'.[143] Perhaps surprisingly, Weber is still arguing
against Rymer's condemnation, and to this end marshals large
chunks of Dryden, Seward, and Colman. He does take issue with
Dryden's censure of the sub-plot and in this speaks for his own era,
finding Bessus 'one of the chief excellencies of the play' but the
'central conceit of Gobrius's plan . . . so offensive as to be intoler-
able to any modern audience'.[144] The play remained off the stage
throughout the nineteenth century and for most of the twentieth,
despite revivals of Renaissance plays, including Beaumont and
Fletcher's *The Maid's Tragedy*, by The Phoenix Society in the 1920s
and later by the Mermaid Theatre and elsewhere in London.[145] With
the opening of The Other Place and then the Swan Theatre at
Stratford, and the reconstructed Globe theatre in London (in 1996),
the drama of Shakespeare's contemporaries enjoyed more frequent
production. To date, however, *A King and No King* has received
only a staged reading at the new Globe, on 16 November 1997.

THE TEXT

A King and No King was entered in the Stationers' Register on 7
August 1618 to Edward Blount. Though the changeover is not
recorded in the SR, Blount seems to have transferred his privilege
to Thomas Walkley, who issued the first quarto in 1619 and was soon
involved in the publication of other King's Men properties: *Philaster*
(1620), *Thierry and Theodoret* (1621), and *Othello* (1622). Walkley's
dedication to the 1619 *A King and No King* indicates the nature of
his copy: a private transcript, probably of the authors' final draft,
made for (or at least in the possession of) Sir Henry Neville. Unlike
the first quarto of *The Maid's Tragedy*, printed the same year but by
a different publisher, Walkley's title-page bears the names of both
authors.

     In the printing house Q1 was composed seriatim, with the
exception of gathering A which contains the title-page, Walkley's
dedication to Neville, and the first four pages of text.[146] From
his bibliographic study, Turner concluded that one compositor set
sheets B to G and another sheets H to (half-sheet) M and A, probably in that order. More recently, Hans Walter Gabler has suggested
a minor modification to Turner's argument for two compositors. On

the basis of five spelling variants, Gabler proposes four different compositors. One set sheet B, another C to D1 or D1v, a third D1 or D1v to H2, and a fourth H2 or H2v to L4v or M1; in addition, M1v to M2v were set largely by the fourth compositor. Evidence for A1–4v is inconclusive, and this final section may have been a collaborative effort.[147]

In seriatim setting (page two after page one, page three after page two, etc.), the compositors would not be under pressure to adjust their copy to fit a prescribed amount of text per page, such as by altering their copy's lineation (spreading prose by printing it as verse or contracting verse to prose) or omitting lines or words. Based on the similarity of his four compositors' work, Gabler concludes that the original manuscript 'must have been a very careful, clear, and consistent copy'.[148] The lineation of Q1 thus probably follows the scribal transcript, though we cannot know what errors or changes the scribe himself introduced. It can sometimes be difficult to tell loose verse from prose, and the scribe may have made guesses that Q1 perpetuated. Turner notes that in two scenes involving Bessus and the Swordmen (4.3 and 5.3) the first is lined largely as verse, the second as prose; he thinks that probably both were originally in an irregular verse designed 'to convey the heroic pretensions of Bessus and these comic characters'.[149] Yet these two scenes do not present the only problem. Q1's verse and, especially, prose are frequently suspect, and the manuscript may not have been so transparent in this regard. Theobald is responsible for much of the lineation printed in modern editions, but, when in doubt, his preference (followed by Bond and to some extent Turner) is verse. As Alden notes of 3.3 (especially passages such as 1–11 or 96–109), 'This and many later speeches of Mardonius are often printed as verse, and they frequently suggest a rhythmical intention; but it is impossible to make regular verse out of them.' Citing Bond's defence of choosing verse (which boldly begins 'In spite of the vigorous protest of the Editors of 1778 [Colman], we follow Theobald in printing this and nearly all the following speeches of Mardonius as verse . . .'), Alden comments that 'In theory this is reasonable enough, but if Beaumont and Fletcher liked such bad blank verse . . . why did they not write it oftener?'[150]

While Q1's lineation is often unsatisfactory, as the above example indicates (another notable instance occurs at 5.2.34–43), editors solve Q1's patches of irregular or broken verse in different ways, ways sometimes based less on the lines themselves than on assumptions about verse drama, about Beaumont and Fletcher's in particular, or about the linguistic decorum appropriate to a character's social status. Rather than burden the collation with such extensive disagreement, I have included an appendix of the most plausible solutions (excluding, of course, those achieved by Theobald's eighteenth-century predilection for smoothing out the metre as well as correcting Q1's grammar). To the scribe, then (and perhaps to authors themselves often disinclined to make sharp distinctions), can probably be traced Q1's lineation puzzles, though presumably the scribe was trying to be as faithful as possible to his original. It is unlikely, for instance, that he introduced the 'ghost' character Mandane, who does not speak and is not spoken to, in the entry direction to 2.1; she was first removed by Dyce. Her name is taken from Beaumont and Fletcher's chief inspiration, Xenophon's *Cyropaedia*, and Turner sensibly proposes that she may originally have been intended as confidant to Panthea, then dropped in favour of Spaconia.[151]

In 1625 Walkley brought out a second quarto, claiming on its title-page to be now 'Printed, according to the true Copie'. Frequently such claims are no more than a marketing ploy, but Q2 differs from Q1 in two significant ways. In addition to correcting some printing errors and reassigning a few speeches, Q2 contains some additional lines in Act 3 (most notably 3.1.153–5 and 3.3.130–2) and a substantial number of 'literary' variants that go beyond the simple righting of obvious wrongs. The more immediately striking difference, however, lies in the stage directions: some are new, others expand existing directions. Berta Sturman proposed that Q2 was printed from a copy of Q1 annotated for performance, and she hypothesised that the original manuscript prompt-book had been lost (perhaps in the fire that destroyed the Globe in 1613).[152] Because of the Q2 additions in Act 3, Turner sensibly concludes that Q2 was influenced not only by theatrical practice but also by consultation with some authoritative manuscript, perhaps the original prompt-book so damaged as to need replacement for a revival.[153]

Evidence of an annotator's prompt-book additions to Q1 are clear. Sixteen entry or exit directions have been added to Q2 (four with *Flourishes* to announce the kings' arrival or departure), and there is one new acting cue (*Beates him* at 5.1.89); other directions have been expanded, by the addition of either the character's name (e.g. Q2 *Exit Bessus*) or a descriptive phrase (Q2 *Enter Tigranes in prison*). The latter might have provided greater clarity for the actor, as might the change in the direction at 3.1.333.1, where Q1's Latin is dropped and the names of those remaining are replaced with those leaving. The considerable degree of linguistic and textual variation between the two quartos is probably attributable to Q2's compositor, however. Q1's forty-eight *um* forms were nearly all changed to *them* (three) or *'em* (forty-four). Q2 was to be a line-for-line reprint of Q1, but the length of the line is three millimetres shorter in Q2; contraction of *them* to *'em* was in some cases used to fit the new line on Q2's page. The Q2 compositor seems to have taken on himself the authority to contract *them* and expand *um* as needed, and he may have taken the same liberty with other forms. Williams concludes that while 'Many substantive variants in Q2 are certainly authoritative and essential to the text', others 'derive from the compositor of Q2'.[154]

The first quarto is therefore the copy-text for this edition, even though it is at least two removes from the authors' final draft, which was transmitted first by the scribe who made the transcript for Neville and then by the Q1 compositors. Q2's fresh, and some of its expanded, stage directions have been adopted as having legitimate authority, if not in Beaumont or Fletcher's hand in this form, then by those who originally staged the play. Other Q2 readings are adopted only if Q1 seems manifestly corrupt—such as eyeskip errors by the scribe or the Q1 compositors or obviously defective speech headings (e.g. 3.1.122–5)—although Q2 in some cases provides a variant reading that may be authentic. Q1 is the first and essentially authoritative quarto, and Q2 may be in part authoritative. Q3–8 and F2 all depend from Q2 and thus carry no independent weight. Indeed, as Williams observes, the deterioration evident in the text's printing history is the more unfortunate because the influential second folio (1679) was set from Q5 (1655), where to save space the printer had run speeches together and turned verse into prose.[155]

I regret that illness prevented me from travelling to a copy of Q1. The present text is based on the Q1 that could come to me, courtesy of Early English Books Online: the copy in the Victoria and Albert Museum (Dyce Collection), on which this edition is based. There are six other known copies of Q1, and it is my good fortune that two previous editors provide excellent collations of the other early texts unavailable to me.[156] Special notice should be taken that the copy of Q1 in the Victoria and Albert Museum's Dyce Collection, on which Dyce based his edition, contains about sixty substantive manuscript corrections in a seventeenth-century hand. They are independent of any printed text, although the authority for these emendations is unknown. They may derive from recollections of a performance, or from a now lost manuscript of the play, one differing from the transcript belonging to Neville and the company's manuscript prompt-book. Some of Dyce's Q1 corrections agree with subsequent seventeenth-century editions (Q2–8); some have been independently proposed by later editors.[157] Where the Dyce manuscript corrections agree with the seventeenth-century editions or with later editors' suggestions, the case for emendation is strong.

NOTES

1 Arthur C. Kirsch, *Jacobean Dramatic Perspectives* (Charlottesville, 1972), p. 4.

2 Glover and Waller, I, pp. xxii, xxv (roman and italic font reversed); see also Sir John Berkenhead's tribute, pp. xli–xliv.

3 In *Court and Country Politics in the Plays of Beaumont and Fletcher* (Princeton, 1990), Philip J. Finkelpearl quotes Giles's son Phineas, writing in 1610 of James's 'promise writ in sand' (p. 17). See also Gordon McMullan, *The Politics of Unease in the Plays of John Fletcher* (Amherst, MA, 1994).

4 Glover and Waller, I, p. xiv.

5 Finkelpearl, *Court and Country Politics*, p. 12. Both Finkelpearl and McMullan discuss at length Beaumont's, and probably through him Fletcher's, ties with Henry Hastings, Fifth Earl of Huntingdon, one of the country Protestant nobles opposed to both James's policies and his profligate court.

6 *Ben Jonson*, ed. C. H. Herford and Percy and Evelyn Simpson, 11 vols (Oxford, 1925–52), III, p. 421.

7 Ibid., VIII, p. 44.

8 *John Dryden 'Of Dramatic Poesy' and Other Critical Essays*, ed. George Watson, 2 vols (London, 1962), I, p. 68.

9 John Aubrey, *Brief Lives*, ed. Oliver Lawson Dick (Ann Arbor, 1957), p. 21.

10 Gerald Eades Bentley, *The Profession of Dramatist in Shakespeare's Time 1590–1642* (Princeton, 1971), p. 199.

11 Neil Carson, 'Collaborative playwriting: the Chettle, Dekker, Heywood syndicate', *Theatre Research International* 14 (1989), 22.

12 Cyrus Hoy, 'The shares of Fletcher and his collaborators in the Beaumont and Fletcher canon', *SB* 11 (1958), 87. Both Hoy's methods and assumptions have been challenged by Jeffrey A. Masten in 'Beaumont and/or Fletcher: collaboration and the interpretation of renaissance drama', *English Literary History* 59 (1992), 341–4, and by McMullen, *The Politics of Unease*, pp. 148–9.

13 E. K. Chambers, *The Elizabethan Stage*, 4 vols (1923; rpt Oxford, 1951), IV, pp. 125–7.

14 For the unusual relationships among these editions see Williams, pp. 174–5.

15 A collaborative comedy written for the Queen's Revels Children, *The Scornful Lady* is usually assigned to *c.* 1610, but its limits are 1610–13, so there may have been one more joint play before Beaumont's departure and Fletcher's brief collaboration with Shakespeare. In late 1612 or early 1613 Beaumont composed *The Masque of the Inner Temple and Gray's Inn* for performance on 20 February 1613, at the celebrations for the wedding of Princess Elizabeth to the Elector Palatine.

16 Xenophon, *Cyropaedia*, trans. Walter Miller, Loeb Classical Library, 2 vols (London, 1914), II, 7–8. Separate elements of the Panthea story, including Araspes's and Cyrus's discussion of love, were gathered together in the eleventh 'novel' of William Painter's *The Palace of Pleasure* (1566–67; rev. ed. of the whole, 1575) and in a sixteenth-century play acted by the Children of the Chapel Royal, *The Warres of Cyrus* (Q 1594).

17 Finkelpearl in fact sees *Philaster*, *The Maid's Tragedy*, and *A King and No King* as a 'trilogy' written 'in the shadow of Xenophon' and intended in part to remind King James of Cyrus's virtues (*Court and Country Politics*, p. 169).

18 Ovid, *Metamorphoses*, trans. A. D. Melville (Oxford, 1986), p. 235.

19 Richard A. Lanham, *The Motives of Eloquence: Literary Rhetoric in the Renaissance* (New Haven, 1976), pp. 58–63; see also Linda S. Kauffman, *Discourses of Desire* (Ithaca, 1986), p. 21.

20 Turner, pp. xiv–xv.

21 Important, though less specific, classical influences in the contemporary fashion for Juvenalian satire and the emphasis in Elizabethan rhetorical education on the Senecan declamation, are discussed by Eugene M. Waith in chaps 2 and 3 of *The Pattern of Tragicomedy in Beaumont and Fletcher* (1952; rpt New Haven, 1969).

22 A version of this tale appears in the Italian *Ducento novelle del Siñore Celio Malespini* (Venice, 1609), 2.36.

23 Turner, p. xiv.

24 Charles R. Forker, ' "A little more than kin, and less than kind": incest, intimacy, narcissism, and identity in Elizabethan and Stuart drama', *Medieval and Renaissance Drama in England* IV (1989), 14. It should be noted that Forker includes instances beyond brother and sister, and some real as well as mistaken attachments.

25 Turner, p. xv.

26 Guarini's *Compendio della poesia tragicomica* appeared with *Il pastor fido* in the 1602 Italian edition; although Fletcher (and others) knew it, it seems not to have been translated in the seventeenth century. G. K. Hunter discusses Guarini's influence in 'Italian tragicomedy on the English stage', in *Dramatic Identities and Cultural Tradition: Studies in Shakespeare and His Contemporaries* (New York, 1978), pp. 133–56.

27 Quotation from Fletcher's epistle is taken from Cyrus Hoy's edition of the play in *Dramatic Works*, III, p. 497.

28 Ibid., p. 492.

29 *The Faithful Shepherdess* was successfully revived in the 1630s at the court of Charles I, where its rarefied atmosphere suited Queen Henrietta Maria's taste for the cult of platonic love.

30 Waith, *The Pattern of Tragicomedy in Beaumont and Fletcher*, pp. 65–6; see also Waith's 'Characterization in John Fletcher's tragicomedies', *Review of English Studies* 29 (1943), 144–53.

31 R. A. Foakes discusses this emphasis on sexuality in 'Tragicomedy and comic form', in A. R. Braunmuller and J. C. Bulman, eds, *Comedy from Shakespeare to Sheridan* (Newark, 1986), p. 78. Other factors that Foakes sees influencing early seventeenth-century tragicomedy include the impact of the private theatres and court masque, and changes in audience as well as theatrical presentation. Foakes's argument builds on the extended discussion of satire in Waith, *The Pattern of Tragicomedy in Beaumont and Fletcher*, pp. 50–62, and 'The English masque and the functions of comedy', in George Hibbard, ed., *The Elizabethan Theatre* VIII (Port Credit, Ontario, 1982), pp. 144–63. See also Verna A. Foster, 'Sex averted or converted: sexuality and tragicomic genre in the plays of Fletcher', *SEL* 32 (1992), 311–22.

32 John T. Shawcross, 'Tragicomedy as genre, past and present', in Nancy Klein Maguire, ed., *Renaissance Tragicomedy: Explorations in Genre and Politics* (New York, 1987), p. 16.

33 James J. Yoch, 'The Renaissance dramatization of temperance: the Italian revival of tragicomedy and *The Faithful Shepherdess*', in Maguire, ed., *Renaissance Tragicomedy*, p. 116.

34 Debora Shugar makes the point succinctly in 'Castigating Livy: the rape of Lucrece and the "Old Arcadia"' (*RenQ* 51 (1998): in 'monarchic regimes, sex is political' (p. 535).

35 For a more general discussion of the relation of early seventeenth-century drama's crossing of traditional limits to the social and political crossing of boundaries that emerged after the Civil War see Molly Smith, *Breaking Boundaries: Politics and Play in the Drama of Shakespeare and His Contemporaries* (Aldershot, 1998).

36 On the 1590s vogue for chivalric romance see: C. R. Baskervill, 'Some evidence for early Romantic plays in England', *Modern Philology* 14 (Aug., Dec. 1916), 229–51, 467–512; Louis B. Wright, *Middle-class Culture in Elizabethan England* (Chapel Hill, NC, 1935), esp. pp. 375–93; Mary Patchell, *The 'Palmerin' Romances in Elizabethan Prose Fiction* (New York, 1947); Lee Bliss, *Francis Beaumont* (Boston, 1987), pp. 37–9. Trickle-down to the popular level is also indicated in lampoons and in the fact that apprentice Rafe in Beaumont's *The Knight of the Burning Pestle* quotes from a volume of the Palmerin cycle and models his knightly career on such romances.

37 See Alexander Leggatt, *Jacobean Public Theatre* (London, 1992), esp. chap. 2, and for the last point A. R. Braunmuller, 'The arts of the dramatist', in A. R. Braunmuller and Michael Hattaway, eds, *The Cambridge Companion to English Renaissance Drama* (Cambridge, 1990), p. 70.

38 Roberta Florence Brinkley, ed., *Coleridge on the Seventeenth Century* (Durham, NC, 1955), p. 655. Danby's critique is developed in *Poets on Fortune's Hill: Studies in Sidney, Shakespeare, Beaumont & Fletcher* (London, 1952), chaps 6 and 7.

39 See 'The Authors', pp. 2–3, and especially the works by Finkelpearl and McMullan cited there. It is worth noting that Charles II is rumoured to have banned performance of *The Maid's Tragedy*, and in the Restora-

tion Edmund Waller rewrote the fifth act to convert it to tragicomedy and avoid regicide.

40 Richard F. Hardin, *Civil Idolatry: Desacralizing and Monarchy in Spenser, Shakespeare, and Milton* (Newark, NJ, 1992), p. 18.

41 John H. Astington argues that it was in fact the success of this play that convinced the most prestigious London adult company to enlist Beaumont and Fletcher's talents when it took over the Blackfriars theatre, despite the apparent commercial failure of both *The Knight of the Burning Pestle* and *The Faithful Shepherdess* ('The popularity of *Cupid's Revenge*', *SEL* 19 (1979), 215–27).

42 Support for Coleridge and Danby should not be drawn uncritically from the cascade of verses prefacing the First Folio, where some enthusiasts laud Beaumont and Fletcher's theatrical style in terms that ally it with the royalist cause. Both the choice of contributors, a roll-call of Cavalier poets, and the nature of the praise must be seen in the political context of 1647 and the attendant temptation to co-opt dead authors to one's own cause. Jeffrey Masten discusses this point at greater length in *Textual Intercourse: Collaboration, Authorship, and Sexualities in Renaissance Drama* (Cambridge, 1997), pp. 143–52; see also P. W. Thomas, *Sir John Berkenhead, 1617–1679: A Royalist Career in Politics and Polemics* (Oxford, 1969), pp. 134–5, and Robert Markley, ' "Shakespeare to thee was dull": the phenomenon of Fletcher's influence', in Robert Markley and Laurie Finke, eds, *From Renaissance to Restoration: Metamorphoses of the Drama* (Cleveland, OH, 1984), pp. 92–5.

43 For Robert Y. Turner, the plays merely 'exploit the anxieties aroused by James's insistence on his power' but in the end 'placate them' (and the censor) by depicting oppressed 'heroic subjects' whose patient suffering confers honour ('Responses to tyranny in John Fletcher's plays', *Medieval and Renaissance Drama in England* 4 (1989), 127).

44 Glenn Burgess, *Absolute Monarchy and the Stuart Constitution* (New Haven, 1996), p. 98; Burgess also notes that this distinction in contemporary works, such as Jean Bodin's *Six Bookes of a Commonweale* (1576, 'Englished' 1606), can be traced back to Aristotle's *Politics*. In *Tragedies of Tyrants: Political Thought and Theater in the English Renaissance* (Ithaca, 1990), Rebecca W. Bushnell surveys the theory, both classical and Renaissance, and popular drama's tyrants from the Morality Plays to Massinger's *The Roman Actor*.

45 *The Political Works of James I*, ed. Charles Howard McIlwain (Cambridge, MA, 1918; rpt 1965), p. 278.

46 Bushnell, *Tragedies of Tyrants*, p. 51. In her chapter 'Sex and tyranny', Sandra Clark argues that incest provides a kind of 'worst-case scenario for testing that logical corollary of absolutist theory which proposes that for a ruler, desire is its own legitimating principle' (*The Plays of Beaumont and Fletcher: Sexual Themes and Dramatic Representation* (Hemel Hampstead, 1994), p. 117). See also 'Tragicomedy and *The Faithful Shepherdess*', pp. 12–13, on lust as a natural subject for tragicomedy and temperance a prime virtue.

47 Carole Levin, ' "Lust being Lord, there is no trust in kings": passion, King John, and the responsibilities of kingship', in Carole Levin and Karen Robertson, eds, *Sexuality and Politics in Renaissance Drama*

(Lewistown, NY, 1991), p. 255. See also Bushnell, *Tragedies of Tyrants*, p. 163.

48 For particulars of their borrowing, see 'Sources', pp. 5–7.

49 Katherine Duncan-Jones, ed., *Sir Philip Sidney* (Oxford, 1989), pp. 218 and 374n.

50 O. B. Hardison, *The Enduring Monument: A Study of the Idea of Praise in Renaissance Literary Theory and Practice* (1962; rpt Westport, CT, 1973), p. 72. Masten notes that, although not published until 1632, the translation apparently circulated at court (*Textual Intercourse*, p. 93).

51 J. W. Williamson, *The Myth of the Conqueror, Prince Henry Stuart: A Study of 17th Century Personation* (New York, 1978), pp. 22–3; shortly after Henry's death, the Venetian ambassador described him as 'athirst for glory if ever any prince was' (qtd, p. 162). Other details of Henry's life and the hopes invested in him are drawn from this work and from Roy Strong, *Henry, Prince of Wales and England's Lost Renaissance* (London, 1986), and David M. Bergeron, *Shakespeare's Romances and the Royal Family* (Lawrence, KA, 1985).

52 In *Intertextuality and Romance in Renaissance Drama: The Staging of Nostalgia* (New York, 1992), Richard Hillman traces the line of inheritance and identification of Prince Henry 'with his heroic forbear [*sic*]' (p. 163). Strong finds the investiture ceremonies a 'thinly veiled focus for a revival of the Elizabethan war party'(*Henry, Prince of Wales*, p. 141).

53 Bergeron quotes descriptions of Princess's Elizabeth to support his suggestion that Beaumont and Fletcher's idealised Panthea may be modelled on her (*Shakespeare's Romances*, p. 60).

54 Williamson, *Myth of the Conqueror*, pp. 51–3, and Strong, *Henry, Prince of Wales*, pp. 179–80. Appropriately, given Henry's interest in using foreign expansion to further religious conversion (via his participation in the Virginia, East India, and Northwest Passage Companies), Beaumont's masque celebrated reforming missionary knights.

55 See Graham Parry, *The Golden Age Restor'd: The Culture of the Stuart Court, 1603–42* (Manchester, 1981), pp. 78–9; Margot Heinemann, 'Political drama', in Braunmuller and Hattaway, eds, *The Cambridge Companion to English Renaissance Drama*, esp. pp. 161–2. Analysing the 'intertextual signs of fantasy and futility' in *Philaster*, Hillman concludes that by the time of Beaumont and Fletcher the 'promise of romance is virtually exhausted' (*Intertextuality and Romance*, p. 171).

56 Other plays clustered in these years (*Philaster*, Shakespeare's late plays) reflect the same concerns. James was not secretive in his deliberations; they were a matter of general interest (and court gossip), and their outcome carried political significance for all of his subjects.

57 Foreign ambassadors as well as domestic observers reported cool obedience on Henry's part and some resistance to his son's eagerness for his new rights and revenues (and possible jealousy) on his father's. The Venetian ambassador's report in June 1610 is quoted in Williamson, *Myth of the Conqueror*, p. 119; see also pp. 127–8, 131, 138.

58 Bergeron, *Shakespeare's Romances*, p. 51; Williamson, *Myth of the Conqueror*, pp. 60–1, 180–4. By some, of course, such traits could be interpreted as the pride and decisiveness befitting the future leader of the Protestant cause both at home and against Catholic Europe.

59 Finkelpearl, *Court and Country Politics*, p. 169. See also Jean-Pierre
   Teissedou, 'L'Asolutisme en question dans *A King and No King*', in Jean-
   Paul Debax and Yves Peyre, eds, *Coriolan: théâtre et politique* (Toulouse,
   1984), pp. 242–3.

60 Perhaps pertinent to Arbace's 'tyrannous' behaviour is Burgess's conclusion that contemporaries worried less about King James's claims of
   divine right than about his arbitrary rule by proclamation (*Absolute
   Monarchy and the Stuart Constitution*, p. 48).

61 Quoting from James's 1610 speeches to Parliament asserting that kings
   were as gods, David Laird concludes that *A King and No King* is
   informed by a linguistic scepticism 'shared with the defenders of English
   Common Law and the more radical members of parliament' ('"A
   curious way of torturing": language and ideological transformation in
   A King and No King', in James Redmond, ed., *Drama and Philosophy*,
   Themes in Drama 12 (Cambridge, 1990), pp. 108–9).

62 Although we do not know how 1.1 was originally staged, in the eighteenth century Arbaces seems clearly to have been played to evoke laugh-
   ter in this scene (see 'Stage history', p. 35).

63 The Morality Play structural model was suggested by Arthur Mizener,
   'The high design of *A King and No King*', *Modern Philology* 38 (1940),
   133–54, and elaborated by Robert K. Turner, Jr, in 'The morality of *A
   King and No King*', *Renaissance Papers* (1961), 93–103 (also the basis for
   Turner's Regents Renaissance edition's analysis).

64 Sandra Clark, *The Plays of Beaumont and Fletcher*, p. 111.

65 In modern terminology, Arbaces suffers a psychic regression. See
   Margaret Mahler, *On Human Symbiosis and the Vicissitudes of Individua-
   tion* (New York, 1968), esp. pp. 53–4, for a discussion of the pre-Oedipal
   identity crisis Beaumont and Fletcher seem to figure in the fears of
   dissolution that rack their young protagonists. Their plays are full of
   ungovernable rivers and swallowing seas, an imagery that gains additional force from Renaissance humoral psychology, where it expresses a
   disturbance in the precarious balance of the four bodily fluids that deter-
   mine one's state of mind as well as physical well-being.

66 In 'The structural uses of incest in English Renaissance drama', *Renaissance Drama*, n.s. XV (1984), Lois E. Bueler concludes that playwrights
   recognised significant opportunities beyond audience titillation:
   structural usefulness in complicating and unravelling plots; thematic
   possibilities for exploring the relation of individual passion to social well-
   being (p. 116). The difficulties initiated by Henry VIII continued under
   Elizabeth and James and insured continued interest; on the pervasive
   recurrence of this issue of incest see Bruce Thomas Boehrer, *Monarchy
   and Incest in Renaissance England: Culture, Kinship, and Kingship*
   (Philadelphia, 1992). In life, as in drama, incest also presented a frustrating yet insurmountable impediment to marriage for an aristocracy
   whose patriarchal need for lineal descendants often clashed with
   complex—and changing—canons of forbidden degrees of consanguin-
   ity or affinity.

67 Keith Thomas, *Man and the Natural World: Changing Attitudes in England
   1500–1800* (London, 1983), p. 38. Thomas notes that incest was not a
   secular crime until the twentieth century.

68 Molly Smith discusses the potential use of incest, exemplified in tragedies by Middleton and Ford, 'as a weapon for undermining traditional orthodoxies such as patriarchy'; rather than a mark of decadence, it may reflect an 'intense preoccupation with the sociopolitical concerns of early Stuart England' (*Breaking Boundaries*, p. 109).

69 In *Anxious Masculinity in Early Modern England* (Cambridge, 1996), Mark Breitenberg suggestively discusses this destructive circularity of forbidden desire in relation to Tarquin in Shakespeare's *The Rape of Lucrece* (p. 99).

70 The dates mentioned in the play are presumably meant to be suggestive rather than literal, but we are told that Gobrius was appointed Lord Protector on the old king's death, when Arbaces was only six, and that, since Arbaces has not seen Panthea since she was nine, he must have gone off to war in his mid-teens. He has proved his valour, but we are probably to assume that the politically advantageous marriage he intends for his sister and Tigranes is his first act of statecraft.

71 For further discussion of lust as a mark of effeminacy see Phyllis Rackin, 'Historical difference/sexual difference', in Jean R. Brink, ed., *Privileging Gender in Early Modern England* (Kirksville, MO, 1993), esp. pp. 46–7, and Michel Foucault, *The History of Sexuality*, vol. 2, trans. Robert Hurley (New York, 1990), pp. 82–6.

72 Richard A. McCabe, *Incest, Drama and Nature's Law 1550–1700* (Cambridge, 1993), p. 200.

73 Clifford Leech, *The John Fletcher Plays* (Cambridge, MA, 1962), p. 80.

74 Masten, *Textual Intercourse*, p. 96.

75 As Sandra Clark notes, though in another context, the 'critique of absolutism . . . does not necessarily extend to a critique of the patriarchal structures of society' (*The Plays of Beaumont and Fletcher*, p. 158).

76 On the discomfort associated with tragicomedy's endings see Foster, 'Sex averted or converted', pp. 318–19.

77 Franco Moretti remarks of *Measure* that its denouement appears 'to abolish the irreversibility of history and render the past everlasting' ('"A huge eclipse": tragic form and the deconsecration of sovereignty', *Genre* 15 (1982), p. 23).

78 On these differences see Lee Bliss, 'Tragicomic romance for the King's Men, 1609–1611: Shakespeare, Beaumont, and Fletcher', in *Comedy from Shakespeare to Sheridan*, pp. 148–64. The charge of cynicism is usually based on analyses that wholly elide Tigranes's importance. Concentrating solely on Arbaces, one might conclude with Michael Neill that in 'Beaumont and Fletcher's libertine skepticism . . . Men finally *are* nothing more than sophistical beasts; and their happiness consists rather in giving way to their beastliness, than in striving to be lords of creation—kings' ('The defence of contraries: skeptical paradox in *A King and No King*', *SEL* 21 (1981), 332).

79 We are reminded twice that putting a false heir on the throne constitutes treason (2.1.47–9; 5.4.244–8), though this is at the end tacitly forgiven in both Arane and Gobrius. Gobrius's success in frustrating Arane's plots is retold at 1.1.479–81.

80 Tragicomic plays that re-inscribe traditional hierarchies need not, of course, be hopelessly starry-eyed about the political or social order. Both

Marston's *The Malcontent* and Shakespeare's *Measure for Measure* avoid death and conclude with a restoration of 'right' order (where birth and merit handily coincide), but their view of human nature is dark and their idealised rulers need all the arts of politic statecraft to effect those happy endings (and, in the case of *Measure,* have not been thought to do so in an entirely satisfying manner).

81 To say with David Laird that 'Gobrius's plotting is intended to expose the young king to what lies beyond his command and thus to curb his arrogance and pride' grants Gobrius a patriotic altruism the play may not intend ('"A curious way of torturing"', p. 110). The only incentive he actually mentions is that 'She sware you should be king' (5.4.230). Laird does cite passages in King James's writings and speech to Parliament in spring 1610 that support a general contention that the play probes 'attitudes and assumptions implicit in the language of power . . . the glittering rhetoric of monarchical absolutism' (p. 108).

82 In 'The multiple plot in Fletcherian tragicomedies', *SEL* 33 (1993), Mark E. Bingham notes the significance of the plot/sub-plot juxtapositions but believes that the 'intended effect' is 'a heightening of the sense of seriousness in the main plot by its extreme distance from the comedy of the Bessus episodes' (p. 415).

83 Foster notes of 4.4 that 'if the moral development of this scene is towards tragedy, its proxemic pattern is decidedly comic' in both their self-deceptions and physical movements ('Sex averted or converted', p. 316).

84 Nicholas F. Radel finds a mode of artificial theatricality typical of Beaumont and Fletcher's tragicomedy, and he interestingly discusses the effect of the speakers' apparent disengagement from reality in '"Then thus I turne my language to you": the transformation of theatrical language in *Philaster*', *Medieval and Renaissance Drama in England* 3 (1986), 129–47.

85 Waith, *The Pattern of Tragicomedy in Beaumont and Fletcher*, p. 34.

86 *A King and No King* openly plays with our expectations; compared to *Philaster*, it is positively rife with indications that things are not what they seem and hence the situation not as dire as it appears. As early as 2.1 Gobrius's and Arane's extensive private conversation leads us to doubt her unnaturalness in trying to kill Arbaces, to wonder why she questions reference to him as 'king', and to hope for later elucidation of the secret plan she suggests Gobrius has a-ripening. Arane virtually disappears until 5.4, but our interest in Gobrius does not. We heard in 1.1 of his letters extolling Panthea, 'grown in beauty and in grace' (1.1.493), and from 3.1 on we hear him speak of her in unexpected but titillatingly erotic language.

87 Chambers, *Elizabethan Stage*, IV, p. 125.

88 Although the lease for the Blackfriars theatre had been signed in August 1608, plague restrictions probably prevented public performances before late 1609 or early 1610.

89 Critics have sometimes assumed that from the beginning Blackfriars plays were written to appeal to patrons both socially superior to and better educated than those at the Globe, but Andrew Gurr argues persuasively that before the 1630s, 'and certainly in the years from 1609

until Burbage died in 1619, the company saw itself as catering to the whole of society, and it offered the same fare at both playhouses' (*Playgoing in Shakespeare's London* (Cambridge, 1987), p. 169).

90 The earlier revival or the 1606 quarto might have given some impetus to the inspiration for Shakespeare's *Cymbeline* and Beaumont and Fletcher's first joint tragicomedy *Philaster*, both usually dated 1609–10. In *The Repertory of Shakespeare's Company* (Fayetteville, AR, 1991), Roslyn Lander Knutson argues that since *Mucedorus* was 'on stage both around 1605–06 and 1610–11 . . . it was in a position to influence the romances and tragicomedies throughout 1607–1613' (pp. 142–3).

91 Chambers, *Elizabethan Stage*, IV, pp. 125–8, and J. Leeds Barroll's Table 2 in Clifford Leech and T. W. Craik, gen. eds, *The Revels History of Drama in English, Volume III: 1576–1613* (London, 1975), pp. 92–3. Knutson sees the King's Men's commercial strategy reflected in their 1612–13 court offerings, where we have such a substantial list of plays: four new plays, at least five continued from 1611–12, and nine in revival (*Repertory of Shakespeare's Company*, p. 143).

92 At court, 10 February 1631 and 10 January 1637. An overwhelming majority of the twenty-two plays acted in the 1636–37 revels season were by Beaumont and Fletcher; for the King's Men's bill see Bentley, *The Jacobean and Caroline Stage*, I, pp. 111, 51–2.

93 Arthur Colby Sprague, *Beaumont and Fletcher on the Restoration Stage* (1926; rpt New York, 1954), p. 10.

94 Ibid., p. 3. Gerald Eades Bentley notes that three weekly journals reported the raid and that 'at least one of the players was arrested and taken to gaol' (Philip Edwards, et al., gen. eds, *The Revels History of Drama in English, Volume IV: 1613–1660* (London, 1981), p. 122).

95 H. E. Rollins, 'A contribution to the history of Commonwealth drama', *Studies in Philology* 18 (1921), 313.

96 See 'The play', pp. 14–16 and n. 42.

97 Sprague, *Beaumont and Fletcher on the Restoration Stage*, p. 14.

98 John Harold Wilson, *The Influence of Beaumont and Fletcher on Restoration Drama* (Columbus, OH, 1928), pp. 8–9.

99 Beaumont and Fletcher's more serious works were not ignored: *The Maid's Tragedy* enjoyed a strong revival pattern as did, to a lesser extent, Fletcher's *Bonduca* and *Valentinian*. Only Jonson's major comedies fared well, while Shakespeare was valued almost exclusively for his tragedies.

100 William Van Lennep, ed., *The London Stage, 1660–1800*, Part I (1660–1700) (Carbondale, IL, 1965), p. 22; Sprague, *Beaumont and Fletcher on the Restoration Stage*, p. 15.

101 Helen McAfee, *Pepys on the Restoration Stage* (New Haven, 1916), pp. 89–90.

102 Sprague, *Beaumont and Fletcher on the Restoration Stage*, p. 20.

103 Ibid., p. 34. The elegy also praises Clun's Falstaff and Iago.

104 John Downes, *Roscius Anglicanus* (1708), ed. Montague Summers (1929; rpt New York, 1968), p. 5. Downes includes the rest of the cast: Tygranes played by Mr Burt, Mardonius by Major Mohun, Gobrius by Mr Wintersel, Lygones by Mr Cartwright, Bessus by Mr Shotterel, Arane by Mrs Corey.

105 'An essay of dramatic poesy', in *Essays of John Dryden*, ed. W. P. Ker, 2 vols (Oxford, 1926), I, p. 81.

106 Wendy Griswold, *Renaissance Revivals: City Comedy and Revenge Tragedy in the London Theatre, 1576–1980* (Chicago, 1986), p. 115.

107 In ' "True Tragicomedies" of the Civil War and Commonwealth', Lois Potter surveys the 'remarkable number of plays written and published in the mid-seventeenth century which described themselves as tragicomedies' (*Renaissance Tragicomedy*, p. 196). In *Secret Rites and Secret Writing: Royalist Literature, 1641–1660* (Cambridge, 1989), Potter studies political allusions to earlier plays, some made simply 'for the sake of their title: *A King and No King*, so relevant to Charles I's situation in the 1640s and Charles II's in the 1650s, is an obvious case' (p. 116). She notes that Edmund Noyes, disapproving of *A King and No King*'s being performed for the Princess Royal in 1654, apparently objects to the satiric implications of the anti-Royalist title rather than the play itself (p. 83). Nahum Tate's *A Duke and No Duke* (1685) offers a later example of capitalising on the provocative title, since this farce, as Dyce pointed out, is borrowed almost wholesale from Sir Aston Cockayne's comedy *Trappolin Suppos'd a Prince* (Dyce, p. 234); so too the anonymous ballad opera *A King and No King, or The Polish Squabble* that played Goodman's Fields theatre in 1733 (Allardyce Nicoll, *A History of English Drama 1660–1900*, 2 vols (1925; rpt Cambridge, 1952), II, p. 377).

108 Nancy Klein Maguire, 'The "whole truth" of Restoration tragicomedy', in *Renaissance Tragicomedy*, pp. 221, 219.

109 Allardyce Nicoll, *A History of Restoration Drama, 1660–1700* (Cambridge, 1923), pp. 306–7.

110 Wintershall [*sic*] again played Gobrius; Mr Cartwright, Lygones; Major Mohun, Mardonius; Mrs Corey, Arane. Bacurius was now played by Mr Lydall, Bessus by Mr Lacy or Mr Shottrell [*sic*], Panthea by Mrs Cox, and Spaconia by Mrs Marshall (Sprague, *Beaumont and Fletcher on the Restoration Stage*, pp. 35–6). The 1675 production may indeed have sparked the publication of Q7.

111 *The Critical Works of Thomas Rymer*, ed. Curt A. Zimansky (New Haven, 1956), pp. 19, 43.

112 Quoted in Sprague, *Beaumont and Fletcher on the Restoration Stage*, p. 38.

113 Besides Kynaston and Mohun, the rest of those listed were new: Bacurius was played by Mr Wiltshire, Bessus by Mr Leigh, Panthea by Mrs Barrer (Barry), Spaconia by Mrs Cook (Sprague, *Beaumont and Fletcher on the Restoration Stage*, pp. 57–8). Interestingly, here and in the earlier cast lists cited in these notes, Mardonius seems to have been played by an ex-soldier, Major Mohan. Mohan died in October 1684.

114 *The London Stage*, Part I, p. 346.

115 Ibid., pp. 355–6.

116 Gerard Langbaine, *An Account of the English Poets*, 1691 (rpt Los Angeles, 1971), p. 210. There may have been a revival around this time, for Q8 appeared in 1693.

117 Wilson, *The Influence of Beaumont and Fletcher on Restoration Drama*, pp. 68–9.

118 'An essay of dramatic poesy', in *The Essays of John Dryden*, I, pp. 80–1.

119 *Tragedies of the Last Age*, in *The Critical Works of Thomas Rymer*, p. 17.

120 Ibid., p. 50.

121 Dryden, 'Preface to *Troilus and Cressida*, containing The grounds of criticism in tragedy', in *The Essays of John Dryden*, p. 212.

122 Ibid., p. 215. For a more detailed account of this shift in the conception of imitation from the Renaissance to Locke, focusing particularly on Dryden, see Rose A. Zimbardo, 'Dramatic imitation of nature in the Restoration's seventeenth-century predecessors' (in *From Renaissance to Restoration*, pp. 57–86).

123 Dryden, 'The grounds of criticism in tragedy', p. 217.

124 Ibid.

125 The historically determined appeal of *A King and No King* is one thread of this volume's analysis of the play. Two essays concerned with this issue are Robert Giddins, '*A King and No King*: monarchy and royalty as discourse in Elizabethan and Jacobean drama', in *Jacobean Poetry and Prose* (New York, 1988), pp. 164–93, and, more interestingly, Stephan P. Flores, '"I am Arbaces, we all fellow subjects": the political appeal of Beaumont and Fletcher's *A King and No King* on the Restoration stage', *Essays in Literature* 20 (1993), 171–96.

126 *The London Stage*, Part II, vol. I (1700–17), p. 69; Sprague, *Beaumont and Fletcher on the Restoration Stage*, p. 86.

127 *The London Stage*, Part II, vol. I (1700–17), pp. 92, 103.

128 Ibid., pp. 121, 138.

129 Ibid., pp. lix–lx; Sprague, *Beaumont and Fletcher on the Restoration Stage*, p. 104.

130 The cast list also includes Boheme as Arbaces, Walker as Tigranes, Ryan as Mardonius, Diggs as Bacurius, Leigh as Gobrius, Mrs Knight as Arane, Mrs Parker as Spaconia, Mrs Brett as Panthea (*The London Stage*, Part II, vol. II (1717–29), p. 767).

131 Ibid., Part III, vol. I (1729–36), p. 332.

132 Theophilus Cibber, *The Lives of the Poets of Great Britain and Ireland* (1753), 4 vols (rpt in one vol., Hildesheim, 1968), pp. 158–9.

133 Robert Gale Noyes, *Ben Jonson on the English Stage, 1660–1776* (Cambridge, MA, 1935), p. 31.

134 Thomas Davies, *Dramatic Miscellanies*, 1784, 3 vols (rpt, New York, 1971), II, pp. 26–8.

135 This report on the alterations appeared in *Public Advertiser*, 15 January 1788 (qtd in *The London Stage*, Part V, vol. II (1783–92), p. 1034). Donald J. Rulfs reproduces a similar description from the *London Chronicle* (12–15 January 1788) that also notes 'the omission of exceptionable passages' ('Beaumont and Fletcher on the London stage 1776–1833', *Publications of the Modern Language Association* 63 (1948), p. 1252).

136 Qtd, without specific date or page number for the *Post*, in Charles Harold Gray, *Theatrical Criticism in London to 1795* (1931; rpt New York 1964), p. 279. The other 'Principal Characters' were Pope as Arbaces, Farren as Tigranes, Aickin as Mardonius, Hull as Gobrius, Fearon as Bacurius, Thompson as Ligones, Wewitzer and Cubitt as Swordmen. Mrs Platt played Queen Mother (Arane), Miss Brunton Panthea, and Mrs Bernard Spaconia. Occasional Prologue, by Henry Sampson

Woodfall, spoken by Mr Farren (*The London Stage*, Part V, vol. II (1783–92), p. 1034).

137 Dyce, p. 234.

138 Bond, p. 247.

139 'Critical reflections on the old English dramatic writers', in *The Dramatic Works of Philip Massinger*, ed. Thomas Coxeter, 4 vols (London, 1761)

140 Colman, p. 71. The last recorded performance before Colman's 1778 edn would have been in 1733. In his 1887 edn, Strachey states that *A King and No King* has not been performed since 1778 (p. 2), but this is almost certainly a misprint for 1788.

141 Colman, p. 108. Colman is forced to concede that it 'would perhaps require a nice hand to make this play thoroughly relished by a modern audience'.

142 Mason, pp. iii–v.

143 Weber, p. 134. Since Weber also asserts that 'no alterations of it have been attempted', he seems unaware of Harris's 1788 version. If Weber's calculations are correct, there may have been a revival around 1760 of which no record remains.

144 Ibid., p. 137.

145 T. W. Craik, ed., *The Maid's Tragedy* (Manchester, 1988), pp. 30–1.

146 I am indebted in the following paragraphs to the work of Turner, both his edition and his article 'Printing of *A King and No King*, Q1', *SB* 18 (1965), 255–61, and to Williams's Textual Introduction (pp. 169–81).

147 Hans Walter Gabler, 'John Beale's compositors in *A King and No King* Q1 (1619)', *SB* 24 (1971), 138–43. Although both intricate and tentative, this account may be correct; as Williams observes, however, 'it could be wished that the distinguishing characteristics of these . . . men were more numerous' (p. 181).

148 Gabler, 'John Beale's compositors', p. 142.

149 Turner, p. xxix.

150 Alden, p. 340.

151 Turner, p. xxix.

152 Berta Sturman, 'The Second Quarto of *A King and No King*, 1625', *SB* 4 (1951–52), 166–70.

153 Turner, p. xxviii.

154 Williams, p. 174; for examples of additional variants between Q1 and Q2 see pp. 172–3.

155 Williams, p. 175 (which also provides a diagram of the stemma of the seventeenth-century editions).

156 Turner's edition offers an Historical Collation of the early editions (to Q8, 1693); he was also able to check the copies of Q1 located in the United States: the Folger Shakespeare Library, the Henry E. Huntington Library, the Harvard University Library, and the Boston Public Library (where, he notes, only Sheets A to D (though not A1, A2) are from Q1, while the rest derive from Q3). Williams added the other two British copies of Q1 for his collation, those in the British Library and the Bodleian Library.

157 See Williams, pp. 176–80, for the manuscript readings and specific comparisons with Q1 and Q2.

A King and no King.

Acted at the *Globe*, by his Maie-
sties Seruants:

Written by *Francis Beamount*, and *Iohn Flecher*.

AT LONDON

Printed for *Thomas Walkley*, and are to bee fold
at his fhoppe at the Eagle and Childe in
Brittans-Burſſe. 1619.

Title-page of the 1619 quarto
(by permission of The Folger Shakespeare Library)

A KING
AND NO KING

[THE PERSONATED PERSONS.

ARBACES, *King of Iberia.*
TIGRANES, *King of Armenia.*
GOBRIUS, *Lord Protector of Iberia and father of Arbaces.*
BACURIUS, *an Iberian lord.*
MARDONIUS } *Captains in the Iberian army.*
BESSUS
LIGONES, *an Armenian statesman, father of Spaconia.*
THREE MEN
A WOMAN
PHILIP, *servant of a Citizen's Wife.*
TWO CITIZENS' WIVES
TWO SWORDMEN
A BOY, *servant of Bessus.*
ARANE, *the Iberian Queen Mother.*
PANTHEA, *her daughter.*
SPACONIA, *an Armenian lady, daughter of Ligones.*
GENTLEMEN, ATTENDANTS, SERVANTS, MESSENGERS, WAITING-
WOMEN]

To the Right Worshipful, and Worthy Knight,
Sir Henry Nevill.

Worthy Sir,
I present, or rather return unto your view, that which formerly
hath been received from you, hereby effecting what you did   5
desire. To commend the work in my unlearned method were
rather to detract from it than to give it any lustre. It sufficeth
it hath your worship's approbation and patronage, to the
commendation of the authors and encouragement of their
further labours. And thus wholly committing myself and it to   10
your worship's dispose, I rest ever ready to do you service, not
only in the like but in what I may.

Thomas Walkley.

---

2. *Sir Henry Nevill*] Nevill(e), of Billingsbear, Berkshire, was born in 1588,
matriculated at Merton College, Oxford, in 1600, proceeded B.A. in 1603,
and by 1614 was a student of law at Lincoln's Inn, one of the Inns of Court
in London. He twice served as a Member of Parliament, was for a time legier
ambassador at Paris, and died in 1629. He was the son of Sir Henry Neville
(1564?–1615), an Elizabethan courtier and diplomat, and father of another
Henry Neville (1620–94), a political figure and miscellaneous writer. C. M.
Gayley thinks the original owner of the manuscript to which Walkley refers
was the elder Sir Henry (*Francis Beaumont, Dramatist* (London, 1914), pp.
145–9).

9–10. *their further labours*] Walkley's prefatory letter was presumably
written in 1619, the year in which he published the play's first quarto; Beaumont had died in 1616. The anomalous phrase may reflect Walkley's acquaintance with the manuscript owner only, not the playwrights. Bond, however,
makes the likely suggestion that it refers to the future publication of other
Beaumont and Fletcher plays. Walkley soon brought out the first quarto of
Philaster (1620), as well as other King's Men plays for which he had acquired
the right of publication, Beaumont and Fletcher's *Thierry and Theodoret*
(1621) and Shakespeare's *Othello* (1622). Walkley is also responsible for the
'corrected' second quartos of Beaumont and Fletcher's *Philaster* (1622) and
A King and No King (1625).

A King and No King

Act I

[I.I]

Enter MARDONIUS *and* BESSUS.

Mardonius. Bessus, the King has made a fair hand on't; h'as
ended the wars at a blow. Would my sword had a close
basket hilt to hold wine and the blade would make knives,
for we shall have nothing but eating and drinking.
Bessus. We that are commanders shall do well enough.   5
Mardonius. Faith, Bessus, such commanders as thou may. I
had as lief set thee *perdue*, for a pudding i' th' dark, as
Alexander the Great.
Bessus. I love these jests exceedingly.
Mardonius. I think thou lovest them better than quarrelling,   10
Bessus; I'll say so much i' thy behalf. And yet thou art
valiant enough upon a retreat; I think thou wouldst kill
any man that stopped thee, an thou couldst.
Bessus. But was not this a brave combat, Mardonius?
Mardonius. Why, didst thou see't?   15
Bessus. You stood with me.
Mardonius. I did so, but me thought thou winkst every blow
they strake.

1.1] *Theobald; not in Q1.* 0.1. *Enter* ... BESSUS.] *Q1; Enter ... Bessus, two
Captaines. Q2.* 13. an] *Q1* (and); if *Q2.*

---

1. *made a fair hand*] made a success of it.
7–8. *lief . . . Great*] readily put you in an important and dangerous
position—if the enemy were only a pudding—as Alexander the Great.
Mardonius's mockery is clear in his qualification of the enemy's fierceness,
but perhaps also in his choice of the military idiom for taking a position in
ambush, 'set perdue'; Bond notes that Cartwright's *Ordinary* (1651) com-
pares a perdue lying out in the field to a fish half hidden by the fennel in
which it is served.
13. *an*] if.
14. *brave*] (1) 'courageous', but also the older meaning particularly appropriate to Bessus's level of appreciation, (2) 'fine, making a good display'.
18. *strake*] struck.

Bessus. Well, I believe there are better soldiers than I that
    never saw two princes fight in lists.   20
Mardonius. By my troth, I think so too, Bessus, many a thou-
    sand; but certainly all that are worse than thou have seen
    as much.
Bessus. 'Twas bravely done of our king.
Mardonius. Yes, if he had not ended the wars. I am glad thou   25
    dar'st talk of such dangerous businesses.
Bessus. To take a prince prisoner in the heart of his own
    country in single combat!
Mardonius. See how thy blood cruddles at this. I think thou
    wouldst be contented to be beaten in this passion.   30
Bessus. Shall I tell you truly?
Mardonius. Ay.
Bessus. I could willingly venter for it.
Mardonius. Um; no venter neither, good Bessus.
Bessus. Let me not live if I do not think it is a braver piece of   35
    service than that I'm so famed for.
Mardonius. Why, art thou famed for any valour?
Bessus. I famed! Ay, I warrant you.
Mardonius. I am very heartily glad on't. I have been with thee
    ever since thou cam'st a' th' wars, and this is the first word   40
    that ever I heard on't. Prithee, who fames thee?
Bessus. The Christian world.
Mardonius. 'Tis heathenishly done of them. In my con-
    science, thou deservest it not.
Bessus. Yes, I ha' done good service.   45
Mardonius. I do not know how thou mayst wait of a man in's
    chamber or thy agility in shifting a trencher, but other-
    wise no service, good Bessus.

---

37. Why, art] *Q2;* Why art *Q1.*   40. a' th'] *Q1;* to th' *Q2.*

---

    20. *in lists*] man-to-man. 'Lists' are the barriers surrounding the ground
for tilting or other knightly combat; by extension, the place of such a martial
contest.
    29. *cruddles*] curdles. According to Weber (1812), this was still the usual
pronunciation of curdles 'in the provinces'.
    30. *passion*] fervour (ironic).
    33. *venter*] venture.
    40. *a' th'*] to the.
    46. *of*] on.
    47. *trencher*] wooden platter.

Bessus. You saw me do the service yourself.

Mardonius. Not so hasty, sweet Bessus. Where was it? Is the   50
place vanished?

Bessus. At Bessus' Desperate Redemption.

Mardonius. Bessus' Desperate Redemption! Where's that?

Bessus. There where I redeemed the day. The place bears my
name.   55

Mardonius. Prithee, who christened it?

Bessus. The soldier.

Mardonius. If I were not a very merrily disposed man, what
would become of thee? One that had but a grain of choler
in the whole composition of his body would send thee of   60
an errand to the worms for putting thy name upon that
field. Did not I beat thee there i' th' head o' th' troops
with a truncheon because thou wouldst needs run away
with thy company when we should charge the enemy?

Bessus. True, but I did not run.   65

Mardonius. Right, Bessus; I beat thee out on't.

Bessus. But came not I up when the day was gone and
redeemed all?

Mardonius. Thou knowst, and so do I, thou meantst to fly,
and, thy fear making thee mistake, thou ranst upon the   70
enemy. And a hot charge thou gav'st, as, I'll do thee right,
thou art furious in running away, and I think we owe thy
fear for our victory. If I were the King and were sure thou
wouldst mistake always and run away upon the enemy,
thou shouldst be general, by this light.   75

Bessus. You'll never leave this till I fall foul.

Mardonius. No more such words, dear Bessus. For though I
have ever known thee a coward and therefore durst never
strike thee, yet if thou proceedst, I will allow thee valiant
and beat thee.   80

---

58. merrily] *Q2* (merily); meerely *Q1*. 69. meantst] *Q2* (meant'st);
mean'st *Q1*.

---

57. *The soldier*] i.e. the soldiery, the troops.

59. *choler*] anger. Choler, or bile, was one of the four humours or chief
bodily fluids whose relative proportion determined one's temperament;
choler disposed one to irascibility.

60–1. *of an*] on an.

62. *head*] front, foremost part.

76. *fall foul*] quarrel, grow angry.

Bessus. Come, come. Our king's a brave fellow.

Mardonius. He is so, Bessus. I wonder how thou com'st to
    know it. But if thou wert a man of understanding, I would
    tell thee he is vainglorious and humble, and angry and
    patient, and merry and dull, and joyful and sorrowful, in   85
    extremities in an hour. Do not think me thy friend for
    this, for if I cared who knew it, thou shouldst not hear it,
    Bessus. Here he is with the prey in his foot.

Senet. Flourish.

Enter ARBACES *and* TIGRANES, *with two* Gentlemen
and Attendants.

Arbaces. Thy sadness, brave Tigranes, takes away
    From my full victory. Am I become   90
    Of so small fame that any man should grieve
    When I o'ercome him? They that placed me here
    Intended it an honour large enough
    For the most valiant living but to dare
    Oppose me single, though he lost the day.   95
    What should afflict you? You are free as I.
    To be my prisoner is to be more free
    Than you were formerly, and never think
    The man I held worthy to combat me
    Shall be used servilely. Thy ransom is   100
    To take my only sister to thy wife—
    A heavy one, Tigranes, for she is
    A lady that the neighbour princes send
    Blanks to fetch home. I have been too unkind
    To her, Tigranes. She but nine year old,   105
    I left her and ne'er saw her since. Your wars

88.1 SD] *Q2; not in Q1.*   88.2. *two* Gentlemen *and*] *Q2 (The two Gentle-*
men); not in Q1.   90. full] *Q2;* fall *Q1.*

---

88. *in his foot*] i.e. like a falcon.
88.1. *Senet. Flourish.*] The senet (also 'sennet') was a set of notes, or
'flourish', on the trumpet or cornet accompanying a ceremonial entrance or
exit. This SD first appears in Q2 and is repeated in subsequent quartos and
F2, though it is omitted by most modern editors; Q2 is also the first to specify
'two Gentlemen' as well as 'Attendants', making this a public entrance
appropriately introduced with a fanfare.
104. *Blanks*] Blank bonds in which Arbaces might insert his own terms
for his sister's marriage.

Have held me long and taught me, though a youth,
The way to victory. She was a pretty child
Then; I was little better. But now fame
Cries loudly on her, and my messengers   110
Make me believe she is a miracle.
She'll make you shrink as I did, with a stroke
But of her eye, Tigranes.
Tigranes.   Is it the course of
Iberia to use their prisoners thus?
Had Fortune thrown my name above Arbaces',   115
I should not thus have talked, for in Armenia
We hold it base. You should have kept your temper
Till you saw home again, where 'tis the fashion
Perhaps to brag.
Arbaces.   Be you my witness, Earth—
Need I to brag? Doth not this captive prince   120
Speak me sufficiently, and all the acts
That I have wrought upon his suffering land?
Should I then boast? Where lies that foot of ground
Within his whole realm that I have not passed
Fighting and conquering? Far then from me   125
Be ostentation. I could tell the world
How I have laid his kingdom desolate
With this sole arm, propped by divinity,
Stripped him out of his glories, and have sent
The pride of all his youth to people graves   130
And made his virgins languish for their loves,
If I would brag. Should I, that have the power
To teach the neighbour world humility,

108–9. child / Then;] *Q1* (childe / Then,); child; / Then *Theobald.*   113.
SH] *Q2 (Tigr.); not in Q1.*

   113. SH *Tigranes.*] The omission of this speech heading in Q1 prompted
Berta Sturman to suggest that 113 was written all on one line in the manuscript from which Q1 was set and that the final word of Arbaces's boast here
was intended as the speech heading for the next speech (*SB* 4 (1951–52),
167–8). Turner argues persuasively that it is more likely 'that the name stood
in the manuscript as part of the text and that the speech prefix was omitted
through eyeskip'.
   121. *Speak* me] Testify.

       Mix with vainglory?
Mardonius [*Aside*].   Indeed, this is none?
Arbaces. Tigranes, no. Did I but take delight   135
       To stretch my deeds, as others do, on words,
       I could amaze my hearers.
Mardonius [*Aside*].   So you do.
Arbaces. But he shall wrong his and my modesty
       That thinks me apt to boast. After an act
       Fit for a god to do upon his foe,   140
       A little glory in a soldier's mouth
       Is well becoming; be it far from vain.
Mardonius [*Aside*]. It's pity that valour should be thus drunk.
Arbaces. I offer you my sister, and you answer
       I do insult—a lady that no suit,   145
       Nor treasure, nor thy crown could purchase thee,
       But that thou foughtst with me.
Tigranes.   Though this be worse
       Than that you spoke before, it strikes not me;
       But that you think to overgrace me with
       The marriage of your sister troubles me.   150
       I would give worlds for ransoms, were they mine,
       Rather than have her.
Arbaces.   See if I insult,
       That am the conqueror and for a ransom
       Offer rich treasure to the conquered,
       Which he refuses, and I bear his scorn!   155
       It cannot be self-flattery to say
       The daughters of your country set by her
       Would see their shame, run home, and blush to death
       At their own foulness. Yet she is not fair
       Nor beautiful; those words express her not.   160
       They say her looks are something excellent

---

147. foughtst] *Q2;* faughst *Q1*.

---

    136. *stretch . . . on*] enlarge . . . with.
    148. *strikes*] (1) impresses (with the metaphor drawn from the process of
minting, where 'strike' = 'imprint an image on a coin or medal'), (2) affects
(an astrological term, where to be 'planet-stricken' is to be suddenly deprived
of life or one of one's faculties).
    159. *foulness*] ugliness.

That wants a name. Yet were she odious,
Her birth deserves the empire of the world,
Sister to such a brother, that hath ta'en
Victory prisoner and throughout the earth   165
Carries her bound, and should he let her loose,
She durst not leave him. Nature did her wrong
To print continual conquest on her cheeks
And make no man worthy for her to take
But me that am too near her; and as strangely   170
She did for me. But you will think I brag.

Mardonius [*Aside*]. I do, I'll be sworn. Thy valour and thy passions severed would have made two excellent fellows in
their kinds. I know not whether I should be sorry thou
art so valiant or so passionate. Would one of 'em were   175
away.

Tigranes. Do I refuse her that I doubt her worth?
Were she as virtuous as she would be thought,
So perfect that no one of her own sex
Would find a want, had she so tempting fair   180
That she could wish it off for damning souls,
I would pay any ransom—twenty times—
Rather than meet her married in my bed.
Perhaps I have a love where I have fixed
Mine eyes, not to be moved, and she on me.   185
I am not fickle.

Arbaces.   Is that all the cause?
Think you, you can so knit yourself in love
To any other that her searching sight
Cannot dissolve it? So, before you tried,
You thought yourself a match for me in fight.   190
Trust me, Tigranes, she can do as much
In peace as I in war; she'll conquer too.
You shall see if you have the power to stand
The force of her swift looks. If you dislike,

162. name. Yet] *Q2;* name yet: *Q1.* 179. one] *Q2;* owne *Q1.* 180.
Would] *Q1;* Could *Q2.* 181. for] *Q2;* her *Q1.* 182. times] *Q1;* lives *Q2.*
192–3. too. / You] *Theobald;* too / You *Q1.*

171. *She*] i.e. Nature.
180. *so . . . fair*] such tempting beauty.
181. *for*] for fear of.

I'll send you home with love and name your ransom   195
   Some other way; but if she be your choice,
   She frees you. To Iberia you must.
Tigranes. Sir, I have learnt a prisoner's sufferance
   And will obey, but give me leave to talk
   In private with some friends before I go.   200
Arbaces. Some two await him forth and see him safe,
   But let him freely send for whom he please,
   And none dare to disturb his conference.
   I will not have him know what bondage is
   Till he be free from me.
                    Exeunt TIGRANES [*and two Attendants*].
                    This prince, Mardonius,   205
   Is full of wisdom, valour, all the graces
   Man can receive.
Mardonius.   And yet you conquered him?
Arbaces. And yet I conquered him and could have done
   Hadst thou joined with him, though thy name in arms
   Be great. Must all men that are virtuous   210
   Think suddenly to match themselves with me?
   I conquered him, and bravely, did I not?
Bessus. And please your majesty, I was afraid at first—
Mardonius. When wert thou other?
Arbaces. Of what?   215
Bessus. That you would not have spied your best advantages,
   for your majesty, in my opinion, lay too high; methinks,
   under favour, you should have lain thus.
Mardonius. Like a tailor at a wake.
Bessus. And then, if't please your majesty to remember, at one   220
   time—by my troth, I wished myself with you.

197. Iberia] *Ileria Q1.*   201. two] *Q1;* to *Q2.*   205. SD *Exeunt . . . Atten-*
dants.] *Weber subst.; Exe. Q1 (after 204 is); Exit Tigranes. Q2 (after is).*   217.
high; methinks,] high me thinkes, *Q1.*

201. *await*] attend.
216. *That*] Because.
217. *lay too high*] assumed too high a fighting stance.
218. *under favour*] with your indulgence.
219. *Like . . . wake*] Mardonius mocks Bessus's advice by suggesting that,
had Arbaces followed it, he would have looked like a tailor at a festival
defending himself against bullies with his yardstick.

Mardonius. 'By my troth', thou wouldst have stunk 'em both
out o' th' lists.
Arbaces. What to do?
Bessus. To put your majesty in mind of an occasion. You lay   225
thus, and Tigranes falsified a blow at your leg, which you
by doing thus avoided; but if you had whipped up your
leg thus and reached him on th' ear, you had made the
blood-royal run about's head.
Mardonius. What country fence-school didst thou learn that
at?   230
Arbaces. Puft! Did I not take him nobly?
Mardonius.   Why you did,
And you have talked enough on't.
Arbaces.   Talked enough!
While you confine my words, by heaven and earth,
I were much better be a king of beasts
Than such a people.—If I had not patience   235
Above a god, I should be called a tyrant
Throughout the world. They will offend to death
Each minute.—Let me hear thee speak again
And thou art earth again. Why, this is like
Tigranes' speech, that needs would say I bragged.   240
Bessus, he said I bragged.
Bessus. Ha, ha, ha.
Arbaces.   Why dost thou laugh?—
By all the world, I'm grown ridiculous
To my own subjects. Tie me to a chair
And jest at me! But I shall make a start   245
And punish some, that other will take heed
How they are haughty. Who will answer me?
He said I boasted.—Speak, Mardonius.
Did I?—He will not answer. O, my temper!
I give you thanks above that taught my heart   250

---

222. 'By my troth'] *This ed. (in quotation marks);* By my Troth *Q1.*   stunk]
Q2; sunke *Q1.*   229. blood-royal] *Q2;* bloud *Q1.*   232. Talked] *Q7;* Talke
Q1.   233. While] *Q1;* Will *Q2.*   words, by] *Q1;* words? By *Langbaine.*

225. *occasion*] opportunity.
226. *falsified*] feinted.
233. *While*] Of the early quartos, only Q1 offers 'While'; Q2–8, followed
by many editors, read 'Will', which then requires '?' after 'words'.

Patience; I can endure his silence. What, will none
Vouchsafe to give me answer? Am I grown
To such a poor respect? Or do you mean
To break my wind? Speak. Speak soon, one of you,
Or else by heaven—
1 Gentleman.   So please your—
Arbaces.   Monstrous!   255
I cannot be heard out; they cut me off
As if I were too saucy. I will live
In woods and talk to trees; they will allow me
To end what I begin. The meanest subject
Can find a freedom to discharge his soul,   260
And not I.—Now it is a time to speak;
I harken.
1 Gentleman. May it please—
Arbaces.   I mean not you.
Did not I stop you once? But I am grown
To balk. But I desire, let another speak.
2 Gentleman. I hope your majesty—
Arbaces.   Thou drawst thy words   265
That I must wait an hour where other men
Can hear in instants. Throw your words away
Quick and to purpose; I have told you this.
Bessus. An't please your majesty—
Arbaces. Wilt thou devour me? This is such a rudeness   270
As yet you never showed me, and I want
Power to command too, else Mardonius

---

252. answer] *Q2;* audience *Q1.*   254. soon, one] *Q1* (soone one*);* some
one *Q2.*   264. To balk. But I desire] *Q1* (balke, but*);* To balke, but I defie
Q2; To talk but idly *Theobald.*   265. drawst] *Q1;* drawl'st *Q2* (draul'st*).*
272. too] *Q2;* mee *Q1;* ye *Weber.*

---

254. *break my wind*] keep me talking till I am out of breath.
264. *To . . . desire*] Theobald's emendation, on Seward's suggestion ('talke
but idlie'), is attractive if Q2's 'I defie' is assumed to be the correct reading.
As Turner points out, however, there is nothing manifestly wrong with Q1 if
'to balk' is understood as 'a thing that is balked' (checked, hindered; cf. *OED*
Balk *v¹* III 5). Q2's 'defie' could easily be a misreading of Q1's 'desire'.
265. *drawst*] draw out. Q2's 'draul'st' may be a valid correction, but it
might also be a misreading or the substitution of a synonym; with the exception of Weber, editors before Turner adopted 'drawl'st'.
272. *too*] Q1's 'me' is probably an unintended echo of the two preceding
instances of 'me' (270, 271).

Would speak at my request.—Were you my king,
I would have answered at your word, Mardonius.
I pray you speak, and truly. Did I boast?   275
Mardonius. Truth will offend you.
Arbaces. You take all great care what will offend me,
    When you dare to utter such things as these.
Mardonius. You told Tigranes you had won his land
    With that sole arm propped by divinity.   280
    Was not that bragging and a wrong to us
    That daily ventured lives?
Arbaces.   O, that thy name
    Were great as mine! Would I had paid my wealth
    It were as great, that I might combat thee!
    I would through all the regions habitable   285
    Search thee and, having found thee, with my sword
    Drive thee about the world till I had met
    Some place that yet man's curiosity
    Hath missed of; there, there would I strike thee dead.
    Forgotten of mankind, such funeral rites   290
    As beasts would give thee thou shouldst have.
Bessus [To the Gentlemen].   The King
    Rages extremely. Shall we slink away?
    He'll strike us.
2 Gentleman [To Bessus]. Content.   [*They move to go.*]
Arbaces. There I would make you know 'twas this sole arm.   295
    I grant you were my instruments and did
    As I commanded you, but 'twas this arm
    Moved you like wheels; it moved you as it pleased.—
    Whither slip you now? What, are you too good
    To wait on me?—Puff! I had need have temper   300
    That rule such people; I have nothing left
    At my own choice. I would I might be private.
    Mean men enjoy themselves, but 'tis our curse
    To have a tumult that, out of their loves,
    Will wait on us whether we will or no.—   305

---

294. SD *They . . . go.*] *This ed.; not in Q1.* 300. Puff!] *Q2 (puffe,); not in
Q1.*

---

300. *Puff!*] Colman, followed by Weber, omits this word, believing it to be
the later insertion (in Q2) of a SD for the actor.
   302. *private*] (1) alone, (2) a private citizen.

Will you be gone?—Why, here they stand like death;
My word moves nothing.
I Gentleman [*To Bessus*].   Must we go?
Bessus.   I know not.
Arbaces. I pray you leave me, sirs.—I'm proud of this,
That they will be entreated from my sight.

> *Exeunt all but* ARBACES *and* MARDONIUS.
> [*Mardonius moves to go.*]

Why now they leave me all.—Mardonius!   310
Mardonius. Sir?
Arbaces. Will you leave me quite alone? Methinks
Civility should teach you more than this,
If I were but your friend. Stay here and wait.
Mardonius. Sir, shall I speak?
Arbaces.   Why, you would now think much   315
To be denied, but I can scarce entreat
What I would have. Do, speak.
Mardonius. But will you hear me out?
Arbaces. With me you article to talk thus? Well,
I will hear you out.   320
Mardonius. Sir, that I have ever lovèd you   [*Kneels.*]
My sword hath spoken for me; that I do,
If it be doubted, I dare call an oath,
A great one, to my witness. And were you
Not my king, from amongst men I should   325
Have chose you out to love above the rest.
Nor can this challenge thanks. For my own sake
I should have doted, because I would have loved
The most deserving man, for so you are.
Arbaces. Alas, Mardonius, rise. You shall not kneel.   330

> [*Raises him.*]

We all are soldiers and all venture lives,
And where there is no difference in men's worths
Titles are jests. Who can outvalue thee?

---

307. SH *I Gentleman.*] *Q2; 2. Gent. Q1.*   309.1. SD *Exeunt . . .* MARDO-
NIUS.] *Q2; not in Q1.*   309.2. SD *Mardonis . . . go.*] *Dyce subst.; not in Q1.*
321. SD] *Weber; not in Q1.*   328. doted] *Q1;* done *Q2.*   330. SD] *Dyce;
not in Q1.*

---

319. *article*] impose conditions, bargain.
327. *challenge*] claim.

Mardonius, thou hast loved me and hast wrong.
Thy love is not rewarded, but believe   335
It shall be better—more than friend in arms,
My father and my tutor, good Mardonius.
Mardonius. Sir, you did promise you would hear me out.
Arbaces. And so I will. Speak freely, for from thee
Nothing can come but worthy things and true.   340
Mardonius. Though you have all this worth, you hold some
    qualities
That do eclipse your virtues.
Arbaces.   Eclipse my virtues?
Mardonius. Yes, your passions, which are so manifold that
    they appear even in this: when I commend you, you hug
    me for that truth; when I speak of your faults, you make   345
    a start and fly the hearing. But—
Arbaces. When you commend me? O, that I should live
To need such commendations! If my deeds
Blew not my praise themselves above the earth,
I were most wretched. Spare your idle praise.   350
If thou didst mean to flatter and shouldst utter
Words in my praise that thou thoughtst impudence,
My deeds should make 'em modest. When you praise,
I hug you! 'Tis so false that wert thou worthy
Thou shouldst receive a death, a glorious death   355
From me. But thou shalt understand thy lies,
For shouldst thou praise me into heaven and there
Leave me enthroned, I would despise thee though
As much as now, which is as much as dust
Because I see thy envy.   360

---

346. hearing. But—] *Q1* (hearing: but,*)*; hearing out. *Theobald;* hearing
on't. *Bond (conj. Mason).*   358. though] *Q1;* then *Langbaine.*

---

358. *though*] Editors split on whether or not to accept Langbaine's emendation ('then'), although most choose Q1's 'though', which could mean 'for
all that, nevertheless, notwithstanding that' (*OED* Though *adv* I and IIa). In
defence of 'then', Williams proposes a possible sequence of errors, since
'though' could in the seventeenth century also be spelled 'thou': manuscript
'then' misread as 'thou', misprinted as Q1's 'though' (and followed by all the
seventeenth-century editions); he notes that the same variant occurs again
at 5.4.166 (Q1 'Thou', Q2 'Then'). Although emendation is unnecessary,
since the seventeenth-century meaning is no longer current and is itself possibly an error, a modern stage production could use 'then'.

Mardonius. However you will use me after, yet
    For your own promise sake hear me the rest.
Arbaces. I will, and after call unto the winds,
    For they shall lend as large an ear as I
    To what you utter. Speak.   365
Mardonius. Would you but leave these hasty tempers, which
    I do not say take from you all your worth,
    But darken 'em, then you would shine indeed.
Arbaces. Well.
Mardonius. Yet I would have you keep some passions, lest   370
    men should take you for a god, your virtues are such.
Arbaces. Why, now you flatter.
Mardonius. I never understood the word. Were you no king
    and free from these wild moods, should I choose a com-
    panion for wit and pleasure, it should be you; or for   375
    honesty to interchange my bosom with, it would be you;
    or wisdom to give me counsel, I would pick out you; or
    valour to defend my reputation, still I would find out you;
    for you are fit to fight for all the world, if it could come
    in question. Now I have spoke. Consider to yourself,   380
    find out a use; if so, then what shall fall to me is not
    material.
Arbaces. Is not material? More than ten such lives
    As mine, Mardonius. It was nobly said;
    Thou hast spoke truth, and boldly, such a truth   385
    As might offend another. I have been
    Too passionate and idle; thou shalt see
    A swift amendment. But I want those parts
    You praise me for. I fight for all the world?
    Give thee a sword, and thou wilt go as far   390
    Beyond me as thou art beyond in years.
    I know thou dar'st and wilt. It troubles me
    That I should use so rough a phrase to thee;
    Impute it to my folly, what thou wilt,
    So thou wilt pardon me. That thou and I   395

---

376. honesty] *Q2;* honest *Q1.*   377. wisdom to] *Q2;* wisdome to / to *Q1.*

376. *interchange my bosom*] exchange confidences.
380. *question*] dispute.
388. *want*] lack.
    parts] qualities.

Should differ thus!
Mardonius.   Why, 'tis no matter, sir.
Arbaces. 'Faith, but 'tis. But thou dost ever take
    All things I do thus patiently, for which
    I never can requite thee but with love,
    And that thou shalt be sure of. Thou and I   400
    Have not been merry lately. Pray thee, tell me
    Where hadst thou that same jewel in thine ear?
Mardonius. Why, at the taking of a town.
Arbaces. A wench, upon my life, a wench, Mardonius,
    Gave thee that jewel.   405
Mardonius. Wench! They respect not me. I'm old and rough,
    and every limb about me, but that which should, grows
    stiffer. I' those businesses I may swear I am truly honest,
    for I pay justly for what I take and would be glad to be
    at a certainty.   410
Arbaces. Why, do the wenches encroach upon thee?
Mardonius. Ay, by this light, do they.
Arbaces. Didst thou sit at an old rent with 'em?
Mardonius. Yes, faith.
Arbaces. And do they improve themselves?   415
Mardonius. Ay, ten shillings to me every new young fellow
    they come acquainted with.
Arbaces. How canst live on't?
Mardonius. Why, I think I must petition to you.
Arbaces. Thou shalt take 'em up at my price.   420

Enter two Gentlemen *and* BESSUS.

---

408. I' those] *Q2;* Ith those *Q1.*   420.1. SD] *Q2; not in Q1.*

408. *honest*] (1) trustworthy, (2) chaste (because of the difficulty of performance suggested in 407–8).

410. *at a certainty*] at a fixed rate (cf. 413, 'at an old rent'). A punning
secondary meaning is that in these transactions Mardonius would like to be
'sure of what he's getting' (since 'pay justly' may imply the possibility of
'repayment' in the form of venereal disease).

411. *encroach*] demand more than a fair price. The metaphor is drawn
from lord and tenant relations, when the lord 'compels the tenant to pay
more rent than he ought' (*OED* Encroach *v* 1b).

415. *improve themselves*] (1) better their lot, (2) raise their charge (continuing the metaphor: 'improve' was a term for raising rents (*OED* Improve
v^2 3)).

420. *my price*] my expense. At 423 Mardonius puns on a second meaning
of 'my price': 'the price I [a king] have to pay'.

Mardonius. Your price?

Arbaces. Ay, at the King's price.

Mardonius. That may be more than I am worth.

1 Gentleman. Is he not merry now?

2 Gentleman. I think not.   425

Bessus. He is, he is. We'll show ourselves.

Arbaces. Bessus, I thought you had been in Iberia by this;
    I bade you haste. Gobrius will want entertainment for
    me.

Bessus. An't please your majesty, I have a suit.   430

Arbaces. Is't not lousy, Bessus? What is't?

Bessus. I am to carry a lady with me—

Arbaces. Then thou hast two suits.

Bessus. And if I can prefer her to the Lady Panthea, your
    majesty's sister, to learn fashions, as her friends term it,   435
    it will be worth something to me.

Arbaces. So many nights' lodgings as 'tis thither, will't not?

Bessus. I know not that, sir, but gold I shall be sure of.

Arbaces. Why, thou shalt bid her entertain her from me, so
    thou wilt resolve me one thing.   440

Bessus. If I can.

Arbaces. Faith, 'tis a very disputable question, and yet I think
    thou canst decide it.

Bessus. Your majesty has a good opinion of my
    understanding.

Arbaces. I have so good an opinion of it: 'tis whether thou
    be valiant.   445

Bessus. Somebody has traduced me to you. Do you see this
    sword, sir?

Arbaces. Yes.

---

428. you haste] *Q2;* you; halfe *Q1.*   434. Panthea] *Q2; Panthan Q1.*   437.
will't] *Q2;* will *Q1.*   438. sir] *Q2; not in Q1.*   442. and] *Q2; not in Q1.*
446. sir?] *Q1;* sir? *Draws. Weber.*

---

428. *want entertainment*] lack accommodation; in a more general sense,
the hospitality appropriate for the King's return.

430. *suit*] (1) petition, (2) set of clothing (the basis of Arbaces's joke at
431), (3) suit of courtship to the lady (Arbaces's rejoinder at 433).

446.] Weber, followed by other editors, here directs Bessus to draw his
sword, although it is unclear from the dialogue where he might sheath it
(editing for a reading public, Weber was generally unconcerned about people
sheathing their swords or getting up off their knees); indicating his sword
would be sufficient illustration.

Bessus. If I do not make my backbiters eat it to a knife within
    this week, say I am not valiant.

Enter Messenger *with a packet.*

Messenger. Health to your majesty!   [*Delivers a letter.*]   450
Arbaces. From Gobrius?
Messenger. Yes, sir.
Arbaces. How does he? Is he well?
Messenger. In perfect health.
Arbaces. Thank thee for thy good news.   455
    A trustier servant to his prince there lives not
    Than is good Gobrius.   [*Reads.*]
1 Gentleman. The King starts back.
Mardonius. His blood goes back as fast.
2 Gentleman. And now it comes again.   460
Mardonius. He alters strangely.
Arbaces. The hand of heaven is on me; be it far
    From me to struggle. If my secret sins
    Have pulled this curse upon me, lend me tears
    Enough to wash me white that I may feel   465
    A childlike innocence within my breast,
    Which once performed, O give me leave to stand
    As fixed as constancy herself, my eyes
    Set here unmoved, regardless of the world,
    Though thousand miseries encompass me.   470
Mardonius [*Aside*]. This is strange.—Sir, how do you?
Arbaces. Mardonius, my mother—
Mardonius.   Is she dead?
Arbaces. Alas, she's not so happy. Thou dost know
    How she hath laboured since my father died

449.1. SD *with a packet*] *Q7; not in Q1.*   450. SD] *Weber; not in Q1.*   455.
news.] *Q1;* news. *Gives money. Weber.*   457. SD] *Weber; not in Q1.*

448. *backbiters*] detractors, carping critics.
455.] Weber here adds '*Gives money*', and this SD was adopted by subsequent editors until Arber and Bond in the early twentieth century. Weber
may have been noting contemporary stage practice, although the last
recorded production before his 1812 edition was in 1778.
469. *here*] i.e. on heaven; or perhaps simply 'set motionless in my head'.
473. *not so happy*] Arbaces presumes that Arane would rather die than
keep her life but be known as both a traitor to the state and an unnatural
mother for trying to have Arbaces killed.

To take by treason hence this loathèd life   475
That would but be to serve her. I have pardoned,
And pardoned, and by that have made her fit
To practise new sins, not repent the old.
She now has hired a slave to come from thence
And strike me here, whom Gobrius, sifting out,   480
Took and condemned and executed there.
The carefulst servant! Heaven let me but live
To pay that man; Nature is poor to me,
That will not let me have as many deaths
As are the times that he hath saved my life,   485
That I might die 'em over all for him.
Mardonius. Sir, let her bear her sins on her own head;
Vex not yourself.
Arbaces.   What will the world
Conceive of me? With what unnatural sins
Will they suppose me laden, when my life   490
Is sought by her that gave it to the world?
But yet he writes me comfort here. My sister,
He says, is grown in beauty and in grace,
In all the innocent virtues that become
A tender, spotless maid. She stains her cheeks   495
With mourning tears to purge her mother's ill,
And 'mongst that sacred dew she mingles prayers,
Her pure oblations for my safe return.
If I have lost the duty of a son;
If any pomp or vanity of state   500
Made me forget my natural offices;
Nay farther, if I have not every night
Expostulated with my wand'ring thoughts,
If aught unto my parent they have erred,
And called 'em back, do you direct her arm   505
Unto this foul, dissembling heart of mine.
But if I have been just to her, send out
Your power to compass me and hold me safe
From searching treason. I will use no means

497. that] *Q2;* her *Q1.*

---

480. *sifting out*] discovering.
501. *offices*] duties.
505. *you*] i.e. the gods.

But prayers, for rather suffer me to see   510
From mine own veins issue a deadly flood
Than wash my dangers off with mother's blood.
Mardonius. I ne'er saw such sudden extremities.   *Exeunt.*

[1.2]

Enter TIGRANES *and* SPACONIA.

Tigranes. Why, wilt thou have me die, Spaconia?
    What should I do?
Spaconia.   Nay, let me stay alone,
    And when you see Armenia again,
    You shall behold a tomb more worth than I.
    Some friend that either loves me or my cause   5
    Will build me something to distinguish me
    From other women. Many a weeping verse
    He will lay on and much lament those maids
    That place their loves unfortunately high,
    As I have done, where they can never reach.   10
    But why should you go to Iberia?
Tigranes. Alas, that thou wilt ask me. Ask the man
    That rages in a fever why he lies
    Distempered there, when all the other youths
    Are coursing o'er the meadows with their loves!   15
    Can I resist it? Am I not a slave
    To him that conquered me?
Spaconia.   That conquered thee?
    Tigranes, he has won but half of thee,

513. SD] *Q2; not in Q1.*

1. die] *Q1;* fly *Weber (conj. Mason).*   9. high] *Q2;* too light *Q1;* too high
Weber.   18. thee] *Q2; not in Q1.*

---

1. *die*] Mason insisted that this word should be 'fly' because Spaconia's
reply indicates that 'she had been exhorting [Tigranes] to flight'. The suggested emendation was adopted by Weber and every subsequent editor until
Turner, who maintains that her first line is ironical and further points out
that Tigranes's next speech indicates that he sees only two choices: either
obey Arbaces or be executed.

15. *coursing*] hunting (usually with greyhounds, by sight).

18–21. *he . . . prisoner*] Bond notes the similarity of Spaconia's sentiment
to the Queen's in *Richard II*, 5.1.27–8: 'Hath Bullingbrook depos'd / Thine
intellect? Hath he been in thy heart?'

Thy body; but thy mind may be as free
As his. His will did never combat thine   20
And take it prisoner.
Tigranes.   But if he by force
Convey my body hence, what helps it me
Or thee to be unwilling?
Spaconia.   O, Tigranes,
I know you are to see a lady there,
To see and like, I fear; perhaps the hope   25
Of her makes you forget me ere we part.
Be happier than you know to wish. Farewell.
Tigranes. Spaconia, stay and hear me what I say.
In short, destruction meet me, that I may
See it and not avoid it, when I leave   30
To be thy faithful lover. Part with me
Thou shalt not. There are none that know our love,
And I have given gold to a captain
That goes unto Iberia from the King
That he would place a lady of our land   35
With the King's sister that is offered me.
Thither shall you, and being once got in
Persuade her by what subtle means you can
To be as backward in her love as I.
Spaconia. Can you imagine that a longing maid,   40
When she beholds you, can be pulled away
With words from loving you?
Tigranes.   Dispraise my health,
My honesty, and tell her I am jealous.
Spaconia. Why, I had rather lose you. Can my heart
Consent to let my tongue throw out such words?   45
And I, that ever yet spoke what I thought,
Shall find it such a thing at first to lie?
Tigranes. Yet do thy best.

Enter BESSUS.

Bessus. What, is your majesty ready?
Tigranes. There is the lady, captain.   50

---

26. me ere we part.] *Theobald;* me; ere we part, *Q1–8;* me, ere we part, *F2.*

29. *that*] so that.

Bessus. Sweet lady, by your leave, I could wish myself more
    full of courtship for your fair sake.
Spaconia. Sir, I shall find no want of that.
Bessus. Lady, you must haste. I have received new letters from
    the King that requires more speed than I expected. He   55
    will follow me suddenly himself and begins to call for
    your majesty already.
Tigranes. He shall not do so long.
Bessus. Sweet lady, shall I call you my charge hereafter?
Spaconia. I will not take upon me to govern your tongue, sir.   60
    You shall call me what you please.   *[Exeunt.]*

---

51. leave, I] *Q1;* leave. *Kisses her.* I *Turner.*   61. SD *Exeunt.*] *Colman; not in
Q1.*   61.1.] *Finis Actus Primi. Q1.*

52. *courtship*] courtly breeding, gallantry. Bessus's kissing her, called for
by Turner's SD, might produce a comic tableau and help prompt her cool
disdain for his courtly affectation (53, 60–1), but he could simply take her
hand, or even her arm, in too familiar a manner.
   53. *I . . . that*] i.e. I shall not miss that because any courtship offered by
you would be too much.
   59. *charge*] Here the primary meaning is 'a thing or person entrusted to
one's care' (*OED* Charge *n* II 14a), but, as at 2.1.164, 'charge' also carries
the demeaning overtones of something 'burdensome, a source of inconve-
nience' (*OED* II 8b).

Act 2

[2.1]

> *Enter* GOBRIUS, BACURIUS, ARANE, PANTHEA, *and*
> *Waiting-women, with Attendance.*

Gobrius. My Lord Bacurius, you must have regard
    Unto the Queen. She is your prisoner;
    'Tis at your peril if she make escape.
Bacurius. My lord, I know't; she is my prisoner
    From you committed. Yet she is a woman,   5
    And, so I keep her safe, you will not urge me
    To keep her close. I shall not shame to say
    I sorrow for her.
Gobrius.   So do I, my lord.
    I sorrow for her that so little grace
    Doth govern her that she should stretch her arm   10
    Against her king, so little womanhood
    And natural goodness as to think the death
    Of her own son.
Arane.   Thou knowst the reason why,
    Dissembling as thou art, and wilt not speak.
Gobrius. There is a lady takes not after you;   15
    Her father is within her, that good man
    Whose tears paid down his sins. Mark how she weeps,
    How well it does become her. And if you
    Can find no disposition in yourself
    To sorrow, yet by gracefulness in her   20

2.1] Actus Secundus Scena Prima. *Q1.* 0.1–2. SD *and Waiting-women,*]
Dyce; and Mandane, waiting women, Q1. 6. safe,] *Q2;* safe: *Q1.*

2.1.0.1.] On the inclusion of *Mandane* in this SD in all editions until Dyce,
see Introduction, p. 6.
  2.1.0.2. *Attendance*] Attendants.
  6. *safe*] unable to cause harm.
  7. *close*] confined, imprisoned.
  12. *think*] intend.
  17. *paid down*] paid for, were sufficient to balance.

Find out the way and by your reason weep.
All this she does for you, and more she needs
When for yourself you will not lose a tear.
Think how this want of grief discredits you,
And you will weep because you cannot weep.   25
Arane. You talk to me as having got a time
    Fit for your purpose, but you know I know
    You speak not what you think.
Panthea.   I would my heart
    Were stone before my softness should be urged
    Against my mother. A more troubled thought   30
    No virgin bears about her: should I excuse
    My mother's fault, I should set light a life
    In losing which a brother and a king
    Were taken from me; if I seek to save
    That life so loved, I lose another life   35
    That gave me being—I shall lose a mother,
    A word of such a sound in a child's ear
    That it strikes reverence through it. May the will
    Of heaven be done, and if one needs must fall,
    Take a poor virgin's life to answer all.   40
Arane. But Gobrius, let us talk.   [*They walk apart.*]
                          You know this fault
    Is not in me as in another woman.
Gobrius. I know it is not.
Arane.   Yet you make it so.
Gobrius. Why, is not all that's past beyond your help?
Arane. I know it is.
Gobrius.   Nay, should you publish it   45
    Before the world, think you 'twill be believed?
Arane. I know it would not.
Gobrius.   Nay, should I join with you,
    Should we not both be torn? And yet both die

---

32. set] *Q2;* let *Q1.*   41. SD] *Weber; not in Q1.*   48. torn] *Q1;* sworn
Theobald.

32. *set light*] value too little.
48. *torn*] torn to pieces, tortured even to death (as traitors). Theobald's
emendation, on Sympson's suggestion ('sworn'), is not far-fetched, but
unnecessary.

Uncredited?
Arane.   I think we should.
Gobrius.   Why then
Take you such violent courses? As for me,   50
I do but right in saving of the King
From all your plots.
Arane.   The King?
Gobrius.   I bade you rest
With patience, and a time would come for me
To reconcile all to your own content;
But by this way you take away my power,   55
And what was done unknown was not by me,
But you. Your urging being done,
I must preserve mine own. But time may bring
All this to light and happily for all.
Arane. Accursèd be this overcurious brain   60
That gave that plot a birth, accursed this womb
That after did conceive to my disgrace.
Bacurius. My Lord Protector, they say there are divers letters
come from Armenia that Bessus has done good service
and brought again a day by his particular valour.   65
Received you any to that effect?
Gobrius. Yes, 'tis most certain.
Bacurius. I'm sorry for't—not that the day was won but that
'twas won by him. We held him here a coward. He did
me wrong once, at which I laughed and so did all the   70
world, for nor I nor any other held him worth my sword.

Enter BESSUS *and* SPACONIA.

Bessus. Health to my Lord Protector! From the king these
letters—and to your grace, madam, these.
               [*Gives letters to Gobrius and Panthea.*]
Gobrius. How does his majesty?

---

71. him] *Q2;* time *Q1.*   73. SD] *Dyce; not in Q1.*

60. *overcurious*] overly ingenious.
63. *divers*] several.
65. *brought . . . day*] recovered the day, won a victory.
71. *him*] Q1's 'time' is not the only example of its confusion of initial *h*
and *t*; cf. 2.1.227, 4.1.67, and 4.2.205.

Bessus. As well as conquest by his own means, and his valiant   75
    commanders', can make him. Your letters will tell you all.
                                    [*Gobrius reads.*]
Panthea. I will not open mine till I do know
    My brother's health. Good captain, is he well?
Bessus. As the rest of us that fought are.
Panthea. But how's that? Is he hurt?   80
Bessus. He's a strange soldier that gets not a knock.
Panthea. I do not ask how strange that soldier is
    That gets no hurt, but whether he have one?
Bessus. He had divers.
Panthea. And is he well again?   85
Bessus. Well again, an't please your grace? Why I was run
    twice through the body and shot i' th' head with a cross
    arrow and yet am well again.
Panthea. I do not care how thou dost. Is he well?
Bessus. Not care how I do! Let a man out of the mightiness   90
    of his spirit fructify foreign countries with his blood for
    the good of his own, and thus he shall be answered. Why,
    I may live to relieve with spear and shield such a lady as
    you distressed.
Panthea. Why, I will care. I am glad that thou art well;   95
    I prithee, is he so?
Gobrius. The King is well and will be here tomorrow.
Panthea. My prayers are heard; now I will open mine.
                                    [*Reads.*]
Gobrius. Bacurius, I must ease you of your charge.—
    Madam, the wonted mercy of the King,   100
    That overtakes your faults, has met with this
    And struck it out. He has forgiven you freely.
    Your own will is your law; be where you please.
Arane. I thank him.
Gobrius.   You will be ready to wait

---

76. SD] *This ed.; not in Q1.*   93–4. as you] *Q2; not in Q1.*   98. SD] *Weber;
not in Q1.*

87–8. *cross arrow*] crossbow bolt.
91. *fructify*] fertilise.
100. *wonted*] customary.
101. *overtakes*] exceeds.
this] i.e. this fault.

Upon his majesty tomorrow?

Arane.   I will.   105

Bacurius. Madam, be wise hereafter. I am glad
    I have lost this office.   *Exit* ARANE.

Gobrius. Good Captain Bessus, tell us the discourse
    Between Tigranes and our king and how
    We got the victory.

Panthea.   I prithee do,   110
    And if my brother were in any danger,
    Let not thy tale make him abide there long
    Before thou bring him off, for all that while
    My heart will beat.

Bessus. Madam, let what will beat, I must tell truth, and thus   115
    it was. They fought single in lists but one to one. As for
    my own part, I was dangerously hurt but three days
    before, else perhaps we had been two to two. I cannot
    tell; some thought we had. And the occasion of my hurt
    was this: the enemy had made trenches—   120

Gobrius. Captain, without the manner of your hurt
    Be much material to this business,
    We'll hear it some other time.

Panthea.   Ay, I prithee
    Leave it, and go on with my brother.

Bessus. I will, but 'twould be worth your hearing. To the lists   125
    they came, and single sword and gauntlet was their fight.

Panthea. Alas!

Bessus. Without the lists there stood some dozen captains of
    either side mingled, all which were sworn, and one of
    those was I. And 'twas my chance to stand near a captain   130

---

107. SD *Exit* ARANE.] *Q2; Exit. Q1.*

108. *discourse*] course of arms, combat (*OED* Discourse 1b, citing this
instance).

116. *in lists*] place of combat (cf. 1.1.20 n).

118–19. *I . . . had*] A good example of Bessus's characteristic strategy of
hesitating over details in order to make the big lie believable (cf. 2.1.155–9,
3.2.76).

121. *without*] unless.

126. *gauntlet*] mailed glove. Turner quotes a 1595 manual of swordsman-
ship, *Vicentio Saviolo, His Practise*, to indicate that 'the single Swoorde and
the glove' was then 'the most in use among Gentlemen' (F3v).

129. *sworn*] i.e. pledged to accept the issue of the single combat.

of the enemy's side called Tiribasus; valiant they said he
was. Whilst these two kings were stretching themselves,
this Tiribasus cast something a scornful look on me and
asked me whom I thought would overcome. I smiled and
told him if he would fight with me he should perceive by   135
the event of that whose king would win. Something he
answered, and a scuffle was like to grow, when one
Zipetus offered to help him. I—

Panthea. All this is of thyself. I prithee, Bessus,
    Tell something of my brother. Did he nothing?   140

Bessus. Why, yes, I'll tell your grace. They were not to fight
    till the word given, which for my own part, by my troth,
    I confess I was not to give.

Panthea. See, for his own part.

Bacurius. I fear yet this fellow's abused with a good report.   145

Bessus. Ay, but I—

Panthea. Still of himself.

Bessus. Cried, 'Give the word', whenas, some of them said,
    Tigranes was stooping, but the word was not given then;
    when one Cosroes, of the enemy's part, held up his finger   150
    to me, which is as much with us martialists as 'I will fight
    with you'. I said not a word nor made sign during the
    combat, but that once done—

Panthea. He slips o'er all the fight.

Bessus. I called him to me. 'Cosroes', said I—   155

Panthea. I will hear no more.

Bessus. No, no, I lie—

Bacurius. I dare be sworn thou dost.

Bessus. 'Captain', said I. 'Twas so.

Panthea. I tell thee, I will hear no further.   160

Bessus. No? Your grace will wish you had.

Panthea. I will not wish it. What, is this the lady
    My brother writes to me to take?

---

143. I confess] *Q2; not in Q1.*   148. whenas,] when as *Q1;* when, as
Theobald.   150. when] *Q1;* yet *Q2.*

---

133. *something a*] a somewhat.
148. *whenas*] at which time, when (*OED* Whenas *conj* 1b). Until Turner
adopted this reading for Q1's 'when as', editors followed Theobald ('when,
as') and substituted Q2's 'yet' for 'when' in 150 to avoid repetition.

Bessus. An't please your grace, this is she.—Charge, will you
    come nearer the princess?   165
Panthea. Y' are welcome from your country, and this land
    Shall show unto you all the kindnesses
    That I can make it. What's your name?
Spaconia.   Thalestris.
Panthea. Y' are very welcome. You have got a letter
    To put you to me that has power enough   170
    To place mine enemy here, then much more you
    That are so far from being so to me
    That you ne'er saw me.
Bessus. Madam, I dare pass my word for her truth.
Spaconia. My truth?   175
Panthea. Why, captain, do you think I am afraid she'll steal?
Bessus. I cannot tell; servants are slippery. But I dare give my
    word for her and for her honesty. She came along with
    me, and many favours she did me by the way; but, by this
    light, none but what she might do with modesty to a man   180
    of my rank.
Panthea. Why, captain, here's nobody thinks otherwise.
Bessus. Nay, if you should, your grace may think your plea-
    sure. But I am sure I brought her from Armenia, and in
    all that way if ever I touched any bare on her above her   185
    knee, I pray God I may sink where I stand.
Spaconia. Above my knee!
Bessus. No, you know I did not, and if any man will say I did,
    this sword shall answer. Nay, I'll defend the reputation of
    my charge whilst I live.—Your grace shall understand, I   190
    am secret in these businesses and know how to defend a
    lady's honour.
Spaconia. I hope your grace knows him so well already,
    I shall not need to tell you he's vain and foolish.
Bessus. Ay, you may call me what you please, but I'll defend   195

---

178. her . . . honesty.] *Q1* (her, . . . honestie:); her; . . . honesty, *Langbaine.*
185. on] *Q1;* of *Q2.*

---

164. *Charge*] Cf. 1.2.59.
174. *truth*] (1) virtue, virginity, (2) integrity. Panthea responds to the
second sense (176); vociferously defending Spaconia's chastity, Bessus
pursues the first sense in the next pun, 'honesty' (178).
185. *bare*] i.e. bare skin.

your good name against the world.—And so I take my
leave of your grace,—and of you, my Lord Protector.—I
am likewise glad to see your lordship well.

Bacurius. O, Captain Bessus, I thank you; I would speak with
 you anon.   200

Bessus. When you please, I will attend your lordship. *Exit.*

Bacurius. Madam, I'll take my leave too.

Panthea. Good Bacurius.   *Exit* [BACURIUS].

Gobrius.   Madam, what writes
 His majesty to you?

Panthea.   O, my lord,
 The kindest words; I'll keep 'em whilst I live 205
 Here in my bosom. There's no art in 'em;
 They lie disordered in this paper just
 As hearty nature speaks 'em.

Gobrius.   And to me
 He writes what tears of joy he shed to hear
 How you were grown in every virtuous way, 210
 And yields all thanks to me for that dear care
 Which I was bound to have in training you.
 There is no princess living that enjoys
 A brother of that worth.

Panthea.   My lord, no maid
 Longs more for anything, or feels more heat 215
 And cold within her breast, than I do now
 In hope to see him.

Gobrius.   Yet I wonder much
 At this: he writes he brings along with him
 A husband for you, that same captive prince.
 And if he love you as he makes a show, 220
 He will allow you freedom in your choice.

Panthea. And so he will, my lord. I warrant you
 He will but offer and give me the power
 To take or leave.

Gobrius.   Trust me, were I a lady,
 I could not like that man were bargained with 225

---

203. SD *Exit* BACURIUS.] *Colman; Exit. Q1 (after 202 too); Exeunt Bessus
and Bacurius.* F2 *(after 203* Bacurius*).*

---

200. *anon*] immediately.
220. *And if*] If.

Before I choose him.

Panthea.   But I am not built
On such wild humours. If I find him worthy,
He is not less because he's offered.

Spaconia [*Aside*]. 'Tis true, he is not; would he would seem
    less.

Gobrius. I think there is no lady can affect   230
Another prince, your brother standing by;
He does eclipse men's virtues so with his.

Spaconia [*Aside*]. I know a lady may; and more, I fear
Another lady will.

Panthea.   Would I might see him.

Gobrius. Why, so you shall. My businesses are great;   235
I will attend you when it is his pleasure
To see you, madam.

Panthea.   I thank you, good my lord.

Gobrius. You will be ready, madam?

Panthea. Yes.   *Exit* GOBRIUS [*with Attendants*].

Spaconia. I do beseech you, madam, send away   240
Your other women and receive from me
A few sad words, which set against your joys
May make 'em shine the more.

Panthea.   Sirs, leave me all.

                                        Exeunt Women.

Spaconia. I kneel a stranger here to beg a thing   [*Kneels.*]
Unfit for me to ask and you to grant;   245
'Tis such another strange ill-laid request
As if a beggar should entreat a king
To leave his sceptre and his throne to him
And take his rags to wander o'er the world

---

227. him] *Q2;* time *Q1.*   232. his] *Q2;* this *Q1.*   239. SD *Exit* GOBRIUS.]
Q2; Exit. Q1 (after 238 madam*).   SD with Attendants.] Dyce; not in Q1.*
243. SD] *Q2; not in Q1.*   244. SD] *Weber; not in Q1.*

226–7. *built . . . humours*] of such an undisciplined, irrational temperament. Panthea here confidently declares herself free of the disposition Mardonius has attributed to Arbaces (1.1.83–6) and Arbaces subsequently demonstrated.

242. *sad*] (1) serious, (2) distressing.

243. *Sirs*] Not infrequently used in addressing women (cf. Philaster to Arethusa and Bellario in *Philaster*, 4.5.53: 'Sirs, feel my pulse').

Hungry and cold.
Panthea.   That were a strange request.   250
Spaconia. As ill is mine.
Panthea.   Then do not utter it.
Spaconia. Alas, 'tis of that nature that it must
      Be uttered—ay, and granted—or I die.
      I am ashamed to speak it; but where life
      Lies at the stake, I cannot think her woman   255
      That will not talk something unreasonably
      To hazard saving of it. I shall seem
      A strange petitioner, that wish all ill
      To them I beg of ere they give me aught,
      Yet so I must. I would you were not fair   260
      Nor wise, for in your ill consists my good.
      If you were foolish, you would hear my prayer,
      If foul, you had not power to hinder me—
      He would not love you.
Panthea.   What's the meaning of it?
Spaconia. Nay, my request is more without the bounds   265
      Of reason yet, for 'tis not in the power
      Of you to do what I would have you grant.
Panthea. Why, then 'tis idle. Prithee, speak it out.
Spaconia. Your brother brings a prince into this land
      Of such a noble shape, so sweet a grace,   270
      So full of worth withal, that every maid
      That looks upon him gives away herself
      To him for ever; and for you to have
      He brings him. And so mad is my demand
      That I desire you not to have this man,   275
      This excellent man, for whom you needs must die
      If you should miss him. I do now expect
      You should laugh at me.
Panthea.   Trust me, I could weep
      Rather, for I have found in all thy words

---

256. talk] *Theobald; take Q1.*

256. *something*] somewhat.
263. *foul*] ugly.
271. *withal*] besides.
276. *needs must*] 'Needs' is here an intensifier, adding the sense of 'necessarily'.

A strange disjointed sorrow.
Spaconia.   'Tis by me   280
    His own desire too, that you would not love him.
Panthea. His own desire! Why, credit me, Thalestris,
    I am no common wooer. If he shall woo me,
    His worth may be such that I dare not swear
    I will not love him; but if he will stay   285
    To have me woo him, I will promise thee
    He may keep all his graces to himself
    And fear no ravishing from me.
Spaconia.   'Tis yet
    His own desire, but when he sees your face,
    I fear it will not be. Therefore, I charge you   290
    As you have pity, stop those tender ears
    From his enchanting voice, close up those eyes
    That you may neither catch a dart from him
    Nor he from you. I charge you as you hope
    To live in quiet, for when I am dead   295
    For certain I shall walk to visit him
    If he break promise with me, for as fast
    As oaths without a formal ceremony
    Can make me, I am to him.
Panthea.   Then be fearless,
    For if he were a thing 'twixt god and man   300
    I could gaze on him, if I knew it sin
    To love him, without passion. Dry your eyes.
    I swear you shall enjoy him still for me;
    I will not hinder you. But I perceive
    You are not what you seem. Rise, rise, Thalestris,   305
    If your right name be so.   [*Spaconia rises.*]
Spaconia.   Indeed, it is not.
    Spaconia is my name, but I desire
    Not to be known to others.
Panthea.   Why, by me
    You shall not. I will never do you wrong;
    What good I can, I will. Think not my birth   310

---

306. SD] *Dyce; not in Q1.*   307. my] *Q2; not in Q1.*

---

280. *by me*] by means of me (i.e. I convey his wishes).
296. *walk*] rise from the grave.
303. *still for me*] always as far as I am concerned.

Or education such that I should injure
A stranger virgin. You are welcome hither.
In company you wish to be commanded,
But when we are alone, I shall be ready
To be your servant.   *Exeunt.*   315

[2.2]

Enter three Men *and a* Woman.

1 Man. Come, come; run, run, run.

2 Man. We shall outgo her.

3 Man. One were better be hanged than carry women out
fiddling to these shows.

Woman. Is the King hard by?   5

1 Man. You heard he with the bottles say he thought we
should come too late. What abundance of people here is!

Woman. But what had he in those bottles?

3 Man. I know not.

2 Man. Why, ink, good man fool.   10

3 Man. Ink? What to do?

1 Man. Why, the King, look you, will many times call for
those bottles and break his mind to his friends.

Woman. Let's take our places quickly; we shall have no room
else.   15

2 Man. The man told us he would walk afoot through the
people.

3 Man. Ay, marry, did he.

315. SD] *Q2; Exit. Q1.*

___

312. *stranger*] foreigner.

2.2.0.1. *Men and a Woman*] References to 'master' (20) and to starting a
fire (146) indicate the status of these crowd-members in this very English
scene—older apprentices or perhaps journeymen; domestic servant—and
suggest appropriate apparel (as does the would-be sophistication of the
Citizens' Wives). The women's clothing might also indicate the scene's
imagined setting in the fields outside the city (22–3).

4. *fiddling*] wasting time.

5. *hard by*] close, at hand.

13. *break*] reveal.

1 Man. Our shops are well looked to now.

2 Man. 'Slife, yonder's my master, I think.   20

1 Man. No, 'tis not he.

                    Enter two Citizens' Wives *and* PHILIP.

1 Citizen's Wife. Lord, how fine the fields be! What sweet living
  'tis in the country.

2 Citizen's Wife. Ay, poor souls, God help 'em. They live as
  contentedly as one of us.   25

1 Citizen's Wife. My husband's cousin would have had me
  gone into the country last year. Wert thou ever there?

2 Citizen's Wife. Ay, poor souls; I was amongst 'em once.

1 Citizen's Wife. And what kind of creatures are they, for love
  of God?   30

2 Citizen's Wife. Very good people, God help 'em.

1 Citizen's Wife. Wilt thou go with me down this summer,
  when I am brought abed?

2 Citizen's Wife. Alas, 'tis no place for us.

1 Citizen's Wife. Why, prithee?   35

2 Citizen's Wife. Why, you can have nothing there. There's
  nobody cries brooms.

1 Citizen's Wife. No!

2 Citizen's Wife. No truly, nor milk.

1 Citizen's Wife. Nor milk! How do they?   40

2 Citizen's Wife. They are fain to milk themselves i' th'
  country.

1 Citizen's Wife. Good lord! But the people there, I think, will
  be very dutiful to one of us?

2 Citizen's Wife. Ay, God knows, will they; and yet they do not   45
  greatly care for our husbands.

1 Citizen's Wife. Do they not? Alas. In good faith, I cannot
  blame them, for we do not greatly care for them ourselves.—Philip, I pray, choose us a place.

Philip. There's the best, forsooth.   50

---

19. looked] *Q2;* looke *Q1.*

---

  20. *'Slife*] A mild curse (contraction of 'God's life').

  41. *fain*] compelled.

1 Citizen's Wife. By your leave, good people, a little.

1 Man. What's the matter?

Philip. I pray you, my friend, do not thrust my mistress so;
  she's with child.

2 Man. Let her look to herself then. Has she not had thrust-   55
  ing enough yet? If she stay shouldering here, she may hap
  to go home with a cake in her belly.

3 Man. How now, goodman squitter-breech. Why do you lean
  so on me?

Philip. Because I will.   60

3 Man. Will you, sir sauce-box?   [*Strikes him.*]

1 Citizen's Wife. Look if one have not struck Philip.—Come
  hither, Philip. Why did he strike thee?

Philip. For leaning on him.

1 Citizen's Wife. Why didst thou lean on him?   65

Philip. I did not think he would have struck me.

1 Citizen's Wife. As God save me, law, thou art as wild as a
  buck. There is no quarrel but thou art at one end or other
  of it.

3 Man. It's at the first end then, for he will never stay the last.   70

---

52. SH *1 Man.*] *Q1;3. Q2.* 53. you] *Q2; not in Q1.* 55–6. thrusting] *Q1;*
showing *Q2–6, F2;* shoving *Q7–8;* shroving *Turner.* 61. SD] *Weber; not in
Q1.*

55–6. *thrusting*] Turner makes a good case for his emendation to 'shroving' ('merrymaking, from the festivity associated with Shrove-tide'), and he
may be right in concluding that the Q1 reading 'is probably a memorial error'
(of 'thrust' at 53) and that Q2's 'showing' results from 'the compositor's misreading of a correct annotation in his copy'. But the double-error rationale
is not necessary, for the line is not gibberish without it. 2 Man's coarse
'thrusting' plays naturally on Philip's prim reprimand (53–4), and 'showing'
might as easily result from the Q2 compositor's trying to carry too many
words in his head and unwittingly conflating 'thrusting' with 'shouldering'.

56. *hap*] chance.

58. *squitter-breech*] pants-fouler (i.e. one suffering with diarrhoea).

61. *sauce-box*] saucy knave.

67. *law*] This exclamation introduced a conventional phrase or called
attention to an emphatic statement (*OED* Law *int*). Theobald emended to
an alternative spelling, 'la'; its frequent use in this form by Shallow, Slender,
and Mistress Quickly in *The Merry Wives of Windsor* may suggest it was a
modish affectation.

1 Citizen's Wife. Well, slipstring, I shall meet with you.
3 Man. When you will.
1 Cititzen's Wife. I'll give a crown to meet with you.
3 Man. At a bawdy house.
1 Citizen's Wife. Ay, you are full of your roguery,—[*Aside*] but   75
       if I do meet you, it shall cost me a fall.

                      Enter one [Man] *running.*

Man. The King, the King, the King, the King! Now, now,
       now, now!

                Flourish. Enter ARBACES, TIGRANES, MARDONIUS,
                              and others.

All. God preserve your majesty!
Arbaces. I thank you all. Now are my joys at full,   80
       When I behold you safe, my loving subjects.
       By you I grow; 'tis your united love
       That lifts me to this height.
       All the account that I can render you

---

71. slipstring] *Q2;* stripling *Q1.*   76.1. SD *Enter . . . running.*] *Flourish.
Enter one running. Q2; not in Q1.*   77. SH *Man.*] *Dyce; 3. Q1; 4. Q2.*   78.1.
SD *Flourish.*] *Q2 (at 76.1); not in Q1.*

---

71. *slipstring*] rogue, one who deserves to be hanged. *OED* citations all
concern youths and suggest the additional sense of 'truant'; only Q1 reads
'stripling'.
    meet] get even. 3 Man, however, responds to another meaning, 'encounter'.
    76. *fall*] yielding to temptation, sin (with a play on her position in the
imagined tryst).
    76.1. SD, 77. SH] Q1 lacks any SD and assigns the speech to 3 Man (*3*).
Although he chooses not to accept Q2 as authoritative, Turner suggests a
hypothetical sequence of events by which, were Q2 correct, Q1 might have
been produced: omission of the SD by the scribe who produced the
copy-text for Q1, followed by the Q1 compositor changing the SH from *4*
to *3* to make sense of what was before him. Instead, Q2 may reflect what
was actually worked out for performance, since its copy-text seems to reflect
consultation with the playhouse prompt-book (see Introduction, p. 42).
Flourish is almost certainly a prompter's addition and, if written ambiguously
in the margin, its attachment to this SD instead of the royal entrance (78.1)
would be an easy mistake. Dyce offers an attractive possibility that retains
Q2's SD but separates its elements, printing *Flourish* after 'fall', as though
the royal party could be heard approaching, followed by the SD for the
running man on a new line. Colman and Weber provide flourishes both here
and at 78.1.

For all the love you have bestowed on me,   85
All your expenses to maintain my war,
Is but a little word. You will imagine
'Tis slender payment; yet 'tis such a word
As is not to be bought without our bloods:
'Tis peace.   90
All. God preserve your majesty!
Arbaces. Now you may live securely in your towns,
Your children round about you; you may sit
Under your vines and make the miseries
Of other kingdoms a discourse for you   95
And lend them sorrows. For yourselves, you may
Safely forget there are such things as tears;
And may you all whose good thoughts I have gained
Hold me unworthy when I think my life
A sacrifice too great to keep you thus   100
In such a calm estate.
All. God bless your majesty!
Arbaces. See all good people, I have brought the man
Whose very name you feared a captive home.
Behold him; 'tis Tigranes. In your hearts   105
Sing songs of gladness and deliverance.
1 Citizen's Wife. Out upon him!
2 Citizen's Wife. How he looks!
Woman. Hang him, hang him, hang him!
Mardonius. These are sweet people.
Tigranes.   Sir, you do me wrong   110
To render me a scornèd spectacle
To common people.
Arbaces.   It was far from me
To mean it so.—If I have aught deserved,
My loving subjects, let me beg of you
Not to revile this prince, in whom there dwells   115
All worth of which the nature of a man
Is capable, valour beyond compare.
The terror of his name has stretched itself
Wherever there is sun. And yet for you

109. SH *Woman.*] Dyce; *3 Weo. Q1.*

I fought with him single and won him too;   120
I made his valour stoop and brought that name,
Soared to so unbelieved a height, to fall
Beneath mine. This, inspired with all your loves,
I did perform, and will for your content
Be ever ready for a greater work.   125

All. The Lord bless your majesty!

Tigranes [*Aside*]. So, he has made me amends now with a
  speech in commendation of himself. I would not be so
  vainglorious.

Arbaces. If there be anything in which I may   130
Do good to any creature, here speak out,
For I must leave you. And it troubles me
That my occasions for the good of you
Are such as calls me from you, else my joy
Would be to spend my days amongst you all.   135
You show your loves in these large multitudes
That come to meet me. I will pray for you.
Heaven prosper you that you may know old years
And live to see your children's children
Eat at your boards with plenty! When there is   140
A want of anything, let it be known
To me, and I will be a father to you.
God keep you all.

All. God bless your majesty! God bless your majesty!

                    Flourish. Exeunt kings and their train.

1 Man. Come, shall we go? All's done.   145

Woman. Ay, for God's sake. I have not made a fire yet.

---

121. brought] *Q2;* made *Q1.*   128. commendation] *Q2;* commendations
Q1.   133. That] *Q2;* Thus *Q1.*   144. God . . . majesty!] *Q2; repetition not
in Q1.*   144.1. SD *Flourish. Exeunt . . . train.*] *Q2 (after 143* all*); Exeunt. Q1
(after* all*).*

---

120. *won*] conquered.

121. *brought*] caused. Q1's 'made' was probably influenced by 'made'
earlier in the same line.

122. *unbelieved*] unbelievable, incredible.

133. *occasions*] affairs. Bond notes that the nature of these 'occasions' is
never explained; he suggests that in Arbaces's announced departure the
authors may have intended 'a fresh illustration of his restlessness' and com-
pares it to 3.1.112: 'yet the time is short'.

2 Man. Away, away; all's done.

3 Man. Content.—Farewell, Philip.

1 Citizen's Wife. Away, you haltersack you.

1 Man. Philip will not fight; he's afraid on's face.   150

Philip. Ay, marry, am I afraid of my face.

3 Man. Thou wouldst be, Philip, if thou sawst it in a glass; it
looks so like a visor.

1 Citizen's Wife. You'll be hanged, sirrah.—

                    Exeunt the three Men *and the* Woman.

Come Philip, walk afore us homeward.—Did not his   155
majesty say he had brought us home peas for all our
money?

2 Citizen's Wife. Yes, marry, did he.

1 Citizen's Wife. They are the first I heard on this year, by my
troth; I longed for some of 'em. Did he not say we should   160
have some?

2 Citizen's Wife. Yes, and so we shall anon, I warrant you, have
every one a peck brought home to our houses. [*Exeunt.*]

---

150. SH *1 Man.*] *Q1*; 2. *Q2.*   151. marry . . . face.] *Q1*; marry; . . . face?
Theobald.   153. so] *Q2; not in Q1.*   154.1. SD] *Exeunt 1, 2, 3, and Women.*
Q1 (after 153 visor*).*   156. all] *Q2; not in Q1.*   163. SD *Exeunt.*] *Theobald;*
not in Q1.   163.1.] *Finis Actus Secundi. Q1.*

    149. *haltersack*] Sack fitted with strings for hanging up, used colloquially
to mean 'gallows-bird'.

    150. *on's*] for his.

    151. *Ay . . . face.*] Most editors have accepted Theobald's transformation
into a question ('Ay . . . face?'), which would fit Philip's apparent habit of
confused but also belligerent dithering and 3 Man's reply. Q1 makes perfect
sense, however, if 'wouldst' is taken in the sense 'ought to, should' (*OED*
Will *v²* II 40b, 41).

    153. *visor*] mask.

    156. *peas*] The pun 'peas'/'peace' may be a nod to Jonson, cf. *Every Man*
Out of His Humour, 4.1.119 (ed. Helen Ostovich, Revels Plays, Manchester,
2001).

    159. *on*] of.

    162. *anon*] immediately.

Act 3

Enter ARBACES *and* GOBRIUS.

Arbaces. My sister take it ill?
Gobrius.   Not very ill.
    Something unkindly she doth take it, sir,
    To have her husband chosen to her hands.
Arbaces. Why, Gobrius, let her. I must have her know
    My will, and not her own, must govern her.   5
    What, will she marry with some slave at home?
Gobrius. O, she is far from any stubbornness—
    You much mistake her—and no doubt will like
    Where you will have her. But when you behold her,
    You will be loath to part with such a jewel.   10
Arbaces. To part with her! Why, Gobrius, art thou mad?
    She is my sister.
Gobrius.   Sir, I know she is,
    But it were pity to make poor our land
    With such a beauty to enrich another.
Arbaces. Pish! Will she have him?   15
Gobrius [*Aside*]. I do hope she will not.—I think she will, sir.
Arbaces. Were she my father and my mother too,
    And all the names for which we think folks friends,
    She should be forced to have him when I know
    'Tis fit. I will not hear her say she's loath.   20
Gobrius [*Aside*]. Heaven bring my purpose luckily to pass;
    You know 'tis just.—Sir, she'll not need constraint,

3.1] Actus Terti Scaena Prima. *Q1.*   16. I do . . . not.] *Q2; not in Q1.*

2. *Something unkindly*] Somewhat resentfully, with some dissatisfaction.
3. *to her hands*] for her.
6. *slave*] contemptible person.
16. *I . . . not*] Q1 alone omits these words; on the textual significance of
their appearance in Q2, see Introduction, p. 42.

She loves you so.

Arbaces.   How does she love me? Speak.

Gobrius. She loves you more than people love their health
That live by labour, more than I could love   25
A man that died for me if he could live
Again.

Arbaces.   She is not like her mother then?

Gobrius. O, no. When you were in Armenia,
I durst not let her know when you were hurt,
For at the first on every little scratch   30
She kept her chamber, wept, and would not eat
Till you were well. And many times the news
Was so long coming that, before we heard,
She was as near her death as you your health.

Arbaces. Alas, poor soul; but yet she must be ruled.   35
I know not how I shall requite her well.
I long to see her; have you sent for her
To tell her I am ready?

Gobrius.   Sir, I have.

Enter 1 Gentleman *and* TIGRANES.

1 Gentleman. Sir, here's the Armenian king.

Arbaces. He's welcome.   40

1 Gentleman. And the Queen-Mother and the Princess wait
without.

Arbaces. Good Gobrius, bring them in.—   *Exit* GOBRIUS.
Tigranes, you will think you are arrived
In a strange land, where mothers cast to poison   45
Their only sons. Think you you shall be safe?

Tigranes. Too safe I am, sir.

Enter GOBRIUS, ARANE, PANTHEA, SPACONIA,
BACURIUS, MARDONIUS, BESSUS, *and* 2 Gentleman.

38.1. SD 1 Gentleman *and*] *Q2; not in Q1.*   39, 41. SH 1 *Gentleman.*] *Q2;*
Gent. Q1.   42. SD] *Q2; not in Q1.*   47.2. SD *and* 2 Gentleman.] *Turner;*
not in Q1; and two Gentlemen. Q2.

36. *requite*] repay, recompense.
45. *cast*] plot.
47. *safe*] Tigranes puns on Arbaces's meaning (unharmed) to express his
own feeling (confined, unable to escape).

Arane. As low as this I bow to you, and would   [*Bows.*]
  As low as is my grave to show a mind
  Thankful for all your mercies.
Arbaces.   O, stand up   50
  And let me kneel! The light will be ashamed
  To see observance done to me by you.
Arane. You are my king.
Arbaces.   You are my mother; rise.
  As far be all your faults from your own soul
                                    [*Raises her.*]
  As from my memory; then you shall be   55
  As white as innocence herself.
Arane.   I came
  Only to show my duty and acknowledge
  My sorrow for my sins; longer to stay
  Were but to draw eyes more attentively
  Upon my shame. That power that kept you safe   60
  From me preserve you still.
Arbaces.   Your own desires
  Shall be your guard.   *Exit* ARANE.
Panthea.   Now let me die!
  Since I have seen my lord the king return
  In safety, I have seen all good that life
  Can show me. I have ne'er another wish   65
  For heaven to grant, nor were it fit I should,
  For I am bound to spend my age to come
  In giving thanks that this was granted me.

---

48. SD] *This ed.; not in Q1; Kneels. Weber.*   49. is] *Q2;* to *Q1.*   54. SD]
Dyce; not in Q1.   61. SD *Exit* ARANE] *Q2; Exit. Q1 (after* still.*).*

---

48. SD *Bows*] Arane may kneel here, as Weber and some other editors
direct, but she says 'bow' and 'to stoop and lower the head' (*OED* Bow *v*[1]
4) would be sufficient. Theobald suggests a precedent for the bowing, kneel-
ing, and rising here in the preliminaries to Volumnia's supplication in *Coriolanus* (5.3.29–31, 50–62), with its shock, for both character and audience, at
seeing a mother enacting a child's 'duty' to her son.

49. *is*] Q1's 'to' is probably a memorial error caused by 'to' in 48 and later
in 49.

62–8. *Now . . . me*] Panthea here matches Arbaces in extreme rhetoric
that verges on the ridiculous, a technique of characterisation that conveys
their youthful innocence as romance protagonists while ensuring the audience's emotional disengagement from either their joy or their anguish.

Gobrius. Why does not your majesty speak?
Arbaces. To whom?   70
Gobrius. To the princess.
Panthea. Alas, sir, I am fearful. You do look
   On me as if I were some loathèd thing
   That you were finding out a way to shun.
Gobrius. Sir, you should speak to her.   75
Arbaces. Ha?
Panthea. I know I am unworthy, yet not ill;
   Armed with which innocence here I will kneel   [*Kneels.*]
   Till I am one with earth, but I will gain
   Some words and kindness from you.   80
Tigranes. Will you speak, sir?
Arbaces [*Aside*].   Speak! Am I what I was?
   What art thou that dost creep into my breast
   And dar'st not see my face? Show forth thyself.
   I feel a pair of fiery wings displayed
   Hither, from thence. You shall not tarry there;   85
   Up and begone! If thou beest love, begone,
   Or I will tear thee from my wounded flesh,
   Pull thy loved down away, and with a quill,
   By this right arm drawn from thy wanton wing,
   Write to thy laughing mother in thy blood   90
   That you are powers belied and all your darts
   Are to be blown away by men resolved,
   Like dust. I know thou fearst my words. Away!
Tigranes [*Aside*]. O, misery! Why should he be so slow?
   There can no falsehood come of loving her,   95
   Though I have given my faith; she is a thing
   Both to be loved and served beyond my faith.
   I would he would present me to her quickly.
Panthea. Will you not speak at all? Are you so far

77–8. ill; / Armed] *Theobald subst.;* ill, / Arm'd, *Q1;* ill-armed *Langbaine.*
78. SD] *Weber.; not in Q1.* 95–6. her, / . . . faith;] *Q1;* her. / . . . faith,
Weber.

---

85. *Hither, from thence*] The 'pair of fiery wings displayed / Hither' are the
blushes now in his cheeks; they come from Cupid's resting-place 'thence',
in his breast.
   90. *thy laughing mother*] Classical poets apply this epithet (*ridens*) to
Venus.

From kind words? Yet to save my modesty,   100
That must talk till you answer, do not stand
As you were dumb. Say something, though it be
Poisoned with anger that may strike me dead.
Mardonius. Have you no life at all? For manhood sake,
Let her not kneel and talk neglected thus.   105
A tree would find a tongue to answer her,
Did she but give it such a loved respect.
Arbaces. You mean this lady? Lift her from the earth;
Why do you let her kneel so long?—Alas,
                                 [Mardonius raises Panthea.]
Madam, your beauty uses to command   110
And not to beg. What is your suit to me?
It shall be granted, yet the time is short
And my affairs are great.—But where's my sister?
I bade she should be brought.
Mardonius [Aside].   What, is he mad?
Arbaces. Gobrius, where is she?   115
Gobrius. Sir?
Arbaces. Where is she, man?
Gobrius. Who, sir?
Arbaces. Who? Hast thou forgot? My sister.
Gobrius. Your sister, sir?   120
Arbaces. Your sister, sir? Someone that has a wit,
Answer. Where is she?
Gobrius.   Do you not see her there?
Arbaces. Where?
Gobrius. There.
Arbaces. There? Where?   125
Mardonius. 'Slight, there. Are you blind?
Arbaces. Which do you mean? That little one?
                           [Indicates Spaconia.]
Gobrius.   No, sir.

---

109. SD] *This ed.; not in Q1; They raise Panthea. Dyce.*   121. Someone] *Q2;*
Gob. Some one *Q1 (on new line).*   122–5. SH *Gobrius. . . . Arbaces. . . .*
Gobrius . . . . Arbaces.] Q2; Arb. . . . Gob. . . . Arb. . . . Gob. Q1.   127. SD]
Turner; not in Q1.

---

107. *respect*] regard, attention.
126. *'Slight*] A cry of impatience (contraction of 'By God's light').

Arbaces. No, sir! Why do you mock me? I can see
   No other here but that petitioning lady.
Gobrius. That's she.
Arbaces.   Away!
Gobrius.   Sir, it is she.
Arbaces.   'Tis false.   130
Gobrius. Is it?
Arbaces.   As hell, by heaven, as false as hell.
   My sister—is she dead? If it be so,
   Speak boldly to me, for I am a man
   And dare not quarrel with divinity;
   But do not think to cozen me with this.   135
   I see you all are mute and stand amazed,
   Fearful to answer me. It is too true
   A decreed instant cuts off every life,
   For which to mourn is to repine. She died
   A virgin though, more innocent than sleep,   140
   As clear as her own eyes, and blessedness
   Eternal waits upon her where she is.
   I know she could not make a wish to change
   Her state for new, and you shall see me bear
   My crosses like a man. We all must die,   145
   And she hath taught us how.
Gobrius.   Do not mistake
   And vex yourself for nothing, for her death
   Is a long life off yet, I hope. 'Tis she;
   And if my speech deserve not faith, lay death
   Upon me, and my latest words shall force   150
   A credit from you.
Arbaces.   Which, good Gobrius?
   That lady dost thou mean?
Gobrius.   That lady, sir.
   She is your sister, and she is your sister
   That loves you so; 'tis she for whom I weep

153–5. She . . . thus.] *Q2; not in Q1.*

135. *cozen*] deceive, cheat.
142. *waits upon*] attends (in the manner of a servant).
150. *latest*] last.
151. *credit*] belief.

To see you use her thus.

Arbaces.   It cannot be.   155

Tigranes [*Aside*]. Pish, this is tedious.

    I cannot hold; I must present myself.

    And yet the sight of my Spaconia

    Touches me as a sudden thunderclap

    Does one that is about to sin.

Arbaces.   Away!   160

    No more of this. Here I pronounce him traitor,

    The direct plotter of my death, that names

    Or thinks her for my sister. 'Tis a lie,

    The most malicious of the world, invented

    To mad your king. He that will say so next,   165

    Let him draw out his sword and sheath it here—

    It is a sin fully as pardonable.

    She is no kin to me, nor shall she be;

    If she were any, I create her none.

    And which of you can question this? My power   170

    Is like the sea, that is to be obeyed

    And not disputed with. I have decreed her

    As far from having part of blood with me

    As the naked Indians. Come and answer me,

    He that is boldest now. Is that my sister?   175

Mardonius [*Aside*]. O, this is fine.

Bessus. No, marry, is she not, an't please your majesty.

    I never thought she was; she's nothing like you.

Arbaces. No; 'tis true, she is not.

Mardonius [*To Bessus*].   Thou shouldst be hanged.

Panthea. Sir, I will speak but once. By the same power   180

    You make my blood a stranger unto yours

    You may command me dead, and so much love

    A stranger may importune, pray you, do.

    If this request appear too much to grant,

    Adopt me of some other family   185

    By your unquestioned word, else I shall live

    Like sinful issues that are left in streets

    By their regardless mothers, and no name

---

173. *having part of*] sharing.

185. *Adopt me of*] Assign me.

Will be found for me.
Arbaces.   I will hear no more.
      [*Aside*] Why should there be such music in a voice   190
      And sin for me to hear it? All the world
      May take delight in this, and 'tis damnation
      For me to do so. [*To her*] You are fair and wise
      And virtuous, I think, and he is blest
      That is so near you as your brother is.   195
      [*Aside*] But you are naught to me but a disease,
      Continual torment without hope of ease.
      Such an ungodly sickness I have got,
      That he that undertakes my cure must first
      O'erthrow divinity, all moral laws,   200
      And leave mankind as unconfined as beasts,
      Allowing them to do all actions
      As freely as they drink when they desire.
      [*To her*] Let me not hear you speak again. [*Aside*] Yet so
      I shall but languish for the want of that   205
      The having which would kill me. [*To them*] No man here
      Offer to speak for her, for I consider
      As much as you can say. [*Aside*] I will not toil
      My body and my mind too. Rest thou there;   [*Sits.*]
      Here's one within will labour for you both.   210
Panthea. I would I were past speaking.
Gobrius.   Fear not, madam,
      The King will alter. 'Tis some sudden rage,
      And you shall see it end some other way.
Panthea. Pray God it do.
Tigranes [*Aside*]. Though she to whom I swore be here, I
      cannot   215
      Stifle my passion longer. If my father

---

209. SD] *Bond subst. (Sinking into his chair of state.); not in Q1.*   212. rage]
Q2; change Q1.

---

      191. *And*] i.e. And yet.
      207. *consider*] already think about.
      209–10. *Rest thou . . . both*] Addressed to his body as he apparently sits,
asserting that his mind ('one within') will now have to 'labour' doubly, for
both tormented mind and exhausted body.
      211. *past speaking*] i.e. unconscious (perhaps even dead, as she begged at
182–3).

Should rise again disquieted with this
And charge me to forbear, yet it would out.
[*Apart to Panthea*] Madam, a stranger and a prisoner begs
To be bid welcome.
Panthea.   You are welcome, sir,   220
        I think, but if you be not, 'tis past me
        To make you so, for I am here a stranger
        Greater than you. We know from whence you come,
        But I appear a lost thing and by whom
        Is yet uncertain, found here in the court   225
        And only suffered to walk up and down
        As one not worth the owning.
Spaconia [*Aside*].   O, I fear
        Tigranes will be caught; he looks, methinks,
        As he would change his eyes with her. Some help
        There is above for me, I hope.   230
Tigranes. Why do you turn away, and weep so fast,
        And utter things that misbecome your looks?
        Can you want owning?
Spaconia [*Aside*].   O, 'tis certain so.
Tigranes. Acknowledge yourself mine—
Arbaces. How now?   [*Rises.*]
Tigranes.   And then see if you want an owner.   235
Arbaces. They are talking.
Tigranes. Nations shall own you for their queen.
Arbaces. Tigranes, art not thou my prisoner?
Tigranes. I am.
Arbaces. And who is this?   240
Tigranes. She is your sister.
Arbaces. She is so.
Mardonius [*Aside*]. Is she so again? That's well.

---

219. SD] *Turner; not in Q1; Comes forward. Weber.*   235. SD] *This ed.; not in*
Q1.

229. *change*] exchange.
235. SD Rises.] Though it is clear when Arbaces sits (209), it is not clear
when he ought to rise; some editors leave him sitting until he kneels (293).
The moment of agitation when he becomes aware of Tigranes and Panthea
in conversation seems the most appropriate for his rising, though it is also
conceivable that earlier he did not actually sit but rather leaned on some
prop and now straightens to attention.

Arbaces. And how dare you then offer to change words with
    her?
Tigranes. Dare do it? Why you brought me hither, sir,   245
    To that intent.
Arbaces.   Perhaps I told you so.
    If I had sworn it, had you so much folly
    To credit it? The least word that she speaks
    Is worth a life. Rule your disordered tongue,
    Or I will temper it.
Spaconia [*Aside*].   Blest be that breath.   250
Tigranes. Temper my tongue! Such incivilities
    As these no barbarous people ever knew.
    You break the law of nature and of nations.
    You talk to me as if I were a prisoner
    For theft. My tongue be tempered? I must speak   255
    If thunder check me, and I will.
Arbaces.   You will?
Spaconia [*Aside*]. Alas, my fortune!
Tigranes. Do not fear his frown; dear madam, hear me.
Arbaces. Fear not my frown? But that 'twere base in me
    To fight with one I know I can o'ercome,   260
    Again thou shouldst be conquerèd by me.
Mardonius [*Aside*]. He has one ransom with him already.
    Methinks 'twere good to fight double or quit.
Arbaces. Away with him to prison.—Now, sir, see
    If my frown be regardless.—Why delay you?   265
    Seize him, Bacurius.—You shall know my word
    Sweeps like a wind, and all it grapples with
    Are as the chaff before it.
Tigranes.   Touch me not.
Arbaces. Help there!
Tigranes. Away!   270

---

244. *change*] exchange.
249. *disordered*] (1) unruly, (2) disobedient (by speaking to Panthea
against his wishes).
250. *temper*] curb.
262. *with*] for.
263. *quit*] nothing.
265. *regardless*] unworthy of respect, safe to disregard.

1 Gentleman. It is in vain to struggle.
2 Gentleman.   You must be forced.
Bacurius. Sir, you must pardon us, we must obey.

                                          [*They seize him.*]

Arbaces. Why do you dally there? Drag him away
   By anything.
Bacurius. Come, sir.   275
Tigranes. Justice, thou oughtst to give me strength enough
   To shake all these off.—This is tyranny,
   Arbaces, subtler than the burning bull's
   Or that famed tyrant's bed. Thou mightst as well
   Search in the depth of winter through the snow   280
   For half-starved people, to bring home with thee
   To show 'em fire and send 'em back again,
   As use me thus.
Arbaces.   Let him be close, Bacurius.

           Exeunt TIGRANES [*guarded by the two* Gentlemen]
                    and BACURIUS.

Spaconia [*Aside*]. I ne'er rejoiced at any ill to him
   But this imprisonment. What shall become   285
   Of me forsaken?
Gobrius.   You will not let your sister
   Depart thus discontented from you, sir?
Arbaces. By no means, Gobrius. I have done her wrong
   And made myself believe much of myself

---

272. SD] *Turner; not in Q1.* 283.1. SD] *Exeunt* TIGRANES . . . *and*
BACURIUS.] *Q2 (Exit . . .); not in Q1. guarded by the two* Gentlemen] *Weber
subst.; not in Q1.*

---

   274. *By anything*] By any means.
   278. *burning bull's*] i.e. Philaris's brazen bull. This tyrant is said to have
punished his enemies by roasting them alive and enjoying their groans as
expressive of the bull's bellowing.
   279. *tyrant's bed*] i.e. Procrustes's bed. According to legend, the Attic
highwayman Procrustes bound his victims to an iron bed and forced them
to fit by either stretching them or lopping off their feet.
   283. *close*] closely confined, secured.
   283.1] Weber's expansion of Q2's SD (*guarded by the two Gentlemen*) visu-
ally reinforces Arbaces's irrational treatment of the prince he had intended
as his sister's husband.

That is not in me. [*To Panthea*] You did kneel to me   290
Whilst I stood stubborn and regardless by
And, like a god incensed, gave no ear
To all your prayers. Behold, I kneel to you.   [*Kneels.*]
Show a contempt as large as was my own,
And I will suffer it; yet at the last,   295
Forgive me.
Panthea.   O, you wrong me more in this
Than in your rage you did. You mock me now. [*Kneels.*]
Arbaces. Never forgive me then, which is the worst
Can happen to me.
Panthea.   If you be in earnest,
Stand up and give me but a gentle look   300
And two kind words, and I shall be in heaven.
Arbaces. Rise you then too.   [*Rises and raises Panthea.*]
                Here I acknowledge thee
My hope, the only jewel of my life,
The best of sisters, dearer than my breath,
A happiness as high as I could think;   305
And when my actions call thee otherwise,
Perdition light upon me.
Panthea.   This is better
Than if you had not frowned. It comes to me
Like mercy at the block, and when I leave
To serve you with my life, your curse be with me.   310
Arbaces. Then thus I do salute thee, and again   [*Kisses her.*]
To make this knot the stronger. [*Aside*] Paradise
Is there. [*To Panthea*] It may be you are still in doubt,
This third kiss blots it out. [*Aside*] I wade in sin
And foolishly entice myself along.—   315
Take her away; see her a prisoner
In her own chamber, closely, Gobrius.
Panthea. Alas, sir, why?

---

293. SD] *Weber; not in Q1.* 297. SD] *Dyce; not in Q1.* 302. SD] *Dyce subst.; not in Q1.* 311. SD] *Dyce; not in Q1.* 314. This] *Q2;* This, this *Q1.*

291. *regardless*] heedless. Arbaces here uses the same word he had with Tigranes (265); in each case he has acted 'like a god incensed' (292), which in a human king is tyranny.

311. *salute*] greet, here with a kiss. As 314 makes clear, Abaces should kiss his 'sister' three times during this speech.

Arbaces. I must not stay the answer.—Do it.

Gobrius.   Good sir—

Arbaces. No more. Do it, I say.   320

Mardonius [*Aside*]. This is better and better.

Panthea. Yet hear me speak.

Arbaces.   I will not hear you speak.—
Away with her. Let no man think to speak
For such a creature, for she is a witch,
A poisoner, and a traitor.   325

Gobrius. Madam, this office grieves me.

Panthea. Nay, 'tis well; the king is pleased with it.

Arbaces. Bessus, go you along too with her. I will prove
All this that I have said, if I may live
So long. But I am desperately sick,   330
For she has given me poison in a kiss—
She had it 'twixt her lips—and with her eyes
She witches people. Go, without a word.—
      Exeunt GOBRIUS, PANTHEA, BESSUS, *and* SPACONIA.
[*Aside*] Why should you that have made me stand in war
Like fate itself, cutting what threads I pleased,   335
Decree such an unworthy end of me
And all my glories? What am I, alas,
That you oppose me? If my secret thoughts
Have ever harboured swellings against you,
They could not hurt you, and it is in you   340
To give me sorrow that will render me
Apt to receive your mercy. Rather so—
Let it be rather so—than punish me
With such unmanly sins. Incest is in me
Dwelling already, and it must be holy   345
That pulls it thence.—Where art, Mardonius?

Mardonius. Here, sir.

Arbaces.   I prithee, bear me if thou canst.

---

319. SH *Gobrius.*] *Q2; Pan. Q1.*   326. SH *Gobrius.*] *Q2; Bac. Q1.*   327.
SH *Panthea.*] *Q2; Gob. Q1.*   333.1. SD] *Q2; Exeunt omnes, præ. Ar. Mar. Q1.*

---

335. *threads*] i.e. threads of life. Arbaces's simile draws on the classical
myth of the three Fates, one of whom spun the thread of a man's life, another
measured it, and a third brought death by cutting it.

347. *bear me*] (1) help support me physically (because 'my legs / Refuse
to bear my body' (349–50)), with a pun on (2) bear with me (in this time of
troubles).

Am I not grown a strange weight?

Mardonius.   As you were.

Arbaces. No heavier?

Mardonius.   No, sir.

Arbaces.   Why, my legs
Refuse to bear my body. O, Mardonius   350
Thou hast in field beheld me, when thou knowst
I could have gone, though I could never run.

Mardonius. And so I shall again.

Arbaces.   O, no, 'tis past.

Mardonius. Pray ye, go; rest yourself.

Arbaces. Wilt thou hereafter when they talk of me,   355
As thou shalt hear nothing but infamy,
Remember some of those things?

Mardonius. Yes, I will.

Arbaces.   I prithee, do, for thou
Shalt never see me so again.

Mardonius.   I warrant ye.

                                        Exeunt.

[3.2]

                     Enter BESSUS.

Bessus. They talk of fame; I have gotten it in the wars and will
afford any man a reasonable pennyworth. Some will say
they could be content to have it, but that it is to be
achieved with danger; but my opinion is otherwise, for if
I might stand still in cannon-proof and have fame fall   5

---

352. *gone . . . run*] Arbaces plays on a now-obsolete meaning of the verb
'to go' ('to walk'), reminding Mardonius of his former courage on the bat-
tlefield, where he could walk and move about (to fight effectively) but was
incapable running (in flight).

359. *warrant*] promise (I shall see you so again). Mardonius may be
promising that Arbaces's feeling of helplessness is temporary and that he will
demonstrate his bravery again; less optimistically, he may mean merely that
he will remember Arbaces's former greatness, no matter what he does now.

2. *afford . . . pennyworth*] yield it to any man at a bargain rate.

3. *but*] except.

5. *cannon-proof*] armour that resists cannonballs.

upon me, I would refuse it. My reputation came princi-
pally by thinking to run away, which nobody knows but
Mardonius, and I think he conceals it to anger me. Before
I went to the wars, I came to the town a young fellow
without means or parts to deserve friends, and my empty   10
guts persuaded me to lie and abuse people for my meat,
which I did, and they beat me. Then would I fast two
days, till my hunger cried out on me, 'Rail still'; then,
methought, I had a monstrous stomach to abuse them
again and did it. In this state I continued till they hung   15
me up by th' heels and beat me with hazel sticks, as if
they would have baked me and have cozened somebody
with me for venison. After this I railed and eat quietly,
for the whole kingdom took notice of me for a baffled,
whipped fellow, and what I said was remembered in mirth   20
but never in anger, of which I was glad. I would it were
at that pass again. After this, God called an aunt of mine
that left two hundred pounds in a cousin's hand for me,
who, taking me to be a gallant young spirit, raised a
company for me with the money and sent me into   25
Armenia with 'em. Away I would have run from them but
that I could get no company, and alone I durst not run.
I was never at battle but once, and there I was running,
but Mardonius cudgelled me; yet I got loose at last, but
was so afraid that I saw no more than my shoulders do   30
but fled with my whole company amongst my enemies
and overthrew 'em. Now the report of my valour is come
over before me, and they say I was a raw young fellow
but now I am improved. A plague of their eloquence;

---

10. *means or parts*] money or talents.
11. *lie . . . meat*] earn dinner by entertaining with slanderous gossip.
13. *Rail*] Inveigh against, scoff.
14. *stomach*] (1) inclination, with pun on (2) appetite.
16. *beat . . . sticks*] i.e. make him tender before cooking.
17–18. *cozened . . . with*] fooled someone into mistaking.
18. *quietly*] undisturbed.
19. *baffled*] disgraced (because hung by the heels, a traditional punishment for recreant knights).
22. *at that pass*] at that juncture.
25. *company*] (1) military regiment, with pun on (2) new group of com-
panions (picked up in 27).

'twill cost me many a beating. And Mardonius might help   35
this too if he would, for now they think to get honour
of me, and all the men I have abused call me freshly
to account—worthily, as they call it—by the way of
challenge.

Enter a Gentleman.

Gentleman. Good morrow, Captain Bessus.   40
Bessus. Good morrow, sir.
Gentleman. I come to speak with you—
Bessus. You are very welcome.
Gentleman. From one that holds himself wronged by you
some three years since. Your worth, he says, is famed, and 45
he nothing doubts but you will do him right, as beseems
a soldier.
Bessus [*Aside*]. A pox on 'em; so they cry all.
Gentleman. And a slight note I have about me for you, for the
delivery of which you must excuse me. It is an office that 50
friendship calls upon me to do and no way offensive to
you, since I desire but right on both sides.
                                    [*Gives him a paper.*]
Bessus. 'Tis a challenge, sir, is it not?
Gentleman. 'Tis an inviting to the field.
Bessus. An inviting? O, cry you mercy! [*Aside*] What a com- 55
pliment he delivers it with! He might as agreeably to my
nature present me poison with such a speech. [*Reads
aside*] Um—reputation; um—call you to an account;
um—forced to this; um—with my sword; um—like a
gentleman; um—dear to me; um—satisfaction.—'Tis   60
very well, sir. I do accept it, but he must await an answer
this thirteen weeks.
Gentleman. Why, sir, he would be glad to wipe off his stain as
soon as he can.
Bessus. Sir, upon my credit, I am already engaged to two   65

39.1. a Gentleman] *Q2; Gent. Q1.*   40. SH *Gentleman.*] *Q1; 3 Gentleman.
(and to exit at 79) Q2–8, F2.*   52. SD] *Weber subst. (a letter); not in Q1.*
57–8. SD] *Weber; not in Q1.*   58–60. um . . . um] *Q1;* um, um, um . . . um,
um, um *Q2.*   65. SH *Bessus.*] *Q2; not in Q1.*

45. *since*] ago.
46. *nothing*] not at all.

hundred and twelve, all which must have their stains
wiped off, if that be the word, before him.

Gentleman. Sir, if you be truly engaged but to one, he shall
stay a competent time.

Bessus. Upon my faith, sir, to two hundred and twelve; and   70
I have a spent body too much bruised in battle, so that I
cannot fight, I must be plain with you, above three
combats a day. All the kindness I can do him is to set him
resolutely in my roll the two hundred and thirteenth man,
which is something, for I tell you I think there will be   75
more after him than before him. I think so. Pray ye
commend me to him and tell him this.

Gentleman. I will, sir. Good morrow to you.

Bessus. Good morrow, good sir.   *Exit* [Gentleman].
Certainly my safest way were to print myself a coward,   80
with a discovery how I came by my credit, and clap it
upon every post. I have received above thirty challenges
within this two hours. Marry, all but the first I put off
with engagement, and by good fortune the first is no
madder of fighting than I, so that that's reserved. The   85
place where it must be ended is four days' journey off,
and our arbitrators are these: he has chosen a gentleman
in travel, and I have a special friend with a quartan ague
likely to hold him this five year for mine; and when his
man comes home, we are to expect my friend's health. If   90
they would send me challenges thus thick, as long as I
lived I would have no other living; I can make seven

---

79. SD *Exit* Gentleman.] *Theobald; Exit: Q1 (after 78 you); Exit 3 Gen. Q2
(after you).* 85. reserved] *Q1;* referred *Q2 (referd).* 87. these] *Q2;* there
Q1. 89. five year] *Q2;* time here *Q1.*

69. *competent*] sufficient (until you are free to satisfy his challenge).
76. *I think so*] Although Dyce supposed this a mistaken repetition of 'I
think' in the line above, Bond argues that it exhibits the 'feigned hesitation
about accuracy' that is Bessus's 'usual cover for a lie'; cf. 2.1.118–19, 155–9.
80. *print*] publish.
81. *discovery*] disclosure, revelation.
credit] reputation.
85. *madder*] more eager.
reserved] set aside, kept in store (as an excuse).
88. *quartan ague*] fever recurring every fourth day.
90. *expect*] await.

shillings a day o' th' paper to the grocers. Yet I learn
nothing by all these but a little skill in comparing of styles.
I do find evidently that there is some one scrivener in this   95
town that has a great hand in writing of challenges, for
they are all of a cut and six of 'em in a hand; and they
all end 'My reputation is dear to me, and I must require
satisfaction.'—Who's there? More paper, I hope. No, 'tis
my lord Bacurius; I fear all is not well betwixt us.   100

                     Enter BACURIUS.

Bacurius. Now, Captain Bessus, I come about a frivolous
    matter caused by as idle a report. You know you were a
    coward.
Bessus. Very right.
Bacurius. And wronged me.   105
Bessus. True, my lord.
Bacurius. But now people will call you valiant, desertlessly, I
    think; yet for their satisfaction, I will have you fight with
    me.
Bessus. O, my good lord, my deep engagements—   110
Bacurius. Tell not me of your engagements, Captain Bessus.
    It is not to be put off with an excuse. For my own part,
    I am none of the multitude that believe your conversion
    from coward.
Bessus. My lord, I seek not quarrels, and this belongs not to   115
    me. I am not to maintain it.
Bacurius. Who then, pray?
Bessus. Bessus the coward wronged you.
Bacurius. Right.
Bessus. And shall Bessus the valiant maintain what Bessus the   120
    coward did?
Bacurius. I prithee, leave these cheating tricks. I swear thou
    shalt fight with me, or thou shalt be beat extremely and
    kicked.

---

93. *to the grocers*] i.e. the grocers would buy the challenges to use as wrap-
ping paper.
95. *scrivener*] professional letter-writer.
97. *a cut*] one style (a metaphor drawn from tailoring, making fashionable clothes to order).
   a hand] one handwriting.

Bessus. Since you provoke me thus far, my lord, I will fight   125
  with you; and, by my sword, it shall cost me twenty
  pounds but I will have my leg well a week sooner
  purposely.
Bacurius. Your leg! Why, what ails your leg? I'll do a cure
  on you; stand up!   [*Kicks him.*]   130
Bessus. My lord, this is not noble in you.
Bacurius. What dost thou with such a phrase in thy mouth? I
  will kick thee out of all good words before I leave thee.
                                        [*Kicks him again.*]
Bessus. My lord, I take this as a punishment for the offence I
  did when I was a coward.   135
Bacurius. When thou wert! Confess thyself a coward still, or,
  by this light, I'll beat thee into sponge.
Bessus. Why, I am one.
Bacurius. Are you so, sir? And why do you wear a sword then?
  Come, unbuckle. Quick!   140
Bessus. My lord—
Bacurius. Unbuckle, I say, and give it me, or, as I live, thy
  head will ache extremely.
Bessus. It is a pretty hilt, and if your lordship take an affec-
  tion to it, with all my heart I present it to you for a new-   145
  year's gift.
        [*Gives him his sword, with a knife attached to the belt.*]
Bacurius. I thank you very heartily. Sweet captain, farewell.
Bessus. One word more. I beseech your lordship to render me
  my knife again.
Bacurius. Marry, by all means, captain. [*Returns knife.*]   150
  Cherish yourself with it and eat hard, good captain; we
  cannot tell whether we shall have any more such. Adieu,
  dear captain.   *Exit.*
Bessus. I will make better use of this than of my sword. A base

---

127. well] *Q2; not in Q1.*   130. SD] *Theobald; not in Q1.*   133. SD] *Weber
subst.; not in Q1.*   146.1. SD] *Weber subst.; not in Q1.*   150. SD] *Weber; not
in Q1.*

145–6. *new-year's gift*] Gifts were customarily exchanged at New Year
rather than at Christmas. The whole speech is an elaborate attempt to trans-
late humiliation into an act of generosity.
  151. *hard*] vigorously, to the limit.

spirit has this vantage of a brave one: it keeps always at   155
a stay; nothing brings it down, not beating. I remember
I promised the King in a great audience that I would
make my backbiters eat my sword to a knife. How to get
another sword I know not, nor know any means left for
me to maintain my credit but impudence. Therefore will   160
I outswear him and all his followers that this is all is left
uneaten of my sword.   *Exit.*

[3.3]

Enter MARDONIUS.

Mardonius. I'll move the King. He is most strangely altered;
   I guess the cause, I fear, too right. Heaven has some secret
   end in't, and 'tis a scourge, no question, justly laid upon
   him. He has followed me through twenty rooms, and ever
   when I stay to await his command, he blushes like a girl   5
   and looks upon me as if modesty kept in his business; so
   turns away from me, but if I go on, he follows me again.

Enter ARBACES.

   See, here he is. I do not use this, yet, I know not how, I
   cannot choose but weep to see him. His very enemies, I
   think, whose wounds have bred his fame, if they should   10
   see him now, would find tears in their eyes.
Arbaces [*Aside*]. I cannot utter it. Why should I keep
   A breast to harbour thoughts I dare not speak?
   Darkness is in my bosom, and there lies
   A thousand thoughts that cannot brook the light.   15
   How wilt thou vex me when this deed is done,
   Conscience, that art afraid to let me name it?
Mardonius. How do you, sir?
Arbaces.   Why, very well, Mardonius.

7.1. SD] *Q2; not in Q1.*   13. thoughts . . . speak?] *Langbaine;* thoughts?
. . . speake: *Q1.*

155–6. *at a stay*] in the same condition.

  1. *move*] urge, appeal to.
  8. *do not use*] am not accustomed to.

How dost thou do?

Mardonius.   Better than you, I fear.

Arbaces. I hope thou art, for, to be plain with thee,   20
Thou art in hell else. Secret scorching flames
That far transcend earthly material fires
Are crept into me, and there is no cure.
Is not that strange, Mardonius; there's no cure?

Mardonius. Sir, either I mistake or there is something hid   25
That you would utter to me.

Arbaces. So there is, but yet I cannot do it.

Mardonius. Out with it, sir. If it be dangerous, I shall not
shrink to do you service. I shall not esteem my life a
weightier matter than indeed it is. I know 'tis subject to   30
more chances than it hath hours, and I were better lose
it in my king's cause than with an ague, or a fall, or sleeping to a thief, as all these are probable enough. Let me
but know what I shall do for you.

Arbaces [*Aside*]. It will not out.—Were you with Gobrius,   35
And bade him give my sister all content
The place affords, and give her leave to send
And speak to whom she please?

Mardonius.   Yes, sir, I was.

Arbaces. And did you to Bacurius say as much
About Tigranes?   40

Mardonius. Yes.

Arbaces. That's all my business.

Mardonius.   O, say not so.
You had an answer of all this before.
Besides, I think this business might be uttered
More carelessly.   45

Arbaces. Come, thou shalt have it out. I do beseech thee,
By all the love thou hast professed to me,
To see my sister from me.

Mardonius.   Well, and what?

---

19. do] *Q2; not in Q1.*   23. Are] *Q2; Art Q1.*   32. a fall] *Q2; fall Q1.*

---

32. *ague*] fever.
43. *of*] to.
45. *more carelessly*] with less caution.
48. *see . . . me*] visit . . . on my behalf.

Arbaces. That's all.
Mardonius.   That's strange. Shall I say nothing to her?
Arbaces. Not a word.   50
     But if thou lov'st me, find some subtle way
     To make her understand by signs.
Mardonius. But what? What should I make her understand?
Arbaces. O, Mardonius, for that I must be pardoned.
Mardonius. You may, but I can only see her then.   55
Arbaces. 'Tis true.   [*Gives a ring.*]
     Bear her this ring then, and, on more advice,
     Thou shalt speak to her. Tell her I do love
     My kindred all. Wilt thou?
Mardonius. Is there no more?
Arbaces.   O, yes. And her the best,   60
     Better than any brother loves his sister.
     That's all.
Mardonius.   Methinks this need not have been
     Delivered with such caution. I'll do it.
Arbaces. There is more yet. Wilt thou be faithful to me?
Mardonius. Sir, if I take upon me to deliver it   65
     After I hear it, I'll pass through fire to do it.
Arbaces. I love her better than a brother ought.
     Dost thou conceive me?
Mardonius.   I hope I do not, sir.
Arbaces. No? Thou art dull. Kneel down before her
     And ne'er rise again till she will love me.   70
Mardonius. Why, I think she does.
Arbaces. But better than she does, another way—
     As wives love husbands.
Mardonius. Why, I think there are few wives that love
     Their husbands better than she does you.   75
Arbaces. Thou wilt not understand me. Is it fit
     This should be uttered plainly? Take it, then,
     Naked as it is. I would desire her love
     Lasciviously, lewdly, incestuously,
     To do a sin that needs must damn us both   80
     And thee too. Dost thou understand me now?

57. *more advice*] further consideration.

Mardonius. Yes. There's your ring again.   [*Returns ring.*]
                                          What have I done
   Dishonestly in my whole life, name it,
   That you should put so base a business to me?
Arbaces. Didst thou not tell me thou wouldst do it?   85
Mardonius. Yes, if I undertook it; but if all
   My hairs were lives, I would not be engaged
   In such a cause to save my last life.
Arbaces [*Aside*]. O guilt, how poor and weak a thing art thou!
   This man that is my servant, whom my breath   90
   Might blow about the world, might beat me here
   Having his cause, whilst I, pressed down with sin,
   Could not resist him.—Dear Mardonius,
   It was a motion misbeseeming man,
   And I am sorry for it.   95
Mardonius. Pray God you may be so. You must understand,
   nothing that you can utter can remove my love and
   service from my prince. But otherwise, I think I shall not
   love you more; for you are sinful, and if you do this crime,
   you ought to have no laws, for after this it will be great   100
   injustice in you to punish any offender for any crime. For
   myself, I find my heart too big; I feel I have not patience
   to look on whilst you run these forbidden courses. Means
   I have none but your favour, and I am rather glad that
   I shall lose 'em both together than keep 'em with such   105
   conditions. I shall find a dwelling amongst some people
   where, though our garments perhaps be coarser, we shall
   be richer far within and harbour no such vices in 'em.
   God preserve you and mend you.
Arbaces. Mardonius! Stay, Mardonius; for though   110
   My present state require nothing but knaves
   To be about me, such as are prepared
   For every wicked act, yet who does know
   But that my loathèd fate may turn about
   And I have use of honest men again?   115
   I hope I may. I prithee, leave me not.

                Enter BESSUS *to them.*

---

82. SD] *Dyce; not in Q1.*

94. *motion*] proposal.

Bessus. Where is the King?

Mardonius. There.

Bessus. An't please your majesty, there's the knife.

Arbaces. What knife?   120

Bessus. The sword is eaten.

Mardonius. Away, you fool. The King is serious
    And cannot now admit your vanities.

Bessus. Vanities! I am no honest man if my enemies have not
    brought it to this. What, do you think I lie?   125

Arbaces. No, no. 'Tis well, Bessus, 'tis very well.
    I am glad on't.

Mardonius. If your enemies brought it to that, your enemies
    are cutlers. Come, leave the King.

Bessus. Why, may not valour approach him?   130

Mardonius. Yes, but he has affairs. Depart, or I shall be some-
    thing unmannerly with you.

Arbaces. No, let him stay, Mardonius, let him stay.
    I have occasions with him very weighty,
    And I can spare you now.   135

Mardonius. Sir?

Arbaces. Why, I can spare you now.

Bessus. Mardonius, give way to the state affairs.

Mardonius. Indeed, you are fitter for his present purpose.
                                                                     Exit.

Arbaces. Bessus, I should employ thee. Wilt thou do't?   140

Bessus. Do't for you? By this air, I will do anything without
    exception, be it a good, bad, or indifferent thing.

Arbaces. Do not swear.

Bessus. By this light, but I will. Anything whatsoever.

Arbaces. But I shall name a thing   145
    Thy conscience will not suffer thee to do.

Bessus. I would fain hear that thing.

---

127. I am] *Q2; Mar.* I am *Q1.*   128. SH *Mardonius.*] *Q2; not in Q1.*
130–2. *Bessus.* Why . . . you.] *Q2; not in Q1.*   141. Do't] *Q2;* Doe *Q1.*

___

125. *brought . . . this*] caused this to happen.
129. *cutlers*] tradesmen who made, sold, and repaired knives.
131–2. *something*] somewhat.
140. *should*] desire to.
146. *suffer*] permit.
147. *fain*] gladly.

Arbaces. Why I would have thee get my sister for me—
 Thou understandst me?—in a wicked manner.
Bessus. O, you would have a bout with her? I'll do't. I'll do't, 150
 i'faith.
Arbaces. Wilt thou? Dost make no more on't?
Bessus. More? No. Why, is there anything else? If there be, tell
 me; it shall be done too.
Arbaces. Hast thou no greater sense of such a sin?   155
 Thou art too wicked for my company,
 Though I have hell within me, and mayst yet
 Corrupt me further. Pray thee, answer me,
 How do I show to thee after this motion?
Bessus. Why, your majesty looks as well, in my opinion, as ever 160
 you did since you were born.
Arbaces. But thou appearest to me after thy grant
 The ugliest, loathed, detestable thing
 That I have ever met with. Thou hast eyes
 Like flames of sulphur which, methinks, do dart 165
 Infection on me, and thou hast a mouth
 Enough to take me in, where there do stand
 Four rows of iron teeth.
Bessus. I feel no such thing. But 'tis no matter how I look; I'll
 do your business as well as they that look better. And 170
 when this is dispatched, if you have a mind to your
 mother, tell me, and you shall see I'll set it hard.
Arbaces. My mother! Heaven forgive me to hear this;
 I am inspired with horror. I hate thee
 Worse than my sin, which, if I could come by, 175
 Should suffer death eternal, ne'er to rise
 In any breast again. Know I will die
 Languishing mad, as I resolve I shall,
 Ere I will deal by such an instrument.

---

149. understandst] *Q2;* understands *Q1.* 150. a bout] *Q7;* about *Q1.*
154. too] *Q2; not in Q1.*

---

150. *bout*] sexual encounter.
159. *show*] appear.
motion] Cf. 3.3.94.
165–8. *flames . . . teeth*] Bond notes that the description seems reminiscent of the Miracle Plays; also 'possibly of *The Faerie Queene*, I.xi.12–4, where the rows of teeth are three'.
172. *set it hard*] go at it vigorously.

Thou art too sinful to employ in this.   180
Out of the world; away!   [*Beats him.*]
Bessus.   What do you mean, sir?
Arbaces. Hung round with curses, take thy fearful flight
 Into the deserts where, 'mongst all the monsters,
 If thou findst one so beastly as thyself,
 Thou shalt be held as innocent.
Bessus.   Good sir—   185
Arbaces. If there were no such instruments as thou,
 We kings could never act such wicked deeds.
 Seek out a man that mocks divinity,
 That breaks each precept, both of God's and man's
 And Nature's too, and does it without lust,   190
 Merely because it is a law and good,
 And live with him, for him thou canst not spoil.
 Away, I say!—   *Exit* BESSUS.
   I will not do this sin.
 I'll press it here till it do break my breast.
 It heaves to get out; but thou art a sin,   195
 And, spite of torture, I will keep thee in.   [*Exit.*]

---

181. SD] *Weber; not in Q1.* 193. SD] *Q1 (after* sin*).* 196. SD *Exit.*]
Langbaine; not in Q1. 196.1.] *Finis Actus Tertii. Q1.*

---

190. *lust*] pleasure (*OED* Lust *n* 1).

Act 4

Enter GOBRIUS, PANTHEA, SPACONIA.

Gobrius. Have you written, madam?
Panthea.   Yes, good Gobrius.
Gobrius. And with a kindness and such winning words
    As may provoke him at one instant feel
    His double fault, your wrong and his own rashness?
Panthea. I have sent words enough, if words may win him   5
    From his displeasure, and such words, I hope,
    As shall gain much upon his goodness, Gobrius.
    Yet fearing, since th' are many and a woman's,
    A poor belief may follow, I have woven
    As many truths within 'em to speak for me   10
    That, if he be but gracious and receive 'em—
Gobrius. Good lady, be not fearful. Though he should not
    Give you your present end in this, believe it,
    You shall feel (if your virtue can induce you
    To labour out this tempest, which I know   15
    Is but a poor proof 'gainst your patience)
    All those contents your spirit will arrive at
    Newer and sweeter to you. Your royal brother
    (When he shall once collect himself and see
    How far he has been asunder from himself,   20
    What a mere stranger to his golden temper)
    Must from those roots of virtue (never dying,

4.1] Actus Quarti Scaena Prima. *Q1.*   12. Though] *Q2;* if *Q1.*   16.
'gainst] *Q2;* against *Q1.*

13. *present end*] immediate goal (i.e. your release).
15. *labour out*] ride out, endure.
16. *proof 'gainst*] trial of.
17. *contents*] contentments.

Though somewhat stopped with humour) shoot again
Into a thousand glories, bearing his fair branches
High as our hopes can look at, straight as justice,   25
Laden with ripe contents. He loves you dearly,
I know it, and I hope I need not further
Win you to understand it.
Panthea.   I believe it.
But howsoever, I am sure I love him dearly,
So dearly that if anything I write   30
For my enlarging should beget his anger—
Heaven be a witness with me, and my faith—
I had rather live entombed here.
Gobrius. You shall not feel a worse stroke than your grief;
I am sorry 'tis so sharp. I kiss your hand   35
And this night will deliver this true story
With this hand to your brother.
Panthea.   Peace go with you;
You are a good man.   *Exit* GOBRIUS.
                              My Spaconia,
Why are you ever sad thus?
Spaconia.   O, dear lady!
Panthea. Prithee, discover not a way to sadness   40
Nearer than I have in me. Our two sorrows
Work like two eager hawks, who shall get highest.
How shall I lessen thine? For mine, I fear,
Is easier known than cured.
Spaconia.   Heaven comfort both
And give yours happy ends, however I   45
Fall in my stubborn fortunes.
Panthea.   This but teaches
How to be more familiar with our sorrows,

---

29. But] *Q2; not in Q1.*   38. SD *Exit* GOBRIUS.] *Q2; Exit. Q1 (after 37*
brother*).*

---

23. *humour*] (1) sap (in the context of the arboreal metaphor), (2) one of
the four humours (here, by implication, an excess of choler; cf. 1.1.59n).
   29. *howsoever*] however he acts.
   31. *enlarging*] release.
   41. *Nearer*] Shorter, more direct.
   42. *eager*] earnestly contending.
   46. *This*] i.e. this mood of resignation (Bond).

That are too much our masters. Good Spaconia,
How shall I do you service?
Spaconia.   Noblest lady,
You make me more a slave still to your goodness   50
And only live to purchase thanks to pay you,
For that is all the business of my life now.
I will be bold, since you will have it so,
To ask a noble favour of you.
Panthea. Speak it; 'tis yours, for from so sweet a virtue   55
No ill demand has issue.
Spaconia. Then, ever-virtuous, let me beg your will
In helping me to see the prince Tigranes,
With whom I am equal prisoner, if not more.
Panthea. Reserve me to a greater end, Spaconia.   60
Bacurius cannot want so much good manners
As to deny your gentle visitation,
Though you came only with your own command.
Spaconia. I know they will deny me, gracious madam,
Being a stranger and so little famed,   65
So utter empty of those excellencies
That tame authority. But in you, sweet lady,
All these are natural, beside a power
Derived immediate from your royal brother,
Whose least word in you may command the kingdom.   70
Panthea. More than my word, Spaconia, you shall carry,
For fear it fail you.
Spaconia.   Dare you trust a token?
Madam, I fear I'm grown too bold a beggar.
Panthea. You are a pretty one, and trust me, lady,
It joys me I shall do a good to you,   75
Though to myself I never shall be happy.

---

59. not] *Q2;* no *Q1.*   67. tame] *Q2;* have *Q1.*   71. word] *Q2;* words *Q1.*

---

50. *still*] continually.

51. *live*] Constructed with 'You make me' in preceding line.

67. *tame*] Cf. 2.1.71 and 4.2.205 for other instances of Q1 misreading initial 't' as 'h'. Q2's changes may reflect authorial correction, though perhaps just common sense, at least in the other cases. Here, Q1's 'have' does make sense, though a weaker and less active one; Bond prints Q1 but in a note suggests that Q2's 'tame' might be a 'rare instance of improvement on the first ed.'.

Here, take this ring, and from me as a token
                                          [*Gives ring.*]
Deliver it; I think they will not stay you.
So all your own desires go with you, lady.
Spaconia. And sweet peace to your grace.
Panthea.   Pray God I find it.   80
                                          Exeunt.

[4.2]

              Enter TIGRANES *in prison.*

Tigranes. Fool that I am, I have undone myself
        And with mine own hand turned my fortune round
        That was a fair one. I have childishly
        Played with my hope so long till I have broke it,
        And now too late I mourn for't. O, Spaconia,   5
        Thou hast found an even way to thy revenge now.
        Why didst thou follow me, like a faint shadow,
        To wither my desires? But, wretched fool,
        Why did I plant thee 'twixt the sun and me
        To make me freeze thus? Why did I prefer her   10
        To the fair princess? O, thou fool, thou fool,
        Thou family of fools, live like a slave still
        And in thee bear thine own hell and thy torment;
        Thou hast deserved it. Couldst thou find no lady
        But she that has thy hopes to put her to   15
        And hazard all thy peace? None to abuse
        But she that loved thee ever, poor Spaconia,
        And so much loved thee that in honesty
        And honour thou art bound to meet her virtues?
        She that forgot the greatness of her griefs   20

---

77. SD] *Dyce; not in Q1.*

0.1. *in prison*] *Q2; not in Q1.*   2. turned] *Q2;* turne *Q1.*

---

    4. *hope*] i.e. hope of happiness ('broke' by shifting his affections from one
woman to another).
    6. *even*] (1) direct, (2) equal in magnitude (to my sin of betrayal).
    10. *prefer*] recommend.
    15. *put her*] i.e. put her in service (cf. 10).
    19. *meet*] equal, requite.

And miseries that must follow such mad passions,
Endless and wild as woman's; she that for thee
And with thee lost her liberty, her name,
And country. You have paid me equal, heavens,
And sent my own rod to correct me with,   25
A woman. For inconstancy I'll suffer;
Lay it on, justice, till my soul melt in me
For my unmanly, beastly, sudden doting
Upon a new face, after all my oaths,
Many and strange ones.   30
I feel my old fire flame again and burn
So strong and violent that should I see her
Again the grief and that would kill me.

Enter BACURIUS *and* SPACONIA.

Bacurius.   Lady,
Your token I acknowledge; you may pass.
There is the king.
Spaconia.   I thank your lordship for it.   35
                              Exit BACURIUS.
Tigranes [Aside]. She comes, she comes. Shame hide me
     ever from her.
Would I were buried or so far removed
Light might not find me out! I dare not see her.
Spaconia. Nay, never hide yourself, for were you hid
Where earth hides all her riches, near her centre,   40
My wrongs without more day would light me to you.
I must speak ere I die. Were all your greatness
Doubled upon you, y' are a perjured man
And only mighty in the wickedness
Of wronging women. Thou art false, false prince;   45
I live to see it. Poor Spaconia lives
To tell thee thou art false, and then no more.
She lives to tell thee thou art more unconstant
Than all ill women ever were together,

---

22. as woman's] *Q1;* in woman *Theobald.*   23. lost] *Q1;* left *Langbaine.*
24. me equal,] *Q2;* me equall *Q1;* me, equal *Theobald.*   29–30. face, . . .
oaths, . . . ones.] *Weber subst.;* face; . . . oathes, . . . ones, *Q1.*   33. me.] *Q2;*
me Ladie. *Q1.*   35. *Bacurius.* Lady] *Q2; Bac.* Your *Q1.*

---

24. *equal*] fairly.

Thy faith as firm as raging overflows   50
That no bank can command, and as lasting
As boys' gay bubbles blown in the air and broken.
The wind is fixed to thee, and sooner shall
The beaten mariner with his shrill whistle
Calm the loud murmurs of the troubled main   55
And strike it smooth again than thy soul fall
To have peace in love with any. Thou art all
That all good men must hate, and if thy story
Shall tell succeeding ages what thou wert,
O, let it spare me in it, lest true lovers,   .   60
In pity of my wrongs, burn thy black legend
And with their curses shake thy sleeping ashes.

Tigranes. O, O!

Spaconia. The destinies, I hope, have pointed out
Our ends alike, that thou mayst die for love,   65
Though not for me; for this assure thyself,
The princess hates thee deadly and will sooner
Be won to marry with a bull, and safer,
Than such a beast as thou art.—[*Aside*] I have struck,
I fear, too deep; beshrow me for't.—Sir,   70
This sorrow works me, like a cunning friendship,
Into the same piece with it.—[*Aside*] He's ashamed;
Alas, I have been too rugged.—Dear my lord,
I am sorry I have spoken anything,
Indeed I am, that may add more restraint   75
To that too much you have. Good sir, be pleased
To think it was a fault of love, not malice,
And do as I will do. Forgive it, prince;

---

64. SH *Spaconia.*] *Q2; not in Q1.*

53. *to*] compared to.
54–6. *beaten . . . again*] Spaconia alludes to the sailor's superstition that
whistling raises the wind (*OED* Whistle *v* 1).
61. *legend*] memorial inscription (on his tomb).
68–9. *bull . . . art*] The bull symbolises bestial male lust (cf. Arbaces at
4.4.136), but here context makes the analogy ironic, since Tigranes's soliloquy has concluded with his rejection of inconstancy, reassertion of his
humanity, and rededication to her.
70. *beshrow*] beshrew, evil befall (a mild curse).
71. *works*] weaves (the metaphor is drawn from embroidering).
like . . . friendship] even as close friends become alike.

I do, and can, forgive the greatest sins
To me you can repent of. Pray, believe me.   80
Tigranes. O, my Spaconia! O, thou virtuous woman!
Spaconia. No more; the King, sir.

Enter ARBACES, BACURIUS, *and* MARDONIUS.

Arbaces. Have you been careful of our noble prisoner
That he want nothing fitting for his greatness?
Bacurius. I hope his grace will quit me for my care, sir.   85
Arbaces. 'Tis well.—Royal Tigranes, health.
Tigranes. More than the strictness of this place can give, sir,
I offer back again to great Arbaces.
Arbaces. We thank you, worthy prince; and pray excuse us,
We have not seen you since your being here.   90
I hope your noble usage has been equal
With your own person. Your imprisonment,
If it be any, I dare say is easy
And shall not outlast two days.
Tigranes.   I thank you.
My usage here has been the same it was,   95
Worthy a royal conqueror. For my restraint,
It came unkindly because much unlooked for,
But I must bear it.
Arbaces. What lady is that, Bacurius?
Bacurius. One of the Princess' women, sir.   100
Arbaces. I feared it. Why comes she hither?
Bacurius. To speak with the Prince, Tigranes.
Arbaces. From whom Bacurius?
Bacurius. From the Princess, sir.
Arbaces. I know I had seen her.   105
Mardonius [*Aside*]. His fit begins to take him now again. 'Tis
a strange fever and 'twill shake us all anon, I fear; would
he were well cured of this raging folly. Give me the wars,
where men are mad and may talk what they list and held

---

105. know] *Q1;* knew *Q2.*

85. *quit*] acquit, pronounce not guilty.
87. *strictness*] (1) physical narrowness, (2) severity.
97. *unkindly*] (1) unnaturally, (2) ungraciously.
109. *list*] please.

the bravest fellows. This pelting, prattling peace is good   110
for nothing. Drinking's a virtue to it.

Arbaces. I see there's truth in no man, nor obedience,
But for his own ends. Why did you let her in?

Bacurius. It was your own command to bar none from him;
Beside, the Princess sent her ring, sir, for my warrant.   115

Arbaces. A token to Tigranes, did she not?
Sirrah, tell truth.

Bacurius.   I do not use to lie, sir;
'Tis no way I eat or live by. And I think
This is no token, sir.

Mardonius [Aside]. This combat has undone him. If he had   120
been well beaten, he had been temperate. I shall never
see him handsome again till he have a horseman's staff
poked through his shoulders or an arm broke with a
bullet.

Arbaces. I am trifled with.   125

Bacurius. Sir?

Arbaces. I know it, as I know thee to be false.

Mardonius [Aside]. Now the clap comes.

Bacurius. You never knew me so, sir. I dare speak it
And durst a worse man tell me, though my better.   130

Mardonius [Aside]. 'Tis well said, by my soul.

Arbaces. Sirrah, you answer as you had no life.

Bacurius. That I fear, sir, to lose nobly.

Arbaces. I say, sir, once again—

---

123. poked] *Q1;* yok'd *Q2.*   129–30. sir. . . . it / . . . better.] *Q1;* sir, . . . it;
/ . . . better—*Colman.*

---

110. *pelting*] paltry, worthless.
prattling] childishly chattering.

111. *to*] compared to.

117. *I . . . use*] I am not accustomed.

122. *handsome*] (1) easy to deal with (*OED* Handsome *a* 1, 5a), (2) seemly,
generous.
staff] lance.

123. *poked*] Q2's 'yoked', adopted in subsequent quartos and by several
later editors, would suggest not just wounding but capture.

128. *clap*] thunder-clap.

130. *durst . . . better*] i.e. would challenge any man who calls me false
because, though of a higher social status, that man would be my inferior in
nobility of mind.

Bacurius. You may say, sir, what you please.   135
Mardonius [*Aside*]. Would I might do so.
Arbaces. I will, sir, and say openly this woman carries letters.
　　By my life, I know she carries letters—this woman does
　　it.
Mardonius. Would Bessus were here to take her aside and   140
　　search her; he would quickly tell you what she carried,
　　sir.
Arbaces. I have found it out; this woman carries letters.
Mardonius [*Aside*]. If this hold, 'twill be an ill world for
　　bawds, chamber-maids, and post-boys. I thank God I   145
　　have none but his letters-patents, things of his own
　　inditing.
Arbaces. Prince, this cunning cannot do it.
Tigranes. Do what, sir? I reach you not.
Arbaces. It shall not serve your turn, Prince.   150
Tigranes. Serve my turn, sir?
Arbaces. Ay, sir, it shall not serve your turn.
Tigranes. Be plainer, good sir.
Arbaces. This woman shall carry no more letters back to
　　your love,
Panthea. By heaven, she shall not; I say she shall not.   155
Mardonius [*Aside*]. This would make a saint swear like a
　　soldier and a soldier like Termagant.
Tigranes. This beats me more, King, than the blows you
　　gave me.
Arbaces. Take 'em away both, and together let 'em be pris-
　　oners, strictly and closely kept or, sirrah, your life shall   160
　　answer it; and let nobody speak with 'em hereafter.

135–6. *Bacurius.* You . . . please. / *Mardonius.* . . . so] *Q1*; Bac. You . . . so
Q2–8, F2. 149. Do] *Q2; not in Q1.*

144. *hold*] continue.
145. *post-boys*] letter-carriers.
146. *letters-patents*] official documents.
147. *inditing*] composition.
149. *reach*] understand.
157. *Termagant*] A boastful and menacing, supposedly Saracen, deity who
appeared in medieval Miracle Plays; Hamlet would have a ranting actor
'whipt for o'erdoing Termagant' (*Ham.* 3.2.13).

Bacurius. Well, I am subject to you and must endure these
    passions.

Spaconia [Aside]. This is the imprisonment I have looked
    for always
    And the dear place I would choose.

        Exit BACURIUS *with* TIGRANES *and* SPACONIA.

Mardonius. Sir, have you done well now?   165

Arbaces. Dare you reprove it?

Mardonius. No.

Arbaces. You must be crossing me.

Mardonius. I have no letters, sir, to anger you
    But a dry sonnet of my corporal's   170
    To an old sutler's wife, and that I'll burn, sir.
    'Tis like to prove a fine age for the ignorant.

Arbaces. How darest thou so often forfeit thy life?
    Thou knowst 'tis in my power to take it.

Mardonius. Yes, and I know you wonnot, or, if you do,   175
    You'll miss it quickly.

Arbaces. Why?

Mardonius. Who shall then tell you of these childish follies
    When I am dead? Who shall put to his power
    To draw those virtues out of a flood of humours   180
    Where they are drowned and make 'em shine again?
    No, cut my head off. Do, kill me.
    Then you may talk, and be believed, and grow,
    And have your too-self-glorious temper rocked
    Into a dead sleep and the kingdom with you,   185
    Till foreign swords be in your throats and slaughter
    Be every where about you, like your flatterers.
    Do, kill me.

Arbaces. Prithee, be tamer, good Mardonius.

---

162. SH *Bacurius.*] *Q1; Tigr. Q2–8, F2.*   171. sutler's] *Q2;* Sadlers *Q1.*
184. rocked] *Theobald;* rott *Q1–8, F2.*   186. Till] *Q2;* Like *Q1.*

---

162. *Bacurius*] All seventeenth-century editions subsequent to Q1, followed by modern editors until Turner, give this speech to Tigranes.

170. *dry*] (1) passionless, (2) unadorned, plain.

171. *sutler's*] camp-victualler.

175. *wonnot*] will not.

179. *put to*] apply.

180. *humours*] passions (cf. 1.1.59n., 1.2.226–7).

Thou knowst I love thee; nay, I honour thee.   190
Believe it, good old soldier, I am all thine,
But I am racked clean from myself. Bear with me;
Woo't thou bear with me, good Mardonius?

Enter GOBRIUS.

Mardonius. There comes a good man. Love him too; he's
    temperate.
You may live to have need of such a virtue;   195
Rage is not still in fashion.
Arbaces.   Welcome, good Gobrius.
Gobrius. My service and this letter to your grace.
                                          [*Gives letter.*]
Arbaces. From whom?
Gobrius. From the rich mine of virtue and all beauty,
Your mournful sister.   200
Arbaces. She is in prison, Gobrius, is she not?
Gobrius. She is, sir, till your pleasure do enlarge her,
                                          [*Kneels.*]
Which on my knees I beg. O, 'tis not fit
That all the sweetness of the world in one,
The youth and virtue that would tame wild tigers   205
And wilder people that have known no manners,
Should live thus cloistered up. For your love's sake
(If there be any in that noble heart)
To her, a wretched lady and forlorn,
Or for her love to you (which is as much   210

---

193. good] *Q1;* my *Q2.*   197. SD] *Dyce; not in Q1.*   202. SD] *Weber; not
in Q1.*   205. tame] *Q2;* have *Q1.*

---

192. *racked*] torn. This figurative sense alludes to the result of having been
tortured on the rack, which pulled apart the joints of the prisoner strapped
to it (cf. 2.1.48).
    193. *woo't*] will.
    good] Editors who adopt Q2's 'my' believe Q1's 'good' to be a memo-
rial error induced by 'good' at 189. This is possible and produces a nicely
egocentric cascade of 'I', 'myself', 'me', 'me', 'my' in 192–3, as well as allit-
eration with 'Mardonius'. Yet Mardonius's immediate observation ('There
comes a good man. Love him too') suggests an intended repetition of 'good',
emphasising the moral issue, that supports Q1.
    196. *still*] always.
    202. *enlarge*] release.

As nature and obedience ever gave),
Have pity on her beauties.
Arbaces. Prithee, stand up. 'Tis true she is too fair
                                        [*Gobrius rises.*]
And all these commendations but her own.
Would thou hadst never so commended her,   215
Or I ne'er lived to have heard it, Gobrius.
If thou but knewst the wrong her beauty does her,
Thou wouldst in pity of her be a liar.
Thy ignorance has drawn me, wretched man,
Whither myself nor thou canst well tell. O, my fate!   220
I think she loves me, but I fear another
Is deeper in her heart. How thinkst thou, Gobrius?
Gobrius. I do beseech your grace, believe it not,
For let me perish if it be not false.
Good sir, read her letter.   [*Arbaces reads.*]   225
Mardonius [Aside]. This love, or what a devil is it, I know not,
begets more mischief than a wake. I had rather be well
beaten, starved, or lousy than live within the air on't. He
that had seen this brave fellow charge through a grove of
pikes but t' other day, and look upon him now, will ne'er   230
believe his eyes again. If he continue thus but two days
more, a tailor may beat him with one hand tied behind
him.
Arbaces. Alas, she would be at liberty,
And there be thousand reasons, Gobrius,   235
Thousands, that will deny it,
Which if she knew, she would contentedly
Be where she is and bless her virtue for it,
And me, though she were closer. She would, Gobrius;
Good man, indeed she would.   240
Gobrius. Then, good sir, for her satisfaction
Send for her and with reason make her know

---

213. SD] *Dyce; not in Q1.*   217. knewst] *Q2;* knew of *Q1.*   225. SD]
Weber; not in Q1.   236. Thousands] *Q2; not in Q1.*

227. *wake*] festival often associated with unruly merrymaking; cf. 1.1.219.
232. *tailor*] Tailors were proverbially unmanly and 'tailor' often used as a
synonym for 'coward'; see the listings under T23 in M. P. Tilley, *A Dictionary of the Proverbs in England in the Sixteenth and Seventeenth Centuries* (Ann
Arbor, MI, 1950).
239. *closer*] confined more closely.

Why she must live thus from you.
Arbaces. I will; go bring her to me.   *Exeunt* [*severally*].

[4.3]

       Enter BESSUS, *and two* Swordmen, *and a Boy.*

Bessus. Y' are very welcome both.—Some stools there, boy,
   And reach a table.—Gentlemen o' th' sword,
   Pray sit without more compliment.—Begone, child.—
                      [*Exit Boy.*]
   I have been curious in the searching of you,
   Because I understood you wise and valiant persons.   5
1 Swordman. We understand ourselves, sir.
Bessus. Nay, gentlemen and my dear friends o' th' sword,
   No compliment, I pray; but to the cause
   I hang upon, which, in few, is my honour.
2 Swordman. You cannot hang too much, sir, for your honour.   10
   But to your cause: be wise and speak truth.
Bessus. My first doubt is my beating by my prince.
1 Swordman. Stay there a little, sir. Do you doubt a beating,
   Or have you had a beating by your prince?
Bessus. Gentlemen o' th' sword, my prince has beaten me.   15
2 Swordman. Brother, what think you of this case?
1 Swordman. If he have beaten him, the case is clear.
2 Swordman. If he have beaten him, I grant the case.
   But how? We cannot be too subtle in this business.
   I say, but how?
Bessus.   Even with his royal hand.   20

244. SD *severally*] *Williams; not in Q1.*

3. SD] *Dyce; not in Q1.*

4.3.0.1] *Swordmen*] Masters in the art of fencing (here used pejoratively
for swaggerers posing as judges in questions of honour).
   2. *reach*] bring.
   4. *curious*] solicitous.
   6. *understand ourselves*] know how to conduct ourselves (punning on 5,
where 'understood you' = 'was informed you were').
   9. *hang upon*] am in expectation about.
   in few] in few words.
   12. *doubt*] point of uncertainty. 1 Swordman takes 'doubt' in another
meaning, 'fear' (13).
   19, 20. *how*] why, for what reason. Bessus, however, understands the word
to mean 'in what manner'.

1 Swordman. Was it a blow of love or indignation?

Bessus. 'Twas twenty blows of indignation, gentlemen,
  Besides two blows o' th' face.

2 Swordman. Those blows o' th' face have made a new case
  on't;
  The rest were but an honourable rudeness.   25

1 Swordman. Two blows o' th' face and given by a worse man,
  I must confess, as we swordmen say, had turned the business. Mark me brother—by a worse man; but being by
  his prince, had they been ten and those ten drawn ten
  teeth, beside the hazard of his nose for ever, all these had   30
  been but favours. This is my flat opinion, which I'll die
  in.

2 Swordman. The King may do much, captain, believe it, for
  had he cracked your skull through like a bottle or broke
  a rib or two with tossing of you, yet you had lost no   35
  honour. This is strange, you may imagine, but this is truth
  now, captain.

Bessus. I will be glad to embrace it, gentlemen.
  But how far may he strike me?

1 Swordman.   There's another,
  A new cause rising from the time and distance,   40
  In which I will deliver my opinion.
  He may strike, beat, or cause to be beaten, for these are
  natural to man. Your prince, I say, may beat you so far
  forth as his dominion reacheth, that's for the distance.
  The time, ten mile a day, I take it.   45

2 Swordman. Brother, you err. 'Tis fifteen mile a day;
  His stage is ten, his beatings are fifteen.

---

35. tossing] *Q2;* crossing *Q1.*   38. gentlemen] *Q2;* gentleman *Q1.*

---

  24. *on't*] of it.
  27. *turned the business*] been decisive.
  35. *tossing*] 'Tossing' seems best to fit the possibility of broken ribs; Turner
defends Q1's 'crossing' (= thwarting, opposing) as an intended euphemism.
  39. *how far*] how extensively. 1 Swordsman, however, comically mistakes
and thinks Bessus asks 'for how long and for what distance' (40).
  47. *stage*] division of a journey between changes to fresh horses. Apparently Arbaces's regular stage is ten miles, but he can go farther when delivering a beating.

Bessus. 'Tis o' the longest, but we subjects must—
1 Swordman. Be subject to it. You are wise and virtuous.
Bessus. Obedience ever makes that noble use on't,   50
    To which I dedicate my beaten body.
    I must trouble you a little further, gentlemen o' th' sword.
2 Swordman. No trouble at all to us, sir, if we may
    Profit your understanding. We are bound
    By virtue of our calling to utter our opinions   55
    Shortly and discreetly.
Bessus. My sorest business is I have been kicked.
2 Swordman. How far, sir?
Bessus. Not to flatter myself in it, all over;
    My sword lost but not forced, for discreetly   60
    I rendered it to save that imputation.
1 Swordman. It showed discretion, the best part of valour.
2 Swordman. Brother, this is a pretty case; pray, ponder on't.
    Our friend here has been kicked.
1 Swordman.   He has so, brother.
2 Swordman. Sorely, he says. Now, had he sit down here   65
    Upon the mere kick, it had been cowardly.
1 Swordman. I think it had been cowardly indeed.
2 Swordman. But our friend has redeemed it in delivering
    His sword without compulsion, and that man
    That took it of him, I pronounce a weak one   70
    And his kicks nullities.
    He should have kicked him after the delivery,
    Which is the confirmation of a coward.
1 Swordman. Brother, I take it you mistake the question.
    For say that I were kicked—
2 Swordman.   I must not say so,   75
    Nor I must not hear it spoke by th' tongue of man.
    You kicked, dear brother? You are merry.

---

49. SH *1 Swordman.*] *Q2 (1.); not in Q1.*   50. SH *Bessus.*] *Q2; 1. Q1.*   60.
lost . . . forced] *Theobald;* forst . . . lost *Q1–8, F2.*

---

57. *sorest*] (1) most grievous, (2) most painful.
58. *How far?*] What distance? Bessus understands the question as 'to what
extent' (59).
63. *pretty*] ingenious, complicated.

1 Swordman. But put the case I were kicked!
2 Swordman.   Let them put it
    That are things weary of their lives and know
    Not honour. Put case you were kicked!   80
1 Swordman. I do not say I was kicked.
2 Swordman. Nor no silly creature that wears his head
    Without a case, his soul in a skin coat.
    You kicked, dear brother!
Bessus. Nay, gentlemen, let us do what we shall do   85
    Truly and honestly.—Good sir, to th' question.
1 Swordman. Why then I say, suppose your boy kicked,
    captain?
2 Swordman. The boy may be supposed; he's liable.
    But kick my brother?
1 Swordman [*To Bessus*]. A foolish forward zeal, sir, in my
    friend.   90
    But to the boy: suppose the boy were kicked?
Bessus. I do suppose it.
1 Swordman.   Has your boy a sword?
Bessus. Surely no. I pray suppose a sword too.
1 Swordman. I do suppose it. You grant your boy was
    kicked, then?
2 Swordman. By no means, captain; let it be supposed still.   95
    This word 'grant' makes not for us.
1 Swordman. I say this must be granted.
2 Swordman. This must be granted, brother?
1 Swordman. Ay, this must be granted.
2 Swordman. Still the 'must'.   100
1 Swordman. I say this must be granted.
2 Swordman. Give me the 'must' again! Brother, you palter.

---

80. case] *Q1;* the case *Q2.*   102. again] *Q2;* againe, againe *Q1.*

    78. *put the case*] suppose.
    83. *Without a case*] unhelmeted.
    skin coat] unprotected body. Bond cites from Halliwell's *Dictionary* the
phrase 'to curry one's skin-coat', meaning to beat severely.
    88. *liable*] (1) likely to be kicked, and in a legal sense as a servant, (2)
subject to kicking.
    102. *palter*] equivocate.

1 Swordman. I will not hear you, wasp.

2 Swordman.   Brother, I say
    You palter. The 'must' three times together!
    I wear as sharp steel as another man,   105
    And my fox bites as deep. 'Musted', my dear brother?
    But to the cause again.

Bessus. Nay, look you, gentlemen—

2 Swordman. In a word, I ha' done.

1 Swordman [*To Bessus*]. A tall man, but untemperate; 'tis
    great pity.—   110
    Once more, suppose the boy kicked.

2 Swordman. Forward.

1 Swordman. And, being thoroughly kicked, laughs at the
    kicker.

2 Swordman. So much for us; proceed.

1 Swordman. And in this beaten scorn, as I may call it,   115
    Delivers up his weapon. Where lies the error?

Bessus. It lies i' th' beating, sir. I found it four days since.

2 Swordman. The error, and a sore one, as I take it,
    Lies in the thing kicking.

Bessus. I understand that well; 'tis sore indeed, sir.   120

1 Swordman. That is according to the man that did it.

2 Swordman. There springs a new branch. Whose was the
    foot?

Bessus. A lord's.

1 Swordman. The cause is mighty, but had it been two lords,
    And both had kicked you, if you laughed, 'tis clear.   125

Bessus. I did laugh, but how will that help me, gentlemen?

1 Swordman. Yes, it shall help you, if you laughed aloud.

Bessus. As loud as a kicked man could laugh, I laughed, sir.

---

106. Musted] *Q2;* musled *Q1.*   113. kicker] *Q2;* kicke *Q1.*   122. foot]
Q2; foole *Q1.*   123. A] *Q2;* Ah *Q1.*   127. SH *1 Swordman.*] *Q1 (1.); 2.*
Q2.

---

103. *I . . . wasp*] Theobald thought this line and the heated exchange over
the use of 'must' to be 'a sneer upon that celebrated quarrelling scene betwixt
Brutus and Cassius' in *Julius Caesar* (4.1.44–50); he also cites Coriolanus's
rage at the tribunes' insulting use of 'shall' in *Coriolanus* (3.1.85ff.).

106. *fox*] sword.

110. *tall*] bold, valiant.

1 Swordman. My reason now. The valiant man is known
   By suffering and contemning; you have   130
   Enough of both, and you are valiant.
2 Swordman. If he be sure he has been kicked enough.
   For that brave sufferance you speak of, brother,
   Consists not in a beating and away
   But in a cudgelled body, from eighteen   135
   To eight and thirty, in a head rebuked
   With pots of all size, daggers, stools, and bedstaves.
   This shows a valiant man.
Bessus. Then I am valiant, as valiant as the proudest,
   For these are all familiar things to me,   140
   Familiar as my sleep or want of money.
   All my whole body's but one bruise with beating;
   I think I have been cudgelled with all nations
   And almost all religions.
2 Swordman. Embrace him, brother; this man is valiant.   145
   I know it by myself, he's valiant.
1 Swordman. Captain, thou art a valiant gentleman;
   To abide upon't, a very valiant man.
Bessus. My equal friends o' th' sword, I must request
   Your hands to this.   150
2 Swordman. 'Tis fit it should be.
Bessus [Calling]. Boy, get some wine and pen and ink
   within.—
   Am I clear, gentlemen?
1 Swordman. Sir, when the world has taken notice what
   We have done, make much of your body, for, I'll pawn   155

---

152. SD] *Dyce subst. (To Boy within); not in Q1; Exit Boy. / Turner.*

130. *contemning*] scorning.
135–6. *eighteen . . . thirty*] 'i.e. during those twenty years when offences
are most commonly resented' (Bond).
136. *rebuked*] punished. Sympson (in Theobald) cites a possible allusion
to Plautus on parasites, *Persa*, 1.2.8, styled 'hard-heads' because accustomed
to having utensils thrown at them (*His cognomentum erat duris capitonibus*).
137. *bedstaves*] Wooden pins fitted to the bedstead to hold the bedding in
place.
148. *To abide upon't*] Depend upon it.
149. *equal*] fair, just (with a possible pun on 'alike in value').
150. *hands*] signatures (for which he needs 'pen and ink' (152)).

My steel, men will be coyer of their legs
Hereafter.
Bessus.   I must request you go along
And testify to the Lord Bacurius,
Whose foot has struck me, how you find my cause.
2 Swordman. We will, and tell that lord he must be ruled,   160
Or there be those abroad will rule his lordship. *Exeunt.*

[4.4]

Enter ARBACES *at one door,* GOBRIUS
and PANTHEA *at another.*

Gobrius. Sir, here's the Princess.
Arbaces.   Leave us then alone,
For the main cause of her imprisonment
Must not be heard by any but herself.—
                                             Exit GOBRIUS.
You are welcome, sister, and I would to God
I could so bid you by another name.—   5
[*Aside*] If you above love not such sins as these,
Circle my heart with thoughts as cold as snow
To quench these rising flames that harbour here.
Panthea. Sir, does it please you I should speak?
Arbaces.   Please me?
Ay, more than all the art of music can   10
Thy speech does please me, for it ever sounds
As thou broughtst joyful, unexpected news.
And yet it is not fit thou shouldst be heard;
I prithee, think so.
Panthea.   Be it so, I will.
I am the first that ever had a wrong   15
So far from being fit to have redress
That 'twas unfit to hear it. I will back
To prison rather than disquiet you,
And wait till it be fit.
Arbaces.   No, do not go,

3. SD] *Q2; not in Q1.*   12. broughtst] *Q2;* broughts *Q1.*

156. *coyer . . . legs*] i.e. they will be more chary of kicking you.

For I will hear thee with a serious thought.   20
I have collected all that's man about me
Together strongly, and I am resolved
To hear thee largely, but I do beseech thee
Do not come nearer to me, for there is
Something in that that will undo us both.   25
Panthea. Alas, sir, am I venom?
Arbaces.   Yes, to me.
Though of thyself I think thee to be in
As equal a degree of heat or cold
As nature can make, yet as unsound men
Convert the sweetest and the nourishingst meats   30
Into diseases, so shall I, distempered,
Do thee. I prithee, draw no nearer to me.
Panthea. Sir, this is that I would: I am of late
Shut from the world, and why it should be thus
Is all I wish to know.
Arbaces.   Why, credit me,   35
Panthea; credit me that am thy brother,
Thy loving brother, that there is a cause
Sufficient, yet unfit for thee to know,
That might undo thee everlastingly
Only to hear. Wilt thou but credit this?   40
By heaven, 'tis true; believe it if thou canst.
Panthea. Children and fools are ever credulous,
And I am both I think, for I believe.
If you dissemble, be it on your head.
I'll back unto my prison; yet methinks   45
I might be kept in some place where you are,
For in myself I find, I know not what
To call it, but it is a great desire
To see you often.
Arbaces. Fie, you come in a step. What do you mean,   50

50–1. step. . . . mean, . . . sister?] *Q1* (step, . . . meane . . . Sister,); step, . . . mean? . . . sister, *Langbaine.*

---

20. *with . . . thought*] thoroughly, carefully.
23. *largely*] at length.
29. *unsound*] unhealthy.
31. *distempered*] (1) diseased (continuing the metaphor), and figuratively (2) disturbed, in turmoil.
33. *that I would*] what I desire.
50. *come in*] approach.

Dear sister? Do not so! Alas, Panthea,
Where I am would you be? Why, that's the cause
You are imprisoned, that you may not be
Where I am.
Panthea. Then I must endure it, sir. God keep you.　　　55
Arbaces. Nay, you shall hear the cause in short, Panthea,
And when thou hearst it, thou wilt blush for me
And hang thy head down like a violet
Full of the morning's dew. There is a way
To gain thy freedom, but 'tis such a one　　　60
As puts thee in worse bondage, and I know
Thou wouldst encounter fire and make a proof
Whether the gods have care of innocents
Rather than follow it. Know I have lost
The only difference betwixt man and beast,　　　65
My reason.
Panthea. 　　　　　Heaven forbid!
Arbaces. 　　　　　　　　Nay, it is gone,
And I am left as far without a bound
As the wild ocean that obeys the winds;
Each sudden passion throws me as it lists
And overwhelms all that oppose my will.　　　70
I have beheld thee with a lustful eye.
My heart is set on wickedness, to act
Such sins with thee as I have been afraid
To think of. If thou dar'st consent to this
(Which, I beseech thee, do not), thou mayst gain　　　75
Thy liberty and yield me a content.
If not, thy dwelling must be dark and close,
Where I may never see thee, for God knows,
That laid this punishment upon my pride,
Thy sight at some time will enforce my madness　　　80
To make a start e'en to thy ravishing.
Now spit upon me and call all reproaches
Thou canst devise together, and at once
Hurl 'em against me, for I am a sickness

81. e'en] *Q2;* eye *Q1.*

---

67. *bound*] boundary (i.e. the limits human reason imposes on behaviour).
69. *lists*] pleases.
81. *start*] sudden, involuntary movement.

As killing as the plague, ready to seize thee. 85
Panthea. Far be it from me to revile the King!
  But it is true that I should rather choose
  To search out death, that else would search out me,
  And in a grave sleep with my innocence
  Than welcome such a sin. It is my fate; 90
  To these cross accidents I was ordained
  And must have patience; and but that my eyes
  Have more of woman in 'em than my heart,
  I would not weep. Peace enter you again!
Arbaces. Farewell, and good Panthea, pray for me— 95
  Thy prayers are pure—that I may find a death,
  However soon, before my passions grow
  That they forget what I desire is sin,
  For thither they are tending. If that happen,
  Then I shall force thee, though thou wert a virgin 100
  By vow to heaven, and shall pull a heap
  Of strange, yet-uninvented sins upon me.
Panthea. Sir, I will pray for you; yet you shall know
  It is a sullen fate that governs us.
  For I could wish as heartily as you 105
  I were no sister to you; I should then
  Embrace your lawful love sooner than health.
Arbaces. Couldst thou affect me then?
Panthea.   So perfectly
  That, as it is, I ne'er shall sway my heart
  To like another.
Arbaces   Then I curse my birth. 110
  Must this be added to my miseries,
  That thou art willing too? Is there no stop
  To our full happiness but these mere sounds,
  'Brother' and 'sister'?
Panthea.   There is nothing else,
  But these, alas, will separate us more 115
  Than twenty worlds betwixt us.
Arbaces.   I have lived

---

112. stop] *Q2;* steppe *Q1.*

---

102. *strange*] (1) rare, exceptional, with the added suggestion of (2) foreign, alien.

To conquer men and now am overthrown
Only by words, 'brother' and 'sister'. Where
Have those words dwelling? I will find 'em out
And utterly destroy them; but they are   120
Not to be grasped. Let 'em be men or beasts
And I will cut 'em from the earth, or towns
And I will raze 'em and then blow 'em up.
Let 'em be seas, and I will drink them off
And yet have unquenched fire left in my breast.   125
Let 'em be any thing but merely voice.
Panthea. But 'tis not in the power of any force
Or policy to conquer them.
Arbaces.   Panthea,
What shall we do? Shall we stand firmly here
And gaze our eyes out?
Panthea.   Would I could do so,   130
But I shall weep out mine.
Arbaces.   Accursèd man,
Thou boughtst thy reason at too dear a rate,
For thou hast all thy actions bounded in
With curious rules when every beast is free.
What is there that acknowledges a kindred   135
But wretched man? Who ever saw the bull
Fearfully leave the heifer that he liked
Because they had one dam?
Panthea.   Sir, I disturb you
And myself too; 'twere better I were gone.
Arbaces. I will not be so foolish as I was.   140
Stay, we will love just as becomes our births,

---

140. SH *Arbaces.*] *Q2; not in Q1.*   141. Stay] *Q2; Arbaces.* Stay *Q1.*

128. *policy*] stratagem.

134. *curious*] elaborate, scrupulously strict.

136–8. *bull . . . dam*] For Arbaces the lusty bull pursuing its sister exemplifies an enviable natural sexual freedom; Spaconia earlier used the bull analogy negatively to emphasise the bestiality of faithless Tigranes (4.2.67–9).

140. *I . . . was*] Q1 appends this line to Panthea's preceding speech; Q2, followed by most later editors, assigns it as here to Arbaces. Certain attribution is impossible, since either character could plausibly voice this sentiment, but Arbaces makes a similar remark below (157–8), and muddled or misaligned SHs are not uncommon elsewhere in Q1 (cf. 3.1.122–5, 319–27; 4.3.48–9; 5.4.338).

No otherwise. Brothers and sisters may
Walk hand in hand together; so will we.
Come nearer. Is there any hurt in this?
Panthea. I hope not.
Arbaces.   'Faith, there's none at all.   145
And tell me truly now, is there not one
You love above me?
Panthea. No, by heaven.
Arbaces. Why yet you sent unto Tigranes, sister.
Panthea. True, but for another. For the truth—   150
Arbaces. No more;
I'll credit thee. I know thou canst not lie;
Thou art all truth.
Panthea.   But is there nothing else
That we may do but only walk? Methinks
Brothers and sisters lawfully may kiss.   155
Arbaces. And so they may, Panthea; so will we,
And kiss again too. We were scrupulous
And foolish, but we will be so no more.   [*They kiss.*]
Panthea. If you have any mercy, let me go
To prison, to my death, to anything.   160
I feel a sin growing upon my blood
Worse than all these, hotter, I fear, than yours.
Arbaces. That is impossible. What should we do?
Panthea. Fly, sir, for God's sake.
Arbaces.   So we must; away!
Sin grows upon us more by this delay.   *Exeunt.*   165

---

149. Why] *Q2; not in Q1.*   156. we] *Q1;* we *They kiss. Williams.*   158. SD]
Bond subst.; not in Q1.   165. Exeunt.] *Q2; not in Q1; Exeunt, severall wayes.*
Q3.   165.1.] *Finis Actus Quarti. Q1.*

---

157. *scrupulous*] i.e. too scrupulous, too careful to behave correctly.

Act 5

5.1

Enter MARDONIUS *and* LIGONES.

Mardonius. Sir, the King has seen your commission and
  believes it,
 And freely by this warrant gives you leave
 To visit Prince Tigranes, your noble master.
Ligones. I thank his grace and kiss his hands.
Mardonius. But is the main of all your business   5
  Ended in this?
Ligones.   I have another, but
 A worse. I am ashamed; it is a business—
Mardonius. You seem a worthy person, and a stranger
 I am sure you are. You may employ me,
 If you please, without your purse. Such offices   10
 Should ever be their own rewards.
Ligones. I am bound to your nobleness.
Mardonius. I may have need of you, and then this courtesy,
 If it be any, is not ill bestowed.
 But may I civilly desire the rest?   15
 I shall not be a hurter, if no helper.
Ligones. Sir, you shall know I have lost a foolish daughter
 And with her all my patience, pilfered away
 By a mean captain of your King's.
Mardonius.   Stay there, sir.

5.1] Actus Quinti Scaena Prima. *Q1.*   2. leave] *Q1;* power *Q2–8, F2.*   8.
seem] *Dyce (conj. Mason);* serve *Q1.*   10. offices] *Q2;* Officers *Q1.*

---

 8. *seem*] In the first clause Q1's 'serve' would go unquestioned, but, given
the whole sentence, Mason's conjecture, adopted by Dyce and most subsequent editors, is inspired. In support of the emendation, Williams notes that
Q1 'contains several *v/m* misreadings from its manuscript copy' (p. 177). The
present text adopts Williams's readings at 3.2.69, Q2 'five' (Q1 'time'); 4.1.67,
Q2 'tame' (Q1 'have'); 4.2.205, Q2 'tame' (Q1 'have'); it does not follow
Williams in amending Q1's 'times' (1.1.182) to Q2's 'lives'.

 10. *offices*] duties, tasks.

If he have reached the noble worth of captain,   20
He may well claim a worthy gentlewoman,
Though she were yours and noble.
Ligones. I grant all that too. But this wretched fellow
Reaches no further than the empty name
That serves to feed him. Were he valiant,   25
Or had but in him any noble nature
That might hereafter promise him a good man,
My cares were something lighter and my grave
A span yet from me.
Mardonius.   I confess such fellows
Be in all royal camps, and have and must be,   30
To make the sin of coward more detested
In the mean soldier, that with such a foil
Sets off much valour. By description
I should now guess him to you. It was Bessus;
I dare almost with confidence pronounce it.   35
Ligones. 'Tis such a scurvy name as Bessus, and now
I think, 'tis he.
Mardonius.   'Captain', do you call him?
Believe me, sir, you have a misery
Too mighty for your age. A pox upon him,
For that must be the end of all his service.   40
Your daughter was not mad, sir?
Ligones.   No, would she had been;
The fault had had more credit. I would do something.
Mardonius. I would fain counsel you, but to what I know not.
He's so below a beating that the women
Find him not worthy of their distaves, and   45
To hang him were to cast away a rope;
He's such an airy, thin, unbodied coward
That no revenge can catch him.

---

28. *something*] somewhat.

31. *sin*] The early annotator of Dyce's copy of Q1 has altered 'sin' to 'name', though as Williams notes, a *s/n* misreading is unlikely.

32–3. *In . . . valour*] 'In the rank and file, whose bravery is more conspicuous by contrast with poltroonery in a man of higher rank' (Bond).

43. *fain*] gladly.

45. *distaves*] The distaff was a cleft wooden pole on which wool was wound before being twisted into thread.

I'll tell you, sir, and tell you truth. This rascal
Fears neither God nor man; h'as been so beaten   50
Sufferance has made him wainscot.
He has had, since he was first a slave,
At least three hundred daggers set in his head,
As little boys do new knives in hot meat.
There's not a rib in's body, o' my conscience,   55
That has not been thrice broken with dry beating,
And now his sides look like to wicker targets,
Every way bended.
Children will shortly take him for a wall
And set their stone-bows in his forehead. He   60
Is of so low a sense, I cannot in
A week imagine what should be done to him.
Ligones. Sure I have committed some great sin,
That this strange fellow should be made my rod.
I would see him, but I shall have no patience.   65
Mardonius. 'Tis no great matter if you have not. If a laming
of him, or such a toy, may do you pleasure, sir, he has it
for you, and I'll help you to him. 'Tis no news to him to
have a leg broke or a shoulder out with being turned a'
th' stones like a tansy. Draw not your sword if you love   70

---

60. He] *Q2; not in Q1.*   66. laming] *Q1;* lamming *Bond (conj. Dyce).*

---

51. *wainscot*] i.e. hardened and coloured like old wood panelling.
52. *slave*] contemptible rascal.
53-4. *set . . . meat*] i.e. his head is nothing more than a piece of meat used
to test a weapon's edge.
56. *dry*] (1) bloodless (with stick or fist), and more vaguely, as an intensifier, (2) hard, severe (cf. 5.3.95-6).
57. *targets*] shield-like structures (to be aimed at in shooting practice).
60. *stone-bows*] cross-bows that shot stones.
in] at (*OED* In *prep* 2b, where 'set' = direct, aim).
61. *low a sense*] (1) vulgar understanding, (2) little feeling (because tough-
ened by beating).
66. *laming*] Bond adopted Dyce's suggestion of 'lamming' (i.e. beating)
and quotes *The Famous Victories* (before 1588): 'I am sure I so belambd him
about the shoulders, that he wil feele it this month.' 'To lam' and 'to lame'
were originally the same; here, the next sentence indicates that modern
'laming' is appropriate.
67. *toy*] trifle.
69-70. *a' th' stones . . . tansy*] like a tansy-flavoured cake cooking on the
hearthstones.

it, for, of my conscience, his head will break it. We use
him i' th' wars like a ram to shake a wall withal. Here
comes the very person of him. Do as you shall find your
temper. I must leave you, but if you do not break him like
a biscuit, you are much to blame, sir.   *Exit.*   75

Enter BESSUS *and* Swordmen.

Ligones. Is your name Bessus?

Bessus. Men call me Captain Bessus.

Ligones. Then, Captain Bessus, you are a rank rascal, without
more exordiums, a dirty, frozen slave; and with the favour
of your friends here, I will beat you.   80

2 Swordman. Pray use your pleasure, sir; you seem to be
A gentleman.

Ligones.   Thus, Captain Bessus, thus.   [*Beats him.*]
Thus twinge your nose, thus kick you, and thus tread you.

Bessus. I do beseech you, yield your cause, sir, quickly.

Ligones. Indeed, I should have told you that first.   85

Bessus. I take it so.

1 Swordman. Captain, 'a should indeed; he is mistaken.

Ligones. Sir, you shall have it quickly and more beating.
You have stolen away a lady, Captain Coward,
And such a one—   *Beats him* [*again*].

Bessus.   Hold, I beseech you, hold, sir!   90
I never yet stole any living thing
That had a tooth about it.—

Ligones. Sir, I know you dare lie—

Bessus. With none but summer whores, upon my life, sir.
My means and manners never could attempt   95
Above a hedge or haycock.

---

75. SD] *Ex. Mardo. Q1.*   75.1. SD] *Q1 (at 75 after 'Ex. Mardo.').*   82. SD]
Weber; not in Q1.   89. SD] *Beates him. Q2; not in Q1.*   94. SH *Bessus.*] *Q2;
not in Q1.*   95. My] *Q2; Bessus. My Q1.*

---

71. *of*] on.
72. *ram*] battering-ram.
withal] with.
79. *exordiums*] preliminaries.
frozen] cold-spirited.
84. *yield*] explain.
96. *haycock*] conical haystack.

Ligones. Sirrah, that quits not me. Where is this lady?
    Do that you do not use to do, tell truth,
    Or, by my hand, I'll beat your captain's brains out,
    Wash 'em, and put 'em in again that will.   100
Bessus. There was a lady, sir, I must confess,
    Once in my charge. The Prince Tigranes gave her
    To my guard for her safety. How I used her
    She may herself report; she's with the Prince now.
    I did but wait upon her like a groom,   105
    Which she will testify, I am sure. If not,
    My brains are at your service when you please, sir,
    And glad I have 'em for you.
Ligones. This is most likely. Sir, I ask your pardon
    And am sorry I was so intemperate.   110
Bessus. Well, I can ask no more. You would think it strange
    Now to have me beat you at first sight.
Ligones. Indeed I would, but I know your goodness can
    Forget twenty beatings. You must forgive me.
Bessus. Yes, there's my hand. Go where you will, I shall   115
    Think you a valiant fellow for all this.
Ligones [*Aside*]. My daughter is a whore;
    I feel it now too sensible. Yet I will see her,
    Discharge myself of being father to her,
    And then back to my country and there die.—   120
    Farewell, captain.
Bessus.   Farewell, sir, farewell.
    Commend me to the gentlewoman, I pray'ee.
                         Exit LIGONES.
1 Swordman. How now, captain; bear up, man.
Bessus. Gentlemen o' th' sword, your hands once more. I have
    Been kicked again, but the foolish fellow is penitent;   125

---

100. that will] *Dyce;* that will I *Q1.*   108. you.] you? *Q1.*   122. SD *Exit*
LIGONES.] *Q2 (after 121* captain*); Exit. Q1 (after* captain*).*

---

97. *quits*] requites, satisfies.
    100. *that will*] Dyce omitted the 'I' in Q1's 'that I will' on the strength of
his copy's annotator's emendation to 'who will' and the stronger verse produced by dropping the "I"; given the 'I' above and below this line, it seems
likely that another crept in at the end of 100.
    108. *glad*] i.e. I am glad.
    118. *sensible*] acutely.

H'as asked me mercy, and my honour's safe.

2 Swordman. We knew that, or the foolish fellow had better
A' kicked his grandsire.

Bessus.   Confirm, confirm, I pray.

1 Swordman. There be our hands again.

2 Swordman. Now let him come and say he was not sorry,   130
And he sleeps for it.

Bessus. Alas, good ignorant old man. Let him go,
Let him go; these courses will undo him.   *Exeunt.*

[5.2]

Enter LIGONES *and* BACURIUS.

Bacurius. My lord, your authority is good, and I am glad it is
so, for my consent would never hinder you from seeing
your own king. I am a minister, but not a governor, of
this state. Yonder is your king. I'll leave you.   *Exit.*

Enter TIGRANES *and* SPACONIA.

Ligones [*Aside*]. There he is indeed, and with him my   5
Disloyal child.

Tigranes [*To Spaconia*]. I do perceive my fault so much that
yet,
Methinks, thou shouldst not have forgiven me.

Ligones. Health to your majesty.

Tigranes. What? Good Ligones, welcome. What business   10
Brought thee hither?

Ligones.   Several businesses.
My public business will appear by this. [*Gives a paper.*]
I have a message to deliver which,
If it please you so to authorise, is
An embassage from the Armenian state   15
Unto Arbaces for your liberty.
The offer's there set down; please you to read it.

---

128. SH *Bessus.*] *Q2; not in Q1.*

4.1. SD] *Q1 (after 5* indeed*).*   12. SD] *Weber; not in Q1.*

---

131. *sleeps*] dies.

2. *my . . . never*] i.e. I would never consent.

Tigranes. There is no alteration happened since
   I came thence?
Ligones.   None, sir; all is as it was.
Tigranes. And all our friends are well?
Ligones.   All very well.   20
                    [*Tigranes reads.*]
Spaconia [*Aside*]. Though I have done nothing but what
      was good,
   I dare not see my father. It was fault
   Enough not to acquaint him with that good.
Ligones. Madam, I should have seen you.
Spaconia. O, good sir, forgive me.   25
Ligones. Forgive you? Why, I am no kin to you, am I?
Spaconia. Should it be measured by my mean deserts,
   Indeed you are not.
Ligones.   Thou couldst prate unhappily
   Ere thou couldst go; would thou couldst do as well!
   And how does your custom hold out here?   30
Spaconia. Sir?
Ligones. Are you in private still, or how?
Spaconia. What do you mean?
Ligones. Do you take money? Are you come to sell sin yet?
   Perhaps I can help you to liberal clients. Or has not the   35
   King cast you off yet? O, thou vile creature, whose best
   commendation is that thou art a young whore! I would
   thy mother had lived to see this; or rather, would I had
   died ere I had seen it. Why didst not make me acquainted
   when thou wert first resolved to be a whore? I would have   40

---

20. SD] *Weber; not in Q1.*

28–9. *Thou . . . well!*] You could talk mischievously before you could walk; would you could be as precocious now!
   30. *custom*] business.
   34–43.] These lines present an excellent example of different assumptions—about metrical propriety in general (and its relation to a character's social status) or Beaumont and Fletcher's in particular—producing different treatments of the early editions' distribution of verse and prose. QQ1, 5, 6, and F2 print the whole speech as prose, as do more recent editors (Alden, and editors since Turner); QQ2–4 and 7, followed by Colman, Dyce, and Strachey, print their last four lines as verse ('I . . . thee'). Webber made his last five lines verse ('When thou . . . thee'); Theobald, followed by Bond and Walley–Wilson, versifies the whole speech.

seen thy hot lust satisfied more privately. I would have
kept a dancer and a whole consort of musicians in mine
own house only to fiddle thee.

Spaconia. Sir, I was never whore.

Ligones.   If thou couldst not
　　Say so much for thyself, thou shouldst be carted.   45

Tigranes. Ligones, I have read it and like it;
　　You shall deliver it.

Ligones.   Well, sir, I will.
　　But I have private business with you.

Tigranes. Speak. What is't?

Ligones. How has my age deserved so ill of you   50
　　That you can pick no strumpets in the land
　　But out of my breed?

Tigranes.   Strumpets, good Ligones?

Ligones. Yes, and I wish to have you know I scorn
　　To get a whore for any prince alive,
　　And yet scorn will not help, methinks. My daughter   55
　　Might have been spared; there were enough beside.

Tigranes. May I not prosper but she's innocent
　　As morning light for me, and I dare swear
　　For all the world.

Ligones.   Why is she with you then?
　　Can she wait on you better than your men?   60
　　Has she a gift in plucking off your stockings?
　　Can she make caudles well, or cut your corns?
　　Why do you keep her with you? For your queen
　　I know you do contemn her; so should I
　　And every subject else think much at it.   65

Tigranes. Let 'em think much, but 'tis more firm than earth
　　Thou seest thy queen there.

---

42. *consort*] company.

45. *carted*] drawn through the streets in an open cart (a traditional punishment for bawds and prostitutes). There is bitter humour in Ligones's
observation, since he of course think that she already deserves carting as a
'whore' (37, 40).

58. *for me*] as far as I'm concerned.

62. *caudles*] A caudle was a hot drink made of gruel mixed with sugar,
wine, lemon peel, and nutmeg.

Ligones. Then have I made a fair hand; I called her whore. If
I shall speak now as her father, I cannot choose but
greatly rejoice that she shall be a queen. But if I should   70
speak to you as a statesman, she were more fit to be your
whore.

Tigranes. Get you about your business to Arbaces;
Now you talk idly.

Ligones.   Yes, sir, I will go.
And shall she be a queen? She had more wit   75
Than her old father when she ran away.
Shall she be a queen? Now, by my troth, 'tis fine;
I'll dance out of all measure at her wedding.
Shall I not, sir?

Tigranes.   Yes, marry, shalt thou.

Ligones. I'll make these withered kexes bear my body   80
Two hours together above ground.

Tigranes. Nay, go. My business requires haste.

Ligones. Good God preserve you; you are an excellent king.

Spaconia. Farewell, good father.

Ligones.   Farewell, sweet, virtuous daughter.
I never was so joyful in my life   85
That I remember. Shall she be a queen?
Now I perceive a man may weep for joy;
I had thought they had lied that said so.   *Exit.*

Tigranes. Come, my dear love.

Spaconia.   But you may see another
May alter that again.

Tigranes.   Urge it no more.   90
I have made up a new strong constancy,
Not to be shook with eyes. I know I have
The passions of a man, but if I meet

---

68. *made . . . hand*] done good work (said ironically).

68–72. *If . . . whore*] See Introduction, p. 8, for the probable source of this
sentiment in Plutarch.

78. *out . . . measure*] excessively (with a pun on 'measure', a slow and
stately dance).

80. *kexes*] dry stalks (i.e. legs).

92. *with eyes*] i.e. by seeing another, no matter how beautiful (alluding to
Spaconia's fear, 89–90).

With any subject that shall hold my eyes
More firmly than is fit, I'll think of thee   95
And run away from it. Let that suffice.   *Exeunt.*

[5.3]

Enter BACURIUS *and a* Servant.

Bacurius. Three gentlemen without to speak with me?
Servant. Yes, sir.
Bacurius. Let them come in.
Servant.   They are entered, sir, already.

Enter BESSUS *and* [*two*] Swordmen.

Bacurius. Now, fellows, your business. [*To Servant*] Are
       these the gentlemen?
Bessus. My lord, I have made bold to bring these gentlemen,   5
       my friends o' th' sword, along with me.
Bacurius. I am afraid you'll fight then.
Bessus. My good lord, I will not; your lordship is mistaken.
       Fear not, lord.
Bacurius. Sir, I am sorry for't.   10
Bessus. I can ask no more in honour.—Gentlemen, you hear
       my lord is sorry.
Bacurius. Not that I have beaten you, but beaten one that will
       be beaten, one whose dull body will require lancing as
       surfeits do the diet, spring and fall. Now to your sword-   15
       men. What come they for, good Captain Stockfish?
Bessus. It seems your lordship has forgot my name.
Bacurius. No, nor your nature neither, though they are things
       fitter, I confess, for anything than my remembrance or
       any honest man's. What shall these billets do? Be piled   20
       up in my woodyard?

14. lancing] *Q1 (*launcing*); a laming Q2; a lamming Weber.   15. fall] Q2;
full Q1.*

---

    1. *without*] outside.
    14. *lancing*] The parallelism of lancing a dull body (bloodletting) and
dieting after surfeit argues for Q1 and against Weber's emendation 'lamming'
(though adopted by Dyce, Strachey, Bond, Walley–Wilson, and Williams).
    16. *Stockfish*] The insult lies in the suggested homology: a stockfish was
a dried fish made tender by beating before being cooked.
    20. *billets*] logs (i.e. the Swordmen).

Bessus. Your lordship holds your mirth still; God continue it.
    But for these gentlemen, they come—
Bacurius. To swear you are a coward. Spare your book; I do
    believe it.   25
Bessus. Your lordship still draws wide. They come to vouch,
    under their valiant hands, I am no coward.
Bacurius. That would be a show indeed worth seeing. Sirrah,
    be wise and take money for this motion; travel with it,
    and where the name of Bessus has been known, or a good   30
    coward stirring, 'twill yield more than a tilting. This will
    prove more beneficial to you, if you be thrifty, than your
    captainship and more natural.—Men of most valiant
    hands, is this true?
2 Swordman. It is so, most renowned.
Bacurius.   'Tis somewhat strange.   35
1 Swordman. Lord, it is strange, yet true. We have examined
    from your lordship's foot there to this man's head the
    nature of the beatings, and we do find his honour is come
    off clean and sufficient. This, as our swords shall help us.
Bacurius. You are much bound to your bilbo-men; I am glad   40
    you are straight again, captain. 'Twere good you would
    think some way to gratify them. They have undergone a
    labour for you, Bessus, would have puzzled Hercules with
    all his valour.
2 Swordman. Your lordship must understand we are no men   45
    o' th' law, that take pay for our opinions. It is sufficient
    we have cleared our friend.
Bacurius. Yet here is something due which I, as touched in
    conscience, will discharge, captain. I'll pay this rent for
    you.   50

---

40. SH *Bacurius.*] *Q2; not in Q1.*

26. *draws wide*] misunderstands.
29. *motion*] puppet-show.
40. *bilbo-men*] swordmen. The Spanish city of Bilbao was noted for manufacturing high-quality swords; Bacurius may also pun on the name for the bar with shackles used to confine prisoners.
41. *straight*] reputable.
43. *Hercules*] Mythical Greek hero famous for strength who was charged with accomplishing twelve seemingly impossible 'labours'.
49. *rent*] hire (further developing the metaphor of payment for goods initiated by 2 Swordsman).

Bessus. Spare yourself, my good lord. My brave friends aim
    at nothing but the virtue.
Bacurius. That's but a cold discharge, sir, for their pains.
2 Swordman. O Lord, my good lord!
Bacurius. Be not so modest; I will give you something.   55
Bessus. They shall dine with your lordship, that's sufficient.
Bacurius. Something in hand the while.—Ye rogues, ye apple-
    squires!
    Do you come hither with your bottled valour, your windy
    froth, to limit out my beatings?   [*Kicks them.*]
1 Swordman. I do beseech your lordship—
2 Swordman.   O, good lord—   60
Bacurius. 'Sfoot, what a many of beaten slaves are here!
    Get me a cudgel, sirrah, and a tough one.
                                        [*Exit* Servant.]
2 Swordman. More of your foot, I do beseech your lordship.
Bacurius. You shall, you shall, dog, and your fellow beagle.
1 Swordman. A' this side, good my lord.   65
Bacurius. Off with your swords, for if you hurt my foot, I'll
    have you flayed, you rascals.
1 Swordman. Mine's off, my lord. [*They take off their swords.*]
2 Swordman. I beseech your lordship stay a little; my strap's
    tied to my codpiece point. Now, when you please.   70
Bacurius. Captain, these are your valiant friends. You long for
    a little too?
Bessus. I am very well, I humbly thank your lordship.
Bacurius. What's that in your pocket, slave? My key, you
    mongrel? Thy buttocks cannot be so hard; out with't,   75
    quickly.
2 Swordman. Here 'tis, sir, a small piece of artillery that a gen-
    tleman, a dear friend of your lordship's, sent me with to

---

58. your windy] *Q1;* you windy *Turner.*   59. SD] *Weber; not in Q1.*   61.
many] *Q1;* bevy *Q2–8, F2.*   62. SD] *Weber; not in Q1.*   68. SD] *Weber; not
in Q1.*   74. slave? My key] *Q1 (*slave, my key*);* slave, my toe *Q2;* hurts my
toe *Q3.*

---

57. *apple-squires*] pimps.
    61. *many*] Q1's spelling, common at the time, of 'meiny' (company).
    70. *codpiece point*] lace fastening the codpiece, the bag on the front of
close-fitting breeches, to the hose.
    74. *slave . . . key*] Q3's 'hurts my toe' persisted in editions through
Whalley–Wilson (1930).

get it mended, sir; for if you mark, the nose is somewhat
loose.   [*Takes out a pistol.*]   80
Bacurius. A friend of mine, you rascal!—I was never wearier
of doing nothing than kicking these two footballs.

Enter Servant.

Servant. Here's a good cudgel, sir.
Bacurius. It comes too late. I am weary; prithee do thou
beat 'em.
2 Swordman. My lord, this is foul play, i' faith, to put a fresh   85
man upon us. Men are but men.
Bacurius. That jest shall save your bones.—Captain, rally up
your rotten regiment and be gone.—I had rather thresh
than be bound to kick these rascals till they cried hold.—
Bessus, you may put your hand to them now, and then   90
you are quit.—Farewell. As you like this, pray visit me
again. 'Twill keep me in good breath.   *Exit* BACURIUS.
2 Swordman. H'as a devilish hard foot. I never felt the like.
1 Swordman. Nor I, and yet I'm sure I ha' felt a hundred.
2 Swordman. If he kick thus i' th' dog-days, he will be dry-   95
founded.—What cure now, captain, besides oil of
bays?
Bessus. Why, well enough, I warrant you. You can go?
2 Swordman. Yes, God be thanked. But I feel a shrewd ache;
sure he has sprang my huckle bone.   100
1 Swordman. I ha' lost a haunch.
Bessus. A little butter, friend, a little butter; butter and parsley
is a sovereign matter. *Probatum est.*

---

80. SD] *Weber; not in Q1.* 82.1. SD] *Q3; not in Q1; Enter Servant, Will.
Adkinson: Q2.* 86. men.] *Q1; men, sir Q2–8, F2.* 87. Captain, rally up]
Q2; up with *Q1.* 92. SD] *Q2; not in Q1.*

---

82. *nothing*] i.e. nothing worth doing.
91. *quit*] released from your debt to them (for swearing you to be valiant).
95. *dog-days*] hottest days of the year, when the Dog Star (Sirius) is above
the horizon.
95–6. *dry-foundered*] lamed. The founder is an inflammation of a horse's
foot, usually from overwork. 'Dry' here is probably used as an intensifier.
96–7. *oil of bays*] liniment made from bayberries.
98. *go*] walk.
100. *sprang*] sprained.
huckle bone] hipbone.
103. *sovereign matter*] i.e. excellent medicine.
Probatum est] It has been proved (Latin).

2 Swordman. Captain, we must request your hands now to
　　our honours.   105
Bessus. Yes, marry, shall ye, and then let all the world come.
　　We are valiant to ourselves, and there's an end.
1 Swordman. Nay, then we must be valiant. O, my ribs!
2 Swordman. O, my small guts! A plague upon these sharp-
　　toed shoes; they are murderers.   *Exeunt.*   110

[5.4]

　　　　　　　Enter ARBACES *with his sword drawn.*

Arbaces. It is resolved. I bore it whilst I could;
　　I can no more. Hell, open all thy gates,
　　And I will thorough them; if they be shut,
　　I'll batter 'em but I will find the place
　　Where the most damned have dwelling. Ere I end,   5
　　Amongst them all they shall not have a sin
　　But I may call it mine. I must begin
　　With murder of my friend, and so go on
　　To an incestuous ravishing, and end
　　My life and sin with a forbidden blow   10
　　Upon myself.

　　　　　　　Enter MARDONIUS.

Mardonius.　　　　What tragedy is near?
　　That hand was never wont to draw a sword
　　But it cried dead to something.
Arbaces.　　　　　　　　Mardonius,
　　Have you bid Gobrius come?
Mardonius.　　　　　　　How do you, sir?
Arbaces. Well, is he coming?
Mardonius.　　　　　　Why, sir, are you thus?   15
　　Why does your hand proclaim a lawless war
　　Against yourself?
Arbaces. Thou answerst me one question with another.

　　2–7. *Hell . . . mine*] These lines are omitted in all the early editions except
Q1.
　　12. *wont*] accustomed.

Is Gobrius coming?
Mardonius.   Sir, he is.
Arbaces.   'Tis well.
I can forbear your questions then. Begone.   20
Mardonius. Sir, I have marked—
Arbaces. Mark less; it troubles you and me.
Mardonius. You are more variable than you were.
Arbaces. It may be so.
Mardonius. Today no hermit could be humblier   25
Than you were to us all.
Arbaces.   And what of this?
Mardonius. And now you take new rage into your eyes,
As you would look us all out of the land.
Arbaces. I do confess it. Will that satisfy?
I prithee, get thee gone.   30
Mardonius. Sir, I will speak.
Arbaces.   Will ye?
Mardonius.   It is my duty.
I fear you will kill yourself. I am a subject,
And you shall do me wrong in't. 'Tis my cause,
And I may speak.
Arbaces.   Thou art not trained in sin,
It seems, Mardonius. Kill myself? By heaven,   35
I will not do it yet, and when I will,
I'll tell thee. Then I shall be such a creature
That thou wilt give me leave without a word.
There is a method in man's wickedness;
It grows up by degrees. I am not come   40
So high as killing of myself; there are
A hundred thousand sins 'twixt me and it
Which I must do. I shall come to't at last,
But, take my oath, not now. Be satisfied
And get thee hence.   45

---

20. I can] *Q2; Mar.* I can *Q1.*   21. SH *Mardonius.*] *Q2; not in Q1.*   37.
thee. Then] *Dyce;* thee then: *Q1.*

---

20. *forbear*] do without.
28. *out . . . land*] into banishment.
34. *trained*] (1) instructed, possibly with overtones of (2) habituated.
40. *by degrees*] Theobald cites Juvenal, *Satires,* 2, 83: *Nemo repente fuit
turpissimus* (No one reaches the depths of turpitude all at once).

Mardonius. I am sorry 'tis so ill.
Arbaces.   Be sorry then.
    True sorrow is alone; grieve by thyself.
Mardonius. I pray you, let me see your sword put up
    Before I go. I'll leave you then.
Arbaces.   Why, so!
                             [Puts up his sword.]
    What folly is this in thee? Is it not   50
    As apt to mischief as it was before?
    Can I not reach it, thinkst thou? These are toys
    For children to be pleased with and not men.
    Now I am safe, you think. I would the book
    Of fate were here; my sword is not so sure   55
    But I should get it out and mangle that,
    That all the destinies should quite forget
    Their fixed decrees and haste to make us new,
    Far-other fortunes. Mine could not be worse.
    Wilt thou now leave me?   60
Mardonius. God put into your bosom temperate thoughts.
    I'll leave you though I fear.
Arbaces.   Go; thou art honest.
                         Exit MARDONIUS.
    Why should the hasty errors of my youth
    Be so unpardonable, to draw a sin
    Helpless upon me?   65

                Enter GOBRIUS.

Gobrius [*Aside*]. There is the King; now it is ripe.
Arbaces. Draw near thou guilty man,
    That art the author of the loathedst crime
    Five ages have brought forth, and hear me speak.
    Curses incurable and all the evils   70
    Man's body or his spirit can receive

---

49. SD] *Weber subst.; not in Q1.*   62. SD *Exit* MARDONIUS.] *Q2; Exit. Q1*
(after fear*)*.

---

    47. *True . . . alone*] Theobald quotes Martial, *Epigrams*, 1.33: *Ille dolet vere qui sine teste dolet* (He sorrows truly who sorrows unseen).
    55. *sure*] firmly fixed, either because (1) in its scabbard, or (2) controlled by the Fates.

        Be with thee!
Gobrius.   Why, sir, do you curse me thus?
Arbaces. Why do I curse thee? If there be a man
        Subtle in curses, that exceeds the rest,
        His worst wish on thee! Thou hast broke my heart.   75
Gobrius. How, sir? Have I preserved you from a child
        From all the arrows malice or ambition
        Could shoot at you, and have I this for pay?
Arbaces. 'Tis true, thou didst preserve me and in that
        Wert crueller than hardened murderers   80
        Of infants and their mothers; thou didst save me
        Only till thou hadst studied out a way
        How to destroy me cunningly thyself.
        This was a curious way of torturing.
Gobrius. What do you mean?   85
Arbaces. Thou knowst the evils thou hast done to me.
        Dost thou remember all those witching letters
        Thou sentst unto me to Armenia,
        Filled with the praise of my beloved sister,
        Where thou extolst her beauty? What had I   90
        To do with that? What could her beauty be
        To me? And thou didst write how well she loved me—
        Dost thou remember this?—so that I doted
        Something before I saw her.
Gobrius.   This is true.
Arbaces. Is it? And when I was returned, thou knowst   95
        Thou didst pursue it till thou woundst me in
        To such a strange and unbelieved affection
        As good men cannot think on.
Gobrius.   This I grant;
        I think I was the cause.
Arbaces.   Wert thou? Nay more,
        I think thou meantst it.
Gobrius.   Sir, I hate a lie   100
        As I love God and honesty; I did.

---

95. And when] *Q2;* and I when *Q1.*   96–7. in / To such] *Q2;* into / Such
Q1.

---

84. *curious*] (1) artful, elaborate, as well as (2) rare.
97. *unbelieved*] incredible.

It was my meaning.
Arbaces.   Be thine own sad judge;
A further condemnation will not need.
Prepare thyself to die.
Gobrius.   Why, sir, to die?
Arbaces. Why wouldst thou live? Was ever yet offender   105
So impudent that had a thought of mercy
After confession of a crime like this?
Get out I cannot where thou hurlst me in,
But I can take revenge; that's all the sweetness
Left for me.   110
Gobrius [*Aside*]. Now is the time.—Hear me but speak.
Arbaces. No. Yet I will be far more merciful
Than thou wert to me. Thou didst steal into me
And never gav'st me warning; so much time
As I give thee now had prevented thee   115
For ever. Notwithstanding all thy sins,
If thou hast hope that there is yet a prayer
To save thee, turn and speak it to yourself.
                                        [*Touches his sword.*]
Gobrius. Sir, you shall know your sins before you do 'em.
If you kill me—
Arbaces.   I will not stay then.
Gobrius.   Know   120
You kill your father.
Arbaces.   How?
Gobrius.   You kill your father.
Arbaces. My father? Though I know it for a lie
Made out of fear to save thy stainèd life,
The very reverence of the word comes cross me
And ties mine arm down.
Gobrius.   I will tell you that   125

---

105. SH *Arbaces.*] *Q1 (c); not in Q1 (u).*   115. thee] *Q1; me Theobald.*
118. SD] *This ed.; not in Q1; Draws his sword. Williams.*

---

115. *thee*] Theobald's emendation to 'me' was followed by subsequent
editors until Turner returned to the Q1 reading. One cannot be certain that
Q1's 'thee' is not the compositor's mistaken repetition of 'thee' earlier in the
same line, but it was not altered in Q2 or other seventeenth-century editions,
and emendation is not necessary. Although Dyce accepted 'me', in his note
he suggested a plausible defence of Q1 as meaning 'had prevented thee from
being able to seduce my affections into such an unlawful channel'.

Shall heighten you again. I am thy father;
I charge thee hear me.
Arbaces.   If it should be so,
As 'tis most false, and that I should be found
A bastard issue, the despisèd fruit
Of lawless lust, I should no more admire   130
All my wild passions. But another truth
Shall be wrung from thee. If I could come by
The spirit of pain, it should be poured on thee
Till thou allowst thyself more full of lies
Than he that teaches thee.

                    Enter ARANE.

Arane.   Turn thee about.   135
I come to speak to thee, thou wicked man;
Hear me, thou tyrant!
Arbaces.   I will turn to thee.
Hear me, thou strumpet! I have blotted out
The name of mother as thou hast thy shame.
Arane. My shame! Thou hast less shame than anything.   140
Why dost thou keep my daughter in a prison?
Why dost thou call her sister and do this?
Arbaces. Cease, thou strange impudence, and answer quickly.
If thou contemnst me, this will ask an answer
                                        [*Draws his sword.*]
And have it.
Arane.   Help me, gentle Gobrius!   145
Arbaces. Guilt dare not help guilt. Though they grow together
In doing ill, yet at the punishment
They sever, and each flies the noise of other.
Think not of help; answer!
Arane.   I will; to what?

---

143. Cease, thou] *Q1;* Cease thy *Q5–6, F2.*   144. SD] *Q8; not in Q1; Points
to his sword. Williams.*

---

130. *admire*] wonder at.
131. *another*] a different.
135. *he*] i.e. Satan, Father of Lies.
144. *contemnst*] scorn.
148. *noise of other*] accusations of the other; possibly, the cries of pain as
the other is punished.

Arbaces. To such a thing as, if it be a truth,   150
　　Think what a creature thou hast made thyself
　　That didst not shame to do what I must blush
　　Only to ask thee. Tell me who I am,
　　Whose son I am, without all circumstance.
　　Be thou as hasty as my sword will be   155
　　If thou refusest.
Arane.　　　　　　Why, you are his son.
Arbaces. His son? Swear; swear, thou worse than woman
　　damned.
Arane. By all that's good, you are.
Arbaces.　　　　　　　　Then art thou all
　　That ever was known bad. Now is the cause
　　Of all my strange misfortunes come to light.   160
　　What reverence expectst thou from a child
　　To bring forth which thou hast offended heaven,
　　Thy husband, and the land? Adulterous witch,
　　I know now why thou wouldst have poisoned me:
　　I was thy lust which thou wouldst have forgot.   165
　　Thou wicked mother of my sins and me,
　　Show me the way to the inheritance
　　I have by thee, which is a spacious world
　　Of impious acts, that I may soon possess it.
　　Plagues rot thee as thou liv'st, and such diseases   170
　　As use to pay lust recompense thy deed!
Gobrius. You do not know why you curse thus.
Arbaces.　　　　　　　　　　Too well.
　　You are a pair of vipers; and behold,
　　The serpent you have got! There is no beast
　　But, if he knew it, has a pedigree   175
　　As brave as mine, for they have more descents,
　　And I am every way as beastly got,

---

161. expectst] Q4; expects Q1.   166. Thou] Q1; Then Q2.

154. *all circumstance*] particular details.
174. *got*] begotten.
176. *brave*] fine.
descents] lines of descent, lineage. The precise meaning here is unclear, but the general sense of 174–9 seems to be that Arbaces sees himself as no better than a beast, begotten lawlessly and unable to trace his lineage back to one noble forebear.

As far without the compass of a law,
As they.
Arane.   You spend your rage and words in vain
And rail upon a guess. Hear us a little.   180
Arbaces. No, I will never hear, but talk away
My breath and die.
Gobrius.   Why, but you are no bastard.
Arbaces. How's that?
Arane.   Nor child of mine.
Arbaces.   Still you go on
In wonders to me.
Gobrius.   Pray you be more patient;
I may bring comfort to you.
Arbaces.   I will kneel   185
                    [*Kneels and puts up sword.*]
And hear with the obedience of a child.
Good father, speak; I do acknowledge you,
So you bring comfort.
Gobrius. First know, our last King, your supposèd father,
Was old and feeble when he married her,   190
And almost all the land, as she, past hope
Of issue from him.
Arbaces.   Therefore, she took leave
To play the whore, because the king was old.
Is this the comfort?
Arane.   What will you find out
To give me satisfaction when you find   195
How you have injured me. Let fire consume me,
If ever I were whore.
Gobrius.   Forbear these starts,
Or I will leave you wedded to despair
As you are now. If you can find a temper,

---

184. Pray you] *Q2;* Pray *Q1.*   185. SD] *This ed.; not in Q1; Kneels. Weber;
Puts up sword. Williams.*   194. SH *Arane.] Q1* (c)*;Arb. Q1* (u)*.*

181–2. *talk . . . breath*] keep talking until I've used up all my breath
(railing at you).
194–6. *What . . . injured me*] Cf. *The Winter's Tale,* 2.1.96–8: 'How will this
grieve you, / When you shall come to clearer knowledge, that / You thus have
publish'd me!'
197. *Forbear*] Refrain from.
199. *find a temper*] calm yourself.

My breath shall be a pleasant western wind   200
  That cools and blasts not.
Arbaces.   Bring it out, good father.
  I'll lie and listen here as reverently   *[Lies down.]*
  As to an angel. If I breathe too loud,
  Tell me, for I would be as still as night.
Gobrius. Our King, I say, was old, and this our Queen   205
  Desired to bring an heir; but yet her husband,
  She thought, was past it, and to be dishonest
  I think she would not. If she would have been,
  The truth is, she was watched so narrowly
  And had so slender opportunity   210
  She hardly could have been. But yet her cunning
  Found out this way: she feigned herself with child;
  And posts were sent in haste throughout the land,
  And God was humbly thanked in every church,
  That so had blessed the Queen, and prayers were made   215
  For her safe going and delivery.
  She feigned now to grow bigger, and perceived
  This hope of issue made her feared and brought
  A far more large respect from every man,
  And saw her power increase and was resolved,   220
  Since she believed she could not have't indeed,
  At least she would be thought to have a child.
Arbaces. Do I not hear it well? Nay, I will make
  No noise at all; but pray you to the point,
  Quick as you can.
Gobrius.   Now when the time was full   225
  She should be brought abed, I had a son
  Born, which was you. This the Queen hearing of,

---

202. SD] *Weber; not in Q1.*   210. opportunity] *Q1;* opportunities *Q2.*

---

202. *Lies down*] It is possible that no physical action is indicated here; 'lie'
could mean 'to keep quiet, remain inactive' (*OED* Lie *v* 21d), but examples
all include the preposition 'by' and the earliest cited date for this usage is
1709. Directorial decision here of course determines whether there is later
movement at 257.
206. *bring*] bring forth.
207. *dishonest*] unchaste, adulterous.
216. *going*] pregnancy (*OED* Go *v* 7).
218. *feared*] (1) revered, (2) dreaded.

Moved me to let her have you, and such reasons
She showed me as she knew would tie
My secrecy. She sware you should be king.   230
And to be short, I did deliver you
Unto her and pretended you were dead,
And in mine own house kept a funeral
And had an empty coffin put in earth.
That night the Queen feigned hastily to labour,   235
And by a pair of women of her own,
Which she had charmed, she made the world believe
She was delivered of you. You grew up
As the King's son till you were six year old.
Then did the King die and did leave to me   240
Protection of the realm and, contrary
To his own expectation, left this Queen
Truly with child indeed of the fair Princess
Panthea. Then she could have torn her hair,
And did alone to me, yet durst not speak   245
In public, for she knew she should be found
A traitor and her talk would have been thought
Madness or anything rather than truth.
This was the only cause why she did seek
To poison you and I to keep you safe,   250
And this the reason why I sought to kindle
Some spark of love in you to fair Panthea,
That she might get part of her right again.
Arbaces. And have you made an end now? Is this all?
If not, I will be still till I am aged,   255
Till all my hairs are silver.
Gobrius.   This is all.
Arbaces. And is it true, say you too, madam?   [*Rises.*]
Arane. Yes, God knows it is most true.
Arbaces. Panthea, then, is not my sister?
Gobrius.   No.

---

230. sware] *Q1*; swore *Q2*.   257. too] *Q2*; *not in Q1*.   257. SD] *Dyce subst.; not in Q1*.

---

237. *charmed*] i.e. whose silence she had procured.
257. *Rises*] If 202 is an implicit SD to lie at Gobrius's feet, this seems a likely moment for Arbaces to rise.

Arbaces. But can you prove this?
Gobrius.   If you will give consent.   260
     Else who dare go about it?
Arbaces.   Give consent!
     Why, I will have them all that know it racked
     To get this from 'em.—All that waitst without
     Come in; whate'er you be, come in and be
     Partakers of my joy.

          Enter MARDONIUS, BESSUS, [*two* Gentlemen,]
               and others.

                         O, you are welcome!   265
     Mardonius, the best news!—Nay, draw no nearer;
     They all shall hear it.—I am found no king!
Mardonius. Is that so good news?
Arbaces.   Yes, the happiest news
     That e'er was heard.
Mardonius.   Indeed, 'twere well for you
     If you might be a little less obeyed.   270
Arbaces. One call the Queen.
Mardonius.   Why, she is there.
Arbaces.   The Queen,
     Mardonius! Panthea is the Queen,
     And I am plain Arbaces.—Go some one;
     She is in Gobrius' house.   *Exit* 1 Gentleman.
               —Since I saw you
     There are a thousand things delivered to me   275
     You little dream of.
Mardonius.   So it should seem.—My lord,
     What fury's this?
Gobrius.   Believe me, 'tis no fury;

260. SH *Gobrius.*] *Q2; not in Q1.*   263. waitst] *waites Q1;* wait *F2.*   265.1.
SD *two* Gentlemen] *Q2 subst. (Gentlemen); not in Q1.*   271. One] *Q2;* On
Q1.   274. SD *Exit* 1 Gentleman.] *Dyce; not in Q1; Exit a Gent. Q2 (after*
276 of).

261. *Else . . . it?*] Otherwise who would dare try to prove this (extraordinary story, dangerous to those who knew the truth and kept the secret)?
     262. *racked*] tortured (cf. 4.2.192).
     264. *whate'er you be*] whoever you are, regardless of your station.
     275. *delivered*] revealed.
     277. *fury*] frenzy, madness.

All that he says is truth.
Mardonius.   'Tis very strange.
Arbaces. Why do you keep your hats off, gentlemen?
    Is it to me? I swear it must not be.   280
    Nay, trust me; in good faith, it must not be.
    I cannot now command you, but I pray you,
    For the respect you bare me when you took
    Me for your king, each man clap on his hat
    At my desire.
Mardonius.   We will, but you are not found   285
    So mean a man but that you may be covered
    As well as we, may you not?
Arbaces.   O, not here;
    You may, but not I, for here is my father
    In presence.
Mardonius.   Where?
Arbaces.   Why there. O, the whole story
    Would be a wilderness to lose thyself   290
    For ever!—O, pardon me, dear father,
    For all the idle and unreverent words
    That I have spoke in idle moods to you.—
    I am Arbaces; we all fellow subjects;
    Nor is the Queen, Panthea, now my sister.   295
Bessus. Why, if you remember, fellow subject Arbaces, I told
    you once she was not your sister; ay, and she looked
    nothing like you.
Arbaces. I think you did, good Captain Bessus.
Bessus [*Aside*]. Here will arise another question now amongst   300
    the swordmen, whether I be to call him to account for
    beating me now he's proved no king.

Enter LIGONES.

Mardonius. Sir, here's Ligones, the agent for the Armenian
    state.
Arbaces. Where is he?—I know your business, good Ligones.
Ligones. We must have our king again, and will.   305

280–1. I . . . trust me] *Q2; not in Q1*.   297. ay, and] *Q2* (I, and); I say *Q1*;
I said *Turner*.   303. state] *Q2*; King *Q1*.

---

   283. bare] bore.

Arbaces. I knew that was your business. You shall have
        Your king again and have him so again
        As never king was had.—Go, one of you,
        And bid Bacurius bring Tigranes hither
        And bring the lady with him that Panthea—   310
        The Queen Panthea—sent me word this morning
        Was brave Tigranes' mistress.   *Exit 2 Gentleman.*
Ligones.   'Tis Spaconia.
Arbaces. Ay, ay, Spaconia.
Ligones.   She is my daughter.
Arbaces. She is so; I could now tell anything
        I never heard. Your king shall go so home   315
        As never man went.
Mardonius.   Shall he go on's head?
Arbaces. He shall have chariots easier than air
        That I will have invented; and ne'er think
        He shall pay any ransom. And thyself,
        That art the messenger, shall ride before him   320
        On a horse cut out of an entire diamond
        That shall be made to go with golden wheels,
        I know not how yet.
Ligones [*Aside*].   Why, I shall be made
        For ever! They belied this king with us
        And said he was unkind.
Arbaces.   And then thy daughter—   325
        She shall have some strange thing; we'll have the kingdom
        Sold utterly and put into a toy
        Which she shall wear about her carelessly,
        Somewhere or other.—

                Enter PANTHEA *and* 1 Gentleman.

                            See the virtuous Queen!—
        Behold the humblest subject that you have   330
        Kneel here before you.   [*Kneels.*]
Panthea.   Why kneel you to me

---

312. SD *Exit 2 Gentleman.*] *Dyce; not in Q1; Exit two Gent. Q2.* 326. thing]
Q2; thinke *Q1.* 329. SD *and* 1 Gentleman] *Q2; not in Q1 (Enter Pan.).*
331. SD] *Weber; not in Q1.*

---

    326. *strange*] rare.
    327. *toy*] trifle, trinket.

That am your vassal?
Arbaces.   Grant me one request.
Panthea. Alas, what can I grant you? What I can
    I will.
Arbaces.   That you will please to marry me,   335
    If I can prove it lawful.
Panthea.   Is that all?
    More willingly than I would draw this air.
Arbaces. I'll kiss this hand in earnest.   [*Rises.*]

[Enter 2 Gentleman.]

2 Gentleman.   Sir, Tigranes
    Is coming, though he made it strange at first
    To see the princess any more.
Arbaces.   The Queen,   340
    Thou meanst.—

    Enter [BACURIUS *with*] TIGRANES *and* SPACONIA.

         O, my Tigranes, pardon me!
    Tread on my neck; I freely offer it.
    And if thou beest so given, take revenge,
    For I have injured thee.
Tigranes.   No, I forgive

---

338. SD *Rises.*] *Dyce subst.; not in Q1.* Enter 2 Gentleman.] *Dyce; not in Q1; Enter* Bacurius *and* 2 Gentleman. *Turner.*   338. SH *2 Gentleman.*] *Q2; Mar. Q1; Bacurius. Turner, conj. Dyce.*   339. at first] *Q2; not in Q1.*   340. SD *Enter* BACURIUS *with* TIGRANES] *Williams; Enter Tig. Q1 (after 340 Queen).* 342–3. it. / ... given,] *Theobald;* it, / ... given; *Q1.*

---

338. *in earnest*] (1) as a pledge, (2) seriously.
338. SD *Enter* 2 *Gentleman. /* SH *2* Gentleman.] Q1 has no SD and assigns the speech to Mardonius who, as Dyce pointed out, has been on stage for some time and could not know this information. Q2 reassigns the speech to *2 Gent.* but lacks a stage direction for his entry, which Dyce supplied and most subsequent editors adopt. In a note Dyce queried whether, in accordance with Arbaces's earlier request to 'Go, one of you, / And bid Bacurius bring Tigranes hither' (308–9), Q1's SH *Mar.* might have been a mistake for *Bac.* Turner accepts this hypothesis, brings Bacurius on (as well as 2 Gentleman), and gives him this speech. Williams agrees on the appropriateness of Bacurius's presence for the final happy tableau, but (more literally following 309) supposes he would accompany Tigranes and Spaconia, and I have accepted his addition of Bacurius to that entry (341).
339. *made it strange*] was reluctant (as a matter of scruple).

And rejoice more that you have found repentance   345
Than I my liberty.
Arbaces.   Mayst thou be happy
In thy fair choice, for thou art temperate.
You owe no ransom to the state, know that.
I have a thousand joys to tell you of
Which yet I dare not utter till I pay   350
My thanks to heaven for 'em. Will you go
With me and help me? Pray you, do.
Tigranes.   I will.
Arbaces. Take then your fair one with you.—And you, queen
Of goodness and of us, O, give me leave
To take your arm in mine.—Come every one   355
That takes delight in goodness; help to sing
Loud thanks for me, that I am proved no king.
                                        [*Exeunt.*]

345. state, know that.] *Q1* (that,); state; know that *Langbaine.* 353. you, queen] *F2;* your Queene *Q1.* 357. SD] *Langbaine (Exeunt omnes.); not in Q1.* 357.1.] FINIS *Q1.*

Appendix

Act 1, scene 1

231–2. Why . . . on't] *Bond; as prose Q1.*

277–8. You . . . these] *Q1;* You . . . care   / . . . utter   / . . . these *Theobald.*

321–9. Sir . . . are.] *Dyce; as prose Q1;* Sir . . . you / . . . do / . . . oath / . . . not / . . . chose / . . . can / . . . should have / . . . most / . . . are *Theobald.*

341–2. Though . . . your virtues] *Theobald; as prose Q1.*

343–6. Yes . . . But] *Q1;* Yes . . . passions / . . . this / . . . truth / . . . start / . . . hearing out *Theobald;* Yes / . . . they / . . . commend you / . . . faults / . . . hearing o't *Bond.*

361–2. However . . . rest] *Theobald; as prose Q1.*

366–8. Would . . . indeed] *This ed.; as prose Q1;* Would . . . leave / . . . say / . . . 'em / . . . indeed *Dyce.*

370–1. Yet . . . such] *Q1;* Yet . . . have / . . . you / . . . such *Bond.*

404. A . . . Mardonius] *Q1;* A wench / . . . Mardonius *Dyce; as prose, Theobald.*

406–10. Wench . . . certainty] *Q1;* Wench . . . me / . . . about me / . . . businesses / . . . pay / . . . glad / . . . certainty *Bond.*

Act 1, scene 2

17–18. That . . . of thee,] *Theobald; as one line Q1.*

Act 2, scene 1

49–52. Why . . . plots] *Q1; as prose, Theobald.*

52–3.] I . . . me] *Colman;* I . . . time / . . . me *Q1.*

104–5. You . . . tomorrow] *Bond;* You . . . ready / . . . tomorrow *Q1; as prose, Theobald.*

106–7. Madam . . . office] *Weber;* Madam . . . hereafter / . . . office *Q1; as prose, Theobald.*

121–3. Captain . . . time] *Weber; as prose Q1.*

123–4. Ay . . . brother] *Turner; as one line Q1;* Ay . . . it / . . . brother *Dyce.*

203–4. Madam . . . you] *This ed.; as one line Q1.*

214–17. My . . . him] *Colman; as prose Q1;* My . . . thing / . . . breast / . . . him F2.

217–19. Yet . . . prince] *Theobald; as prose Q1.*

224–6. Trust . . . him] *Theobald; as two lines* Trust . . . like / . . . him *Q1.*

226–8. But . . . offered] *Theobald;* But . . . humours / . . . less / . . . offered *Q1.*

Act 2, scene 2.

127–9. So . . . vainglorious] *Q1;* So . . . me / . . . commendations / . . . vainglorious *Weber.*

Act 3, scene 1

16. I . . . sir] *This ed.;* I . . . not / . . . sir *Theobald.*

26–7. A . . . Again.] *Theobald; as one line Q1.*

44–6. Tigranes . . . safe] *Q1;* Tigranes you / . . . land / . . . sons / . . . safe *Turner.*

61–2. Your . . . guard] *Theobald; as one line Q1.*

62–8. Now . . . me] *Q1;* Now . . . since I / . . . safety / . . . me / . . . grant / . . . bound / . . . thanks / . . . me *Theobald.*

121–2. Your . . . she] *Theobald; as one line Q1.*

235. And . . . owner] *Q1;* And . . . then / . . . owner *Theobald.*

244. And . . . her] *Q1;* And how / . . . her *Theobald;* And . . . change / . . . her *Turner.*

258. Do . . . me] *Q1;* Do . . . frown / . . . me *Theobald.*

272. Sir . . . obey] *Q1;* Sir . . . us / . . . obey *Theobald.*

273–4. Why . . . anything] *Q1;*   Why . . . there   / . . . anything *Theobald.*

295–6. And . . . me] *Weber; as one line Q1.*

319. I . . . it] *Q1;* I . . . answer / Do it *Theobald.*

327. Nay . . . it] *Q1;* Nay . . . well / . . . it *Weber.*

355–7. Wilt . . . things] *Q1;* Wilt . . . hereafter / . . . hear / . . . some / . . . things *Turner.*

358–9. I . . . again] *This ed.; as one line Q1;* I . . . see / . . . again *Weber;* I . . . do / . . . again *Dyce.*

Act 3, scene 3

1–11. I'll . . . eyes] *Q1;* I'll . . . altered / . . . has / . . . scourge / . . . me / . . . stay / . . . girl / . . . modesty / . . . me / . . . again / . . . yet / . . . weep / . . . think / . . . see / . . . eyes *Theobald.*

18–19. Why . . . do] *Theobald; as one line Q1.*

27. So . . . it] *Q1;* So . . . is / . . . it *Theobald.*

28–34. Out . . . you] *Q1;* Out . . . sir / . . . shrink / . . . esteem / . . . indeed / . . . chances / . . . lose it / . . . or / . . . these / . . . know / . . . you *Theobald.*

39–40. And . . . Tigranes] *Q1;* And . . . to / . . . Tigranes *Theobald.*

46–8. Come . . . me] *Q1;* Come . . . out / . . . hast / . . . me *Theobald.*

49. That's . . . her] *Q1;* That's strange / . . . her *Theobald.*

53. But . . . understand] *Q1;* But . . . should / . . . understand *Theobald;* But what? / . . . understand *Turner.*

54. O . . . pardoned] *Q1;* O Mardonius / . . . pardoned *Theobald.*

55. You . . . then] *Q1;* You may / . . . pardoned *Theobald.*

60–2. O . . . all] *Colman;* O . . . best / . . . all *Q1.*

62–3. Methinks . . . it] *Bond; as three lines* Methinks this / . . . caution / . . . it *Q1;* Methinks . . . not / . . . it *Theobald; as prose, Colman.*

64. There . . . me] *Theobald;* There . . . yet / . . . me *Q1.*

69–70. No . . . me] *Q1;* No . . . dull / . . . again / . . . me *Turner.*

72–3. But . . . husbands] *Q1;* But . . . does / . . . husbands *Bond.*

74–5. Why . . . you] *This ed.; as prose Q1;* Why . . . wives / . . . you *Theobald;* Why / . . . husbands / . . . you *Bond;* Why . . . are / . . . than / . . . you *Turner.*

144. By . . . whatsoever] *Theobald;* By . . . will / . . . whatsoever *Q1.*

150–1. O . . . i' faith] *Theobald;* O . . . her / . . . i'faith *Q1.*

160–1. Why . . . born] *Q1;* Why . . . opinion / . . . born *Theobald.*

182–3. Hung . . . monsters] *Theobald; as prose Q1.*

Act 4, scene 1

34–7. You . . . brother] *Theobald; as prose Q1.*

Act 4, scene 2

36–7. She . . . removed] *Theobald; as prose Q1.*

101. I . . . hither] *Q1;* I . . . it / . . . hither *Theobald.*

106–11. His . . . it] *Colman; as verse:* His . . . again / . . . all *as prose:*
Anon . . . it *Q1;* His . . . again / . . . all / . . . cured of / . . . men /
. . . held / . . . peace / . . . to't *Theobald.*

115. Beside . . . warrant] *Colman; as two lines* Beside . . . sir / . . .
warrant *Q1.*

137–9. I . . . it] *Q1;* I . . . openly / . . . life / . . . it *Weber.*

163–4. This . . . choose] *Theobald; as prose Q1;* This . . . looked /
. . . choose *Williams.*

175–6. Yes . . . quickly] *Bond; as prose Q1.*

241–3. Then . . . you] *Q1;* Then . . . for / . . . with / . . . live / . . . you
Theobald.

Act 4, scene 3

26–32. Two . . . in] *Q1;* Two . . . man, / . . . turned / . . . man / . . .
ten / . . . hazard / . . . favours / . . . in *Weber.*

33–7. The King . . . captain] *Q1;* The King . . . it / . . . bottle / . . .
you / . . . strange / . . . captain *Weber.*

42–5. He . . . it] *Q1;* He . . . beaten / . . . man / . . . forth / . . .
distance / . . . it *Weber;* He . . . beaten / . . . prince / . . . his / . . .
distance / . . . it. *Turner.*

55–6. By . . . discreetly] *Q1;* By . . . utter / . . . discreetly *Turner.*

59–61. Not . . . imputation] *Colman; as prose Q1.*

78–80. Let . . . kicked] *Weber; as prose Q1;* Let . . . it / . . . not / . . .
kicked *Dyce.*

82–4. Nor . . . brother] *Weber; as prose Q1;* Nor no silly / . . . case /
. . . brother *Turner.*

88–9. The boy . . . brother] *Theobald; as prose Q1.*

95–6. By . . . us] *Q1;* By . . . still / . . . us *Weber.*

97. I . . . granted] *Q1;* I . . . must / . . . granted *Bond.*

99. Ay . . . granted] *Q1;* Ay / . . . granted *Bond.*

101. I . . . granted] *Q1;* I say / . . . granted *Bond.*

102. Give . . . palter] *Q1;* Give . . . again / . . . palter *Bond.*

103–5. Brother . . . man] *Williams; as prose Q1;* Brother / . . .
together / . . . man *Weber;* Brother . . . times / . . . man *Bond.*

117. It . . . since] *Colman;* It . . . Sir / . . . since *Q1;* It . . . it / . . .
since *Theobald.*

118–19. The . . . kicking] *Q1;* The . . . one / . . . kicking *Williams.*

126. I . . . gentlemen] *Weber;* I . . . laugh / . . . Gentlemen *Q1.*

149–50. My . . . this] *Theobald; as one line Q1.*

152. Boy . . . within] *Q1;* Boy / . . . within *Weber.*

154–7. Sir . . . hereafter] *Bond; as three lines* Sir . . . done / . . . steel
/ . . . hereafter *Q1;* Sir . . . what / . . . for / . . . of / . . . hereafter
Turner; Sir . . . world / . . . done / . . . steel / . . . hereafter *Williams.*
157–9. I . . . cause.] *Bond; as prose Q1;* I . . . testify / . . . me / . . .
cause *Weber;* I . . . go / . . . Bacurius / . . . cause. *Turner.*

Act 4, scene 4

55. Then . . . you] *Q1;* Then . . . sir / . . . you *Weber.*
129–30. What . . . out] *Theobald; as prose Q1.*
149. Why . . . sister] *Q1;* Why yet / . . . sister *Theobald.*
150. True . . . truth] *Q1;* True / . . . truth *Theobald.*

Act 5, scene 1

1–3. Sir . . . master] *Bond; as prose Q1.*
5–6. But . . . this] *Q1; as prose, Theobald;* But . . . ended / . . . this
Walley–Wilson; But is / . . . this *Turner.*
6–7. I . . . business] *This ed.; as prose Q1;* I . . . worse / . . . business
Bond; I . . . ashamed / . . . business *Turner.*
8–11. You . . . rewards] *Bond; as prose Q1;* You . . . person / . . . me /
. . . offices / . . . rewards *Turner;* You . . . stranger / . . . if / . . .
offices / . . . rewards *Williams.*
12. I . . . nobleness] *Q1;* I . . . bound / . . . nobleness *Bond.*
36–7. 'Tis . . . he] *Dyce; as prose Q1;* 'Tis . . . Bessus / . . . he *Weber.*
51–4. Sufferance . . . meat] *Williams; as three lines* Sufferance . . .
had / . . . daggers / . . . meat *Q1;* Sufferance . . . had / . . . slave /
. . . head / . . . meat *Weber.*
60–2. And . . . him] *Dyce; as two lines* And . . . sense / . . . him *Q1.*
66–75. 'Tis . . . sir] *Q1;* 'Tis . . . If / . . . do / . . . and / . . . him / . . .
out / . . . not / . . . conscience / . . . wars / . . . withal / . . . do / . . .
you / . . . biscuit / . . . sir *Theobald.*
78–80. Then . . . you] *Q1;* Then . . . Bessus / . . . exordiums / . . .
favour / . . . you *Theobald.*
81–2. Pray . . . gentleman] *Dyce; as one line Q1.*
82–3. Thus . . . you] *Weber; as prose Q1.*
109–10. This . . . intemperate] *Q1;*   This . . . Sir   / . . . I   / . . .
intemperate *Theobald; as prose, Colman.*
111–12. Well . . . sight] *Q1;* Well . . . more   / . . . you   / . . . sight
Theobald; as prose, Colman.
113–14. Indeed . . . me] *Turner;* Indeed . . . forget   / . . . me *Q1;*
Indeed . . . know / . . . must / . . . me *Theobald; as prose, Colman.*

115–16. Yes . . . this] *Turner;* Yes . . . think / . . . this *Q1;* Yes . . . will
/ . . . this *Theobald; as prose, Colman.*

121–2. Farewell . . . pray'ee] *Theobald; as prose Q1.*

124–6. Gentlemen . . . safe] *Q1; as prose, Theobald;* Gentlemen . . .
more / . . . penitent / . . . safe *Turner.*

127–8. We . . . grandsire] *Dyce;* We . . . kicked / . . . grandsire *Q1; as
prose, Theobald.*

130–1. Now . . . it] *Q1;* Now . . . come / . . . it *Theobald; as prose,
Colman.*

132–3. Alas . . . him] *Q1; as prose, Theobald.*

Act 5, scene 2

5–6. There . . . child] *Turner;* There . . . indeed / . . . child *Q1; as
prose, Theobald;* There . . . is / . . . child *Weber.*

7–8. I . . . me] *Q1;* I . . . fault / . . . have / . . . me *Turner.*

10–11. What . . . hither] *Q1;*   What . . . Ligones   / . . . hither
Theobald.

18–19. There . . . thence] *Theobald;*   There . . . happened   / . . .
thence *Q1.*

34–43. Do . . . thee] *Q1;* Do . . . yet / . . . clients / . . . thou / . . . is /
. . . mother / . . . died / . . . acquainted / . . . whore / . . . satisfied /
. . . dancer / . . . musicians / . . . thee *Theobald; as prose:* Do . . .
whore? *as verse:* I . . . satisfied / . . . dancer / . . . musicians / . . .
thee *Weber.*

44–5. If . . . carted] *Theobald; as prose Q1.*

66–9. Then . . . whore] *Colman; as five verse lines* Then . . . whore /
. . . choose / . . . if / . . . fit / . . . whore *Q1;* Then . . . fair / . . . speak
/ . . . greatly / . . . I / . . . fit / . . . whore *Theobald.*

82. Nay . . . haste] *Q1;* Nay go / . . . haste *Theobald.*

83. Good . . . king] *Q1;* Good . . . you / You . . . king *Theobald.*

Act 5, scene 3

5–6. My . . . me] *Q1;* My . . . gentlemen / . . . me *Weber.*

7. I . . . then] *Q1;* I am / . . . then *Weber.*

8–9. My . . . lord] *Q1;* My . . . not / . . . lord *Theobald.*

11–12. I . . . sorry] *Q1;* I . . . Gentlemen / . . . sorry *Weber.*

13–16. Not . . . Stockfish] *This ed.; as prose:* Not . . . lancing *as verse:*
As . . . fall / Now . . . Stockfish *Q1;* Not . . . you / . . . be beaten /
. . . lamming / . . . fall / . . . sword-men / . . . Stockfish *Colman;*
Not . . . have / . . . be beaten / . . . lancing / . . . fall / . . . swordmen

/ . . . Stockfish *Dyce; as prose:* Not . . . fall *as verse:* Now . . .
Captain / Stock-fish *Williams.*

18–21. No . . . woodyard] *Q1;* No . . . are / . . . anything / . . . man's
/ . . . woodyard *Theobald.*

22–3. Your . . . come] *Q1;* Your . . . it / . . . come *Weber.*

24–5. To . . . it] *Q1;* To . . . book / . . . it *Weber;* To swear / . . . it
Dyce.

26–7. Your . . . coward] *Q1;* Your . . . vouch / . . . coward *Theobald.*

28–34. That . . . true] *Q1;* That . . . Sirs / . . . with't / . . . known /
. . . than / . . . you / . . . captainship / . . . hands / . . . true *Weber.*

36–9. Lord . . . us] *Q1;* Lord . . . true / . . . there / . . . beatings / . . .
off / . . . us *Theobald.*

40–4. You . . . valour] *Q1;* You . . . bilbo-men / . . . good / . . . them
/ . . . Bessus / . . . valour *Theobald.*

45–7. Your . . . friend] *Q1;* Your . . . men / . . . opinions / . . . friend
Weber.

48–50. Yet . . . you] *Q1;* Yet . . . touched / . . . pay / . . . you *Weber.*

51–2. Spare . . . virtue] *Q1;* Spare . . . lord / . . . virtue *Weber.*

57–9. Something . . . beatings] *Q1;* Something . . . apple-squires /
. . . valour / . . . beatings *Theobald.*

61–2. 'Sfoot . . . one] *Theobald; as prose Q1.*

66–7. Off . . . rascals] *Q1;* Off . . . swords / . . . flayed / . . . rascals
Theobald; Off . . . foot / . . . rascals *Dyce.*

69–70. I . . . please] *Q1;* I . . . strap's / . . . please *Weber;* I beseech /
. . . tied / . . . please *Turner.*

71–2. Captain . . . too] *Q1;* Captain . . . friends / . . . too *Weber;*
Captain . . . long / . . . too *Bond.*

73. I . . . lordship] *Q1;* I . . . well / . . . lordship *Turner.*

74–6. What's . . . quickly] *Q1;* What's . . . mongrel / . . . quickly
Weber; What's . . . in / . . . Thy / . . . quickly *Turner.*

77–80. Here . . . loose] *Q1;* Here . . . artillery / . . . lordship's / . . .
mark / . . . loose *Weber;* Here . . . sir / . . . gentleman / . . . with /
. . . mark / . . . loose *Dyce;* Here . . . artillery / . . . lordship's / . . .
sir / . . . loose *Turner.*

81–2. A . . . footballs] *Q1;* A . . . rascal / . . . nothing / . . . foot-balls
Weber; A . . . never / . . . than / . . . footballs *Turner.*

84. It . . . 'em] *Q1;* It . . . prithee / . . . them *Weber;* It . . . late / . . .
'em *Turner.*

85–6. My . . . men] *Q1;* My . . . play / . . . us / . . . men *Weber;* My
. . . put / . . . men *Dyce.*

99–100. Yes . . . bone] *Q1;* Yes . . . ache / . . . huckle-bone *Weber.*

102–3. A . . . *est*] *Q1*; A . . . butter / . . . matter / . . . *est* / *Weber*.

104–5. Captain . . . honours] *Q1*;   Captain . . . request   / . . . honours *Weber*.

106–7. Yes . . . end] *Q1*; Yes . . . ye / . . . valiant / . . . end *Weber*.

108. Nay . . . ribs] *Q1*; Nay . . . must / . . . ribs *Dyce*.

109–10. O . . . murderers] *Q1*; O . . . guts / . . . murderers *Weber*.

Act 5, scene 4

13–14. Mardonis . . . come] *Theobald; as one line Q1*.

22. Mark . . . me] *Q1*; Mark . . . you / . . . me *Theobald*.

23. You . . . were] *Q1*; You are / . . . were *Dyce*.

25–6. Today . . . all] *Q1*; Today . . . be / . . . all *Theobald*.

46–7. Be . . . thyself] *Q1*; Be . . . alone / . . . thyself *Theobald*.

49–50. Why . . . not] *Q1*; as one line, *Theobald*.

66. There . . . ripe] *Q1*; There . . . King / . . . ripe *Weber*.

98–9. This . . . cause] *Theobald; as one line Q1*.

99–100. Wert . . . it] *Theobald; as one line Q1*.

120–1. Know . . . father] *Theobald*; Know . . . father. *Arb*. How? / *Gob*. You . . . father *Q1*.

125–7. I . . . me] *Theobald; as two lines* I . . . thy / . . . me *Q1*.

157. His . . . damned] *Theobald; as two lines* His son / . . . damned *Q1*.

158–60. Then . . . light] *Theobald; as two lines* Then . . . is / . . . light *Q1*.

183–4. Still . . . me] *Theobald; as one line Q1*.

184–5. Pray . . . you] *Theobald; as one line Q1*.

258. Yes . . . true] *Q1*; Yes / . . . true *Theobald*.

260–1. If . . . it] *Colman; as one line Q1*; If . . . go / About it *Theobald*.

268–9. Yes . . . heard] *Theobald; as one line Q1*.

271–2. The Queen . . . Queen] *Theobald; as one line Q1*.

284–5. Me . . . desire] *Theobald; as one line Q1*.

288–9. You . . . presence] *Theobald; as one line Q1*.

303. Sir . . . state] *Theobald; as two lines* Sir . . . Ligones / . . . King. *Q1*.

331–2. Why . . . vassal] *Theobald*; Why . . . you / . . . vassal *Q1*.

333–4. Alas . . . I will] *Theobald*; Alas . . . you / . . . I will *Q1*.

338–40. Sir . . . more] *Theobald; as two lines* Sir . . . strange / To . . . more *Q1* (at first *not in Q1*).

Index

Page numbers refer to the Introduction, dedication and appendix; act-scene-line numbers refer to the Commentary. When a gloss is repeated in the annotations, only the initial occurrence is indexed.

CPSIA information can be obtained at www.ICGtesting.com
Printed in the USA
BVOW06s0525110615

404004BV00013B/62/P